A PRACTICAL GUIDE TO THE INSURANCE ACT 2015

DAVID KENDALL AND HARRY WRIGHT

PRACTICAL INSURANCE GUIDES

A Practical Guide to the Insurance Act 2015
By David Kendall and Harry Wright
(2017)

A Guide to Reinsurance Law
Edited by Robert Merkin
(2007)

Insurance Law: An Introduction
Edited by Robert Merkin
(2004)

Tackling Insurance Fraud: Law and Practice
by Carol Boland
(2004)

Reinsurance: London Market Practice
Second edition
by Carol Boland
(1996)

A PRACTICAL GUIDE TO THE INSURANCE ACT 2015

DAVID KENDALL, M.A., L.L.B. (Hons.)
Solicitor of the Senior Courts of England and Wales;
Visiting Professor, Queen Mary University of London.
Partner, Cooley (UK) LLP, London.

AND

HARRY WRIGHT, M.A.
of Gray's Inn, Barrister, 7 King's Bench Walk.

Routledge
Taylor & Francis Group
LONDON AND NEW YORK

First published 2018
by Informa Law from Routledge

2 Park Square, Milton Park, Abingdon, Oxfordshire OX14 4RN
52 Vanderbilt Avenue, New York, NY 10017

Routledge is an imprint of the Taylor & Francis Group, an informa business

First issued in paperback 2019

British Library Cataloguing in Publication Data
A catalogue record for this book is available from the British Library

Library of Congress Cataloging in Publication Data
Names: Kendall, David (Insurance lawyer), author. | Wright, Harry (Lawyer), author.
Title: A practical guide to the Insurance Act 2015 / by David Kendall and Harry Wright.
Description: First edition. | Abingdon, Oxon ; New York, NY : Informa Law from Routledge, 2018. | Includes index. | Includes Law Commision note and text of act.
Identifiers: LCCN 2017013153| ISBN 9781138290204 (hbk) | ISBN 9781315189161 (ebk)
Subjects: LCSH: Great Britain. Insurance Act 2015. | Insurance law--Great Britain.
Classification: LCC KD1854.582015 .K46 2018 | DDC 346.41/086--dc23LC record available at https://lccn.loc.gov/2017013153

ISBN: 978-1-138-29020-4 (hbk)
ISBN: 978-0-367-88636-3 (pbk)

Typeset in Times New Roman
by Servis Filmsetting Ltd, Stockport, Cheshire

TABLE OF CONTENTS

FOREWORD

This entirely new work comes at an opportune time. Most of the Insurance Act 2015 came into force on 12 August 2016, for insurances or variations effected after that date. The final piece in the jigsaw is section 13A. Added by the Enterprise Act 2016, this came into force on 4 May 2017, and will, for the first time in English law, give insureds a (not uncontroversial) right to claim damages for late payment of claims.

The Marine Insurance Act 1906 could serve as a case study of the compatibility of codification with the common law method. On the one hand, it achieved certainty, based on pre-existing common law authority. On the other hand, it introduced rigidity, being treated as a template for all types of insurance law, not merely marine. This rigidity built into law some conspicuous inequities which proved impervious to subsequent common law modification. Particularly stringent from the point of view of insureds were the operation of the principle of utmost good faith (especially in connection with the insured's duty of disclosure and insurers' remedy of avoidance *ab initio*) and the draconian effects of warranties and 'basis of the contract' clauses. These aspects of English insurance law may sometimes have encouraged a less rigorous approach to original underwriting ('underwriting at the claims stage'). They could certainly allow insurers to raise technical defences when their real concerns about a claim were more fundamental, but unprovable. In that respect, the stringency of English insurance law could even be deployed by foreign competitors as a marketing tool against use of the London market. The law relating to fraudulent claims was also not free from doubt, and there were voices speaking in favour of a right along the lines of what is now section 13A.

From the middle of the last century onwards, a series of efforts thus took place to achieve more or less far-reaching reform. But it was a 2002 report of a committee of the British Insurance Law Association, chaired by Mr Adrian Hamilton QC, which led to the Law Reform Commission returning to the subject and in due course making proposals which gave rise to the present wide-ranging changes affecting all branches of insurance. The Act went through Parliament under the special procedure designed for uncontroversial Law Commission proposals. But, perhaps inevitably, the effect of some of its provisions is open to discussion and will certainly give rise in due course to litigation.

That is the great value of this book. David Kendall and Harry Wright provide a clear analysis of the Act's perhaps deceptively simple terms (if one may use that phrase in this context, without being misunderstood). The Act reshapes the duty of disclosure as a duty of fair presentation, redefines the knowledge relevant in that connection (introducing new concepts such as 'reasonable search', 'senior management' and 'confidential information'), reshapes the effects of breach of the duty of fair presentation, of warranties and basis of contract clauses, clarifies the law on fraudulent claims and introduces the entirely new remedy of a claim for damages for late payment. In all of these areas, its effects will need working out in practice.

There is thus every reason to welcome warmly a work in which the authors deploy experience and expertise, to set the Act against the background of the previous statutory text and case law and examine how familiar and new situations will now fall to be resolved. The authors write clearly, informatively and analytically, with footnotes referring both to case law and other relevant commentaries. Their work will be of great use to all who effect or place insurances, to the insurance market, to legal practitioners and to academics alike. It should assist as much to avoid problems as to solve them when they arise. It is a pleasure warmly to commend the work to all who need to deal with English insurance law in any of these contexts.

Lord Mance
Justice of the Supreme Court
of the United Kingdom

FOREWORD

The Marine Insurance Act 1906 and leading subsequent cases are in the DNA of the Lloyd's and London insurance market, even if not consciously so at all times with all practitioners, because market practice has grown around that law. Disputes have informed and modified market practice and contract wordings over the years. The Insurance Act 2015, amended by the Enterprise Act 2016, therefore brings a sea change. Some fear, understandably, that we will be at sea for some time before the new law settles down. We await the first significant cases on the Act. In the meantime, a very good way for market practitioners to minimise the risk that it will be they who feature in these cases is to read this book.

The Lloyd's Market Association (LMA) was in the thick of the consultation process preceding the new legislation and gave evidence to the House of Lords Special Public Bill Committee. Both the authors advised the LMA at crucial times and were heavily involved in authoring and reviewing our market guidance and related model clauses. The LMA supported some of the cornerstones of the Law Commissions' reform programme, but was concerned about various provisions which have made it into the statute book. This book puts it all into clear, balanced and refreshing perspective – the background and development of the Act, the more difficult and controversial parts, how these relate to the law before 12 August 2016 (when the Insurance Act came into force), and therefore how practitioners may approach the new law.

I recommend this book to those engaged in broking and underwriting insurance business, to those designing standard insurance products and preparing and reviewing bespoke contracts at time of placement in the market, and of course to those responsible in organisations for buying insurance and reinsurance cover. This book will also be of great interest to legal advisers and the academic world.

Kees van der Klugt
Director of Legal & Compliance
Lloyd's Market Association

GLOSSARY / ABBREVIATIONS

AIRMIC	Association of Insurance and Risk Managers in Industry and Commerce
BIBA	British Insurance Brokers' Association
BILA	British Insurance Law Association
BILA 2002 Report	Insurance Contract Law Reform, Recommendations to the Law Commission. A Report of the Sub-Committee of the British Insurance Law Association, 1 September 2002
CIDRA 2012	Consumer Insurance (Disclosure and Representations) Act 2012
Explanatory Notes	HM Treasury's Explanatory Notes to the Insurance Act 2015, 12 February 2015
FCA	Financial Conduct Authority
Insurance Act /the Act	Insurance Act 2015 (Chapter 4)
IUA	International Underwriting Association
July 2014 Report	The Joint Law Commissions' Report on Insurance Contract Law: Business Disclosure; Warranties; Insurers' Remedies for Fraudulent Claims; and Late Payment, CM 8898, July 2014
Law Commissions	The Law Commission of England and Wales and the Scottish Law Commission
Law Commission's 1980 Report	Insurance Law: Non-Disclosure and Breach of Warranty Law Com No 104 (1980 Cmnd 8064)
Law Com No 201	Law Commissions' Consultation Paper No 201 – Insurance Contract Law: Post Contract Duties and Other Issues, December 2011
Law Com No 293	Ninth Programme of Law Reform (2005)
Law Commissions' 2007 Joint Consultation Paper	The Joint Law Commissions' Joint Consultation and Discussion Paper on Insurance Contract Law: Misrepresentation, Non-Disclosure and Breach of Warranty by the Insured, CP182, June 2007
Law Com No 319	The Joint Law Commissions' Report on Consumer Insurance Law: Pre-Contract Disclosure and Misrepresentation, CM 7758, December 2009
Law Com No 204	The Business Insured's Duty of Disclosure and the Law of Warranties (June 2012) Law Commission Consultation Paper No 204

Law Commissions' 2012 Joint Consultation Paper	The Joint Law Commissions' Joint Consultation and Discussion Paper on Insurance Contract Law: The Business Insured's Duty of Disclosure and the Law of Warranties, CP204, June 2012
Law Com No 353	Insurance Contract Law: Business Disclosure; Warranties; Insurers' Remedies for Fraudulent Claims; and Late Payment
Law Reform Committee's 1957 Report	Law Reform Committee (1957) Cmnd 62
LMA	Lloyd's Market Association
Marine Insurance Act	Marine Insurance Act 1906 [6 Edw. 7 Ch. 41]

TABLE OF CASES

TABLE OF LEGISLATION

Regulations, orders and rules

European Union

Australia

New Zealand

[illegible]	[illegible]

Regulations, orders and rules

[illegible]

Insurance Companies [illegible]

[illegible]

European Union

[illegible]

Directive [illegible]

[illegible]

Australia

[illegible]

New Zealand

[illegible]

TABLE OF LAW COMMISSION PAPERS AND REPORTS

Consultation papers

Issues papers

CHAPTER 1

Background to the Insurance Act

Overview

1.1 This is a book about the Insurance Act 2015 and its impact on English law. The Insurance Act is the first comprehensive statutory reform of non-consumer insurance law since the Marine Insurance Act 1906, which essentially codified the existing common law. It is the product of extensive efforts by the Law Commissions of England and Wales, and Scotland, to reform UK insurance law,[1] a process begun more than 50 years ago.[2]

1.2 The Insurance Act makes very significant changes to insurance law in the United Kingdom, and (it is expected) to the business of buying, underwriting and broking insurance contracts governed by the laws of the United Kingdom. It has been variously described as a 'thorough overhaul' of UK insurance law;[3] 'the most significant reform of the nation's insurance law' for 250 years;[4] and (less promisingly) as in some respects 'uncertain and obscure';[5] and a 'risky sacrifice of the … prized certainty of business insurance law'.[6]

1.3 The Act is intended to level the playing field between the parties to a contract of insurance, which was previously seen as unduly favourable to the insurer.[7] It therefore makes a number of changes which ought to favour the insured, most obviously the abolition of avoidance as the sole remedy for breach of the duty of utmost good faith, and its replacement with proportionate remedies for breach of a (new) duty of fair presentation. In addition, the Act transforms insurance warranties so that breach will no longer discharge the insurer's liability automatically and permanently. It also

1 That is to say the laws of either England and Wales, Scotland or Northern Ireland. Technically, there is of course no such thing as United Kingdom law, and the phrase is used herein as shorthand for the laws of each of the constituent parts of the United Kingdom of Great Britain and Northern Ireland.

2 In 1954, Lord Kilmuir asked the Law Reform Committee (predecessor to the Law Commission) to consider various aspects of insurance law, and the Committee reported in 1957: see (1957) Cmnd 62.

3 David Hertzell, 'The Insurance Act 2015 Background and Philosophy' in Malcolm Clarke and Barış Soyer (eds), *The Insurance Act 2015: A New Regime for Commercial and Marine Insurance Law* (hereafter Clarke & Soyer 2016) (Informa, London, 2016), 1.

4 Sir Bernard Rix, 'Conclusion General reflections on the law reform' in Clarke & Soyer 2016, 107.

5 *Arnould's Law of Marine Insurance and Average*, supp. to the 18th edn (hereafter *Arnould*, supp. to 18th edn) (Sweet & Maxwell, London, 2015), para.1.1–02.

6 Paul Jaffe, 'Reform of the Insurance Law of England and Wales – Separate Laws for the Different needs of Businesses and Consumers' in BILA Journal No 123 (October 2013) 33 (albeit commenting on the Law Commissions' proposals as they stood at the time of writing, not the Insurance Act).

7 July 2014 Report, para.1.6.

heralds the potential availability of damages where an insurer fails to pay a claim within a reasonable time. These are fundamental changes.

1.4 The Insurance Act has gone substantially further than addressing merely those areas of insurance law most obviously in need of attention. It has also brought about a comprehensive reform of the law governing the knowledge of the insured and the insurer for the purposes of the duty of fair presentation. This is important, since an insured is required to disclose only material matters which it knows or is taken to know, and is not required to disclose matters known to the insurer. The law on knowledge therefore underpins the new duty of fair presentation. Whereas the aim of the Act was to advance the interests of insureds, reforms to the law on knowledge appear to add to the insured's burden, or at least to uncertainty over what the insured must disclose. The Act also introduces a new restriction whereby an insurer will be unable to rely upon breach of any risk mitigation term in order to limit or discharge its liability, if the breach was irrelevant to the actual loss which has occurred (for example, there may be no reliance on breach of a burglar alarm warranty where the loss was caused by a flood). This provision will apply not only to warranties, but to a potentially wide range of terms which, if complied with, would tend to reduce the risk of loss. These too are fundamental changes.

1.5 This book is intended to assist those participating in the business of insurance (whether as buyers, insurers or brokers), or practising in the field of insurance law, to navigate and understand the meaning and practical effect of the changes brought about by the Insurance Act. It is written in something of a vacuum of authority since, at the time of writing, not a single decision based upon the Insurance Act has been handed down.[8] It might, therefore, be considered premature, but the need for those carrying on the business of insurance appeared to the authors to warrant a tentative attempt to explain the new law, particularly those aspects which are obscure and likely to cause problems.

Recent history of insurance law reform in the UK

1.6 Since it was first considered by the Law Reform Committee in 1954, it has taken more than 50 years for statutory reform of non-consumer insurance law in the United Kingdom to be realised. From 1978, this process has been driven by the Law Commissions, though the movement for reform pre-dates their existence, which did not come about until 1965.[9] The recent process of reform can be traced to 1954, when Viscount Kilmuir (then Lord Chancellor) invited the Law Commissions' predecessor, the Law Reform Committee, to consider certain aspects of insurance law. In 1957, the Committee published its Fifth Report, recommending a softening of the duty of utmost good faith through amendment of the test for materiality, so that no fact should be deemed material unless it would have been considered material by a

---

8 Though see the following on the likely effect of the Insurance Act 2015 on fraudulent claims: *Versloot Dredging BV and another v HDI Gerling Industrie Versicherung AG and others* [2016] UKSC 45, [2016] 3 WLR 543, [102] (Lord Sumption); and on remedies for breach of the duty of fair presentation: *Involnert Management Inc v Aprilgrange Ltd & Ors* [2015] EWHC 2225 (Comm), [2015] 2 Lloyd's Rep 289, [186] (Leggatt J).

9 Law Commissions Act 1965.

reasonable insured. Additionally, it was proposed that no misrepresentation should be actionable if the insured could prove that the statement in question was true to the best of his knowledge and belief. These reforms were never enacted.

1.7 There followed a period of inactivity until 1978, when the Law Commission of England and Wales was asked to consider insurance law reform by Lord Elwyn-Jones, the Lord Chancellor. The Law Commission reported in 1980,[10] having considered matters including non-disclosure and misrepresentation, warranties and basis clauses. The 1980 Report proposed statutory reform through a draft 'Insurance Law Reform Bill', which included the following reforms of note:

(i) The insured would be required to disclose material matters which it knows or is assumed to know. The insured would be assumed to know a material matter if it would have been ascertainable by reasonable enquiry and if a reasonable person applying for the insurance in question would have ascertained it. The insured would be required to disclose a matter only if it is one which a reasonable person in the position of the insured would disclose to his insurers, having regard to the nature and extent of the insurance cover sought, and the circumstance in which it was sought.[11]

(ii) In a proposal form, the insured would be required to answer questions to the best of his knowledge and belief, having made such enquiries as were reasonable in the circumstances.[12]

(iii) A term would be capable of being a warranty only if it were material to the risk. There would be a rebuttable presumption that any term possessing the attributes of a warranty was material to the risk.[13] The warranty would also need to be provided to the insured, in writing, within a reasonable time of it being given by the insured, failing which the insurer would be precluded from relying on breach of the warranty.[14]

(iv) An insured would be entitled to recover if it could show that, notwithstanding a breach of warranty, the warranty was intended to safeguard against the risk of a particular type of loss, and the actual loss was of a different type; or, even if the loss was of a type which the warranty was intended to safeguard against, the insured's breach could not have increased the risk that the loss would occur in the way in which it did in fact occur. In either case, the insurer would be entitled to repudiate the contract for the future, on account of the breach of warranty.[15] In addition, basis clauses would have been rendered ineffective.[16]

1.8 A major limitation of the 1980 recommendations was that none of them would have applied to Marine, Aviation or Transport insurance.[17] As will be seen, many of the reforms proposed in the Law Commission's 1980 Report and the Insurance Law Reform Bill bear striking similarities to provisions in the Insurance Act. In spite of

10 Law Com No 104 (1980) (hereafter, 'Law Commission's 1980 Report').
11 Law Commission's 1980 Report, paras 4.43–4.53, Insurance Law Reform Bill, cl.2.
12 Ibid., paras 4.61 & 4.82, Insurance Law Reform Bill cl. 6(4).
13 Ibid., paras 6.12–6.13, Insurance Law Reform Bill cll 8(1) & 8(3).
14 Ibid., para.6.14, Insurance Law Reform Bill, cl.8(2).
15 Ibid., paras 6.15–6.22, Insurance Law Reform Bill cl.10(5).
16 Ibid., paras 7.1–7.11, Insurance Law Reform Bill cl.9.
17 As defined in the Insurance Companies (Classes of General Business) Regulations 1999, SI 1955/1522.

the numerous and detailed recommendations, no reform was enacted. There followed a long period of relative silence on the subject of insurance law reform by the Law Commission, which appears to have been brought to an end by a 2002 report by a sub-committee of the British Insurance Law Association, which concluded that there was a need for reform.[18] The BILA sub-committee recommended (in summary) that the Law Commission's 1980 recommendations should be implemented,[19] with certain moderations and additions (such as the introduction of proportionate remedies for breach of the duty of utmost good faith,[20] and treating sums payable under an insurance contract as a debt, with an implied term requiring insurers to pay the debt within a reasonable time).[21] The report, contributed to by senior judges, counsel, and academics, was described by the Law Commissions as a 'major factor' in their decision to return to the area of insurance law in 2005,[22] when insurance law reform was again considered with a new intensity.

Consideration of reform in the new millennium

1.9 The Law Commissions returned to the subject of insurance law reform in March 2005, indicating that they would perform a review of insurance law.[23] In January 2006, the Law Commissions published a Scoping Paper seeking views from interested parties about the areas of insurance law which were in need of attention. Over the following six years, the Law Commissions undertook a herculean review of UK Insurance Law, publishing a series of Issues Papers, Consultation Papers and a Final Report covering a multitude of topics:

- Issues Paper 1: Misrepresentation and Non-Disclosure (September 2006).
- Issues Paper 2: Warranties (November 2006).
- Issues Paper 3: Intermediaries and Pre-contract Information (March 2007).
- Consultation Paper No 182: Misrepresentation, Non-Disclosure and Breach of Warranty by the Insured (June 2007).[24]
- Issues Paper 4: Insurable Interest (January 2008).
- Issues Paper 5: Micro-Businesses (April 2009).
- Consumer Insurance Law: Pre-Contract Disclosure and Misrepresentation (December 2009).[25]
- Issues Paper 6: Damages for Late Payment and the Insurer's Duty of Good Faith (March 2010).
- Issues Paper 7: The Insured's Post-Contract Duty of Good Faith (July 2010).
- Issues Paper 8: The Broker's Liability for Premiums: Should Section 53 be Reformed? (July 2010).

---

18 BILA, *Insurance Contract Law Reform – Recommendations to the Law Commissions,* BILA (2002), para.4.
19 Ibid., paras 4–5.
20 Ibid., para.17.3, especially para.17.3.4.
21 Ibid., paras 4–5, 17.3 & 17.6.2.
22 July 2014 Report, paras 1.8–1.9
23 Law Com No 293, p.3.
24 Law Commissions' 2007 Joint Consultation Paper.
25 Law Com No 319.

- Issues Paper 9: The Requirement for a Formal Marine Policy: Should Section 22 be Repealed? (October 2010).
- Consultation Paper No 201: Insurance Contract Law: Post Contract Duties and Other Issues (December 2011).[26]
- Consultation Paper No 204: The Business Insured's Duty of Disclosure and the Law of Warranties (June 2012).[27]

1.10 Even a heavily abridged summary of the Law Commissions' papers on insurance law reform would fill many pages, and could not do justice to the depth of research and consideration undertaken. The accumulated learning from the papers referred to above was condensed into the Law Commissions' final (420-page) report of July 2014: 'Insurance Contract Law: Business Disclosure; Warranties; Insurers' Remedies for Fraudulent Claimant; and Late Payment',[28] which accompanied the draft Insurance Bill and Explanatory Notes. Extensive reference is made to the July 2014 Report in this book, as well as the other papers referred to above.[29] The paragraphs below attempt to summarise the problems which the Law Commissions identified in the final July 2014 Report, which the Insurance Act is intended to remedy.

The problems of the old law

1.11 The Law Commissions considered (with some justification, it is submitted) that the old law was unduly favourable to insurers, and opposed to the interests of insureds. The principal source of this problem was the Marine Insurance Act 1906, which the Law Commissions considered to have two fundamental shortcomings. The first was one of policy, in that the 1906 Act deliberately placed the insurer in the dominant position in a number of respects, chiefly the effect of breaching a warranty, and the pre-contractual duty of utmost good faith.[30] The second was one of drafting, namely the fact that the 1906 Act was written in such 'clear and forthright terms', which was thought to 'hamper the ability of judges to develop the law'.[31] It has been noted that the same criticism cannot be levelled at certain parts of the Insurance Act.[32] In all, therefore, the Law Commissions considered that whilst there was much in the 1906 Act worth preserving, certain aspects had become outdated, and increased the likelihood that insurance may fail to respond as expected, or at all.[33] This was seen as increasing the risk of insurance disputes, which caused delay, expense and uncertainty. There was also concern that unless the law was reformed, international trust in UK insurance in the international marketplace would be undermined.[34]

26 Law Com No 201.
27 Law Commissions' 2012 Joint Consultation Paper.
28 July 2014 Report.
29 The status of Law Commission papers as aids to constructions is considered below: see below, para.1.23 *et seq*.
30 July 2014 Report, para.1.25.
31 David Hertzell, 'The Insurance Act 2015 Background and Philosophy' in Clarke & Soyer 2016, 3.
32 *Arnould*, supp. to 18th edn, para.1.1–02.
33 July 2014 Report, para.1.3
34 Ibid.

Duty of utmost good faith and avoidance

1.12 The Law Commissions' leading criticism of the old law was the nature of the duty of utmost good faith and (above all) the sole remedy of avoidance for its breach. The Law Commissions identified two problems about the nature of the duty: it was not properly understood and was too onerous; and two undesirable consequences of the duty: the phenomena of data-dumping and underwriting at the claims stage. Under the old law, the duty of utmost good faith required the insured to disclose every material circumstance which it knew or ought to know before entering into a contract of insurance. The Law Commissions considered this to be a duty 'so wide and undefined that the policyholder can rarely be certain that they have complied with it'.[35] In medium-sized and large companies, in which material information could be very diffuse, there was said to be a lack of understanding of what a company knows or ought to know;[36] whose knowledge was relevant;[37] and what was a material matter for disclosure. This was thought to be causing widespread failure to disclose material information.[38] The duty of disclosure under the old law was also characterised as being too onerous, especially for medium-sized and large businesses, because every material circumstance may be of a significant or even 'insurmountable' volume.[39] This was caused in part by the volume of information now available to insureds and insurers, which has grown exponentially since the 1906 Act, meaning the old law was seen as increasingly anachronistic.[40]

1.13 A combination of the uncertainty about what was a material circumstance and what knowledge was relevant for the purposes of the duty of disclosure was said to cause 'data-dumping', which is the disclosure by an insured of vast quantities of unstructured information in an attempt to safeguard against the prospect of non-disclosure.[41] This phenomenon was blamed in part on the failure of the 1906 Act to make any provision on the way in which the insured must give disclosure to the insurer.[42] Aside from the obvious practical difficulties of data-dumping for the insurer, the Law Commissions were concerned that the practice could be used to 'bury' important information in a mountain of unprocessed and irrelevant material.[43] As well as data-dumping, the old law was said in certain cases to cause 'underwriting at the claims stage'. This was when an insurer would accept a poor-quality risk presentation without asking questions unless and until a claim arose,[44] whereupon the disclosure would be reviewed in detail in attempt to find a way to avoid the policy and therefore the claim for non-disclosure or misrepresentation.[45]

1.14 In spite of these misgivings about the nature of the insured's pre-contractual duty of utmost good faith and the problems to which it gave rise, the Law Commissions' central concern (shared by many) was the sole remedy of avoidance. It was described

35 Ibid., para.1.27.
36 Ibid., paras 3.11(2) and 5.8.
37 Ibid., para.5.15.
38 Ibid., para.5.10.
39 Ibid., para.5.14.
40 Ibid., paras 1.18 and 3.2.
41 Ibid., paras 3.7 and 5.28.
42 Ibid., para.5.28.
43 Ibid., para.5.29.
44 Ibid., para.5.37.
45 Ibid., paras 1.27 and 3.11(3).

variously as 'draconian',[46] 'all or nothing'[47], and a remedy that 'over protects' the insurer.[48] Avoidance did not discriminate based upon severity of the breach, but instead applied regardless of whether the misrepresentation or non-disclosure was fraudulent or innocent.[49] It also gave no room for consideration of what the insurer would actually have done differently, had the insured fulfilled its duty (such as charging a higher premium, or imposing different terms).[50] Finally, given the 'all or nothing' nature of avoidance, it created an inequality of arms which enabled insurers to use the threat of avoidance as a negotiating tool to reduce the cost of settlement.[51] These problems with avoidance could not be remedied by the common law, since the strictures of the 1906 Act provided that avoidance was the only remedy for breach of the duty of utmost good faith.[52] The Law Commissions therefore concluded that statutory reform relating to the duty of utmost good faith was essential.

Warranties and basis clauses

1.15 Shortly behind avoidance was the problem caused by the old law on breach of warranty. The Law Commissions criticised the fact that an insurer could rely upon a breach of warranty as discharging its liability even when the breach had been remedied by the time of loss, or if the breach of warranty did not cause or contribute to the actual loss.[53] For example, breach of a burglar alarm warranty would discharge the insurer from liability for loss caused by a flood or fire, even though the breach of warranty had nothing to do with the loss.[54] As with avoidance, this problem was created by the Marine Insurance Act 1906, which formerly provided in clear terms that breach of warranty led to automatic discharge of the insurer's liability, and the insured could not rely upon the defence that it had remedied its breach of warranty. Although the Law Commissions recognised that cases in which a technical breach of warranty was relied upon were 'very rare', it was thought that arguments based upon a breach of warranty may be used as a bargaining tool in order to drive down the cost of settlement of a claim.[55]

1.16 The Law Commissions considered that a specific instance of the injustice of warranties was seen in basis clauses, which typically took the form of a declaration by the insured that the statements contained in the insurance proposal formed the '*basis of the contract*'. Under the old law, this amounted to a warranty that all of the matters stated in the proposal were true. It followed that if any of the matters was incorrect, the insured was in breach of warranty and the insurer's liability was permanently discharged. Such clauses have long been criticised by the Law Commissions,[56] chiefly

46 Ibid., para.1.27.
47 Ibid., para.5.41.
48 Ibid., para.5.42.
49 Ibid., para.11.15.
50 Ibid., para.11.16.
51 Ibid., paras 5.42 and 11.19.
52 Sir Bernard Rix, 'Conclusion General reflections on the law reform', in Clarke and Soyer 2016, 115.
53 July 2014 Report, para.1.28.
54 Ibid., para.12.4(3).
55 Ibid., para.1.28.
56 Law Commission's 1980 Report, para.7.2.

because they enabled an insurer to evade liability for any error in the proposal, no matter how immaterial.[57] They were also thought to be little understood by insureds.[58] The Law Commissions therefore proposed their abolition.

Fraudulent claims

1.17 The Law Commissions have acknowledged that insurance fraud is a serious and expensive problem, and that the civil law must play a crucial role as a deterrent.[59] It was therefore considered necessary to have a clear statement of the consequences of insurance fraud as a matter of civil law, in order to act as a deterrent to wrongdoers.[60] However, the Law Commissions considered the law in this area to be somewhat confused,[61] as a result of tension between the common law rule that a fraudster forfeits (only) the fraudulent claim[62] (including any part of it that is genuine[63]), and the 1906 Act, which permitted the insurer to avoid the entire contract *ab initio* for breach of the duty of utmost good faith (suggesting that previous and future claims would also be affected).[64] In practice, the confusion was more theoretical than real, and the courts did not generally permit insurers to avoid in the context of fraudulent claims,[65] although there was some residual uncertainty over the point.[66] There was in addition uncertainty about the effect of a fraudulent claim on subsequent claims which were made in good faith. It was generally acknowledged that the making of a fraudulent claim amounted to a repudiatory breach of contract which gave the insurer a right to terminate, but the policy continued until such right was exercised, and any claim arising before the right was exercised had to be paid.[67] The contrary view was that the making of a fraudulent claim brought the contract to an end automatically, meaning any claim post-dating the fraud did not need to be paid. The Law Commissions saw fit to clarify the law on fraudulent claims, and have done so in the Insurance Act 2015.

Damages for late payment of an insurance claim

1.18 The Law Commissions criticised the fact that formerly, under English Law at least,[68] an indemnity insurer could not be liable for foreseeable loss caused by its

57 July 2014 Report, para.13.6 *et seq*.

58 Ibid., para.1.29.

59 July 2014 Report, paras 19.1–19.3.

60 Ibid., para.21.5.

61 Ibid., paras 1.31 & 20.1.

62 *Manifest Shipping Co Ltd v Uni-Polaris Insurance Co Ltd (The Star Sea)* [2001] UKHL 1, [2003] 1 AC 469, [62]–[67] (Lord Hobhouse).

63 *Galloway v Guardian Royal Exchange (UK) Ltd* [2999] Lloyd's Rep IR 209, 214 (Millett LJ).

64 Marine Insurance Act 1906, s.17.

65 For example, *Agapitos v Agnew (No 1) (The Aegeon)* [2002] EWCA Civ 247, [2003] QB 556, [45] (Mance LJ); *Axa General Insurance Ltd v Gottlieb* [2005] EWCA Civ 112, [2005] 1 All ER (Comm) 445.

66 *Manifest Shipping Co Ltd v Uni-Polaris Insurance Co Ltd (The Star Sea)* [2001] UKHL 1, [2003] 1 AC 469, [110] (Lord Scott).

67 *Axa General Insurance Ltd v Gottlieb* [2005] EWCA Civ 112, [2005] 1 All ER (Comm) 445, [22] (Mance LJ).

68 The position was otherwise in Scotland: *Strachan v The Scottish Boatowners Mutual Insurance Association* 2010 SC 367.

failure to pay a valid claim within a reasonable time.[69] For example, a factory owner whose premises were put out of action by vandals and whose insurance claim was disputed for a long time was forced to sell his business at a loss, yet he could not recover that loss when the insurers eventually accepted that the claim was valid.[70] Generally speaking, this was likely to be of greatest disadvantage to smaller insureds which were incapable of reinstating damage unless timely payment of an insurance claim was made (as in *Sprung*).[71]

1.19 The problem brought about by the old law was a product of the legal fiction whereby an indemnity insurer's duty is characterised as being to hold the insured harmless against the insured peril. In other words, the insurer is treated as having promised that the insured ship will not sink, or that the insured building will not burn down. If the insured peril causes loss, the insurer is liable in damages for breach of its duty to hold the insured harmless,[72] and English Law does not permit a party to claim damages for a failure to pay damages.[73] Whilst commenting that the legal fiction does not accord with the parties' understanding of the nature of their duties under a contract of insurance,[74] the Law Commissions have not sought to do away with the hold harmless fiction.[75] This reflects a recognition that the fiction serves a useful purpose, not least in providing certainty as to when the limitation period starts to run, and for the calculation of interest. Nonetheless, the Law Commissions criticised the bar on damages for late payment as unfair, as well as being out of line with the law in Scotland, other jurisdictions, and ordinary principles of contract.[76] They concluded that an insured should have a remedy where an insurer has acted unreasonably in delaying or refusing payment of a claim.[77]

Parliamentary passage of the Insurance Bill

1.20 The Insurance Act, like the Consumer Insurance (Disclosure and Representations) Act 2012, was enacted following the special procedure for uncontroversial Law Commission bills. This permits a bill to be introduced into the House of Lords and considered by a Special Public Bills Committee, thereby spending less time on the floor of the House of Lords and the Commons, and standing a substantially better prospect of being enacted. The Special Public Bills Committee procedure hands the conduct of the committee stage to a select committee, which can take written and oral evidence, before going through the bill clause by clause and considering amendments. Whilst any bill can be scrutinised in this way, the procedure is usually reserved for technical measures which are not controversial in party-political terms, such as

69 *Sprung v Royal Insurance (UK) Ltd* [1999] 1 Lloyd's Rep IR 111; *Apostolos Konstantine Ventouris v Trevor Rex Mountain (The Italia Express) (No 3)* [1992] 2 Lloyd's Rep 281.
70 *Sprung v Royal Insurance (UK) Ltd* [1999] 1 Lloyd's Rep IR 111.
71 July 2014 Report, para.26.9.
72 *Firma C-Trade SA v Newcastle Protection and Indemnity Association (The Fanti); Secony Mobil Oil Inc v West of England Shipowners Mutual Association (The Padre Island)* [1991] 2 AC 1, 35 (Lord Goff).
73 *The President of India v Lips Maritime Corporation (The Lips)* [1988] AC 395, 425 (Lord Brandon).
74 July 2014 Report, para.26.5.
75 Ibid., para.25.9.
76 Ibid., para.1.32.
77 Ibid., para.24.4.

uncontroversial Law Commission bills. However, the concept of an 'uncontroversial' bill is not defined for these purposes,[78] and appears to have been applied in the context of the Insurance Act with some fluidity, as will be seen. When it was introduced into the House of Lords, the Insurance Bill[79] was identified as being suitable for the special procedure described above. The original Bill attached to the July 2014 Report contained two provisions which proved difficult, however: clause 11 (on 'terms relevant to particular descriptions of loss'),[80] and clause 14 (on damages for late payment of an insurance claim).[81]

1.21 In essence, clause 11 provided that where a term would tend to reduce the risk of loss of a particular kind (if complied with), the insurer could not rely upon breach of such a term if the actual loss was of a different kind. After the Law Commissions published the July 2014 Report and draft Bill, there was significant opposition to clause 11 on the basis that it was uncertain[82] and too broad in scope.[83] The Treasury therefore asked the Law Commissions to redraft the provision. The Law Commissions produced a new draft clause 11 on 7 November 2014,[84] but the Government Minister (Lord Newby) appears to have considered even that revised clause as too controversial, when it was considered in the Special Public Bills Committee on 2 December 2014:

> *The Chairman [Lord Woolf]*: Do the Government intend to pursue the Law Commission's November 2014 revision of the clause governing terms not relevant to the loss?
>
> *Lord Newby*: The same arguments apply to this provision as to the first one.[85] Again, there was not a consensus among stakeholders on this. Certainly, members of the Committee will have seen the evidence submitted by the QC who had a number of arguments as to why he thought this was inappropriate or very difficult. At the moment, the Law Commission does not feel that there is consensus … [86]

1.22 In view of this, on 18 December 2014 the Special Public Bill Committee published a version of the Bill which did not include the revised version of clause 11.[87] Seemingly without explanation, there was a change of heart over Christmas, and the version of the Bill as amended at report stage, which was published on 9 January 2015, did include the revised version of clause 11.[88] Apparently, nothing had happened in the intervening period to make the formerly controversial clause 11 somehow uncontroversial. In any event, the Bill (including clause 11) was brought from the House of Lords on 16 January 2015, and received Royal Assent on 12 February 2015.

1.23 By contrast, the original clause 14 did not survive. Clause 14 of the Insurance Bill would have introduced into every contract of insurance an implied term requiring payment of sums due in respect of a claim within a reasonable time, breach of which

78 House of Lords Special Public Bill Committee, *Insurance Bill [HL]*, HL Paper 81, p.124.
79 HL Bill 2014–2015.
80 July 2014 Report, p.356 (Insurance Bill, cl.11).
81 Ibid., p.357 (Insurance Bill, cl.14).
82 HL Paper 81, p.78 (Memorandum submitted by the Law Commission, David Hertzell, para.17).
83 HL Paper 81, p.78 (Memorandum Submitted by BILA, para.39).
84 HL Paper 81, p.46.
85 i.e. the provisions on damages for late payment, which were considered too controversial for inclusion. See HL Paper 81, p.4.
86 HL Paper 81, p.6:
87 HL Bill 72 2014–2015.
88 HL Bill 76 2014–2015.

would have sounded in damages.[89] This reform was opposed during consultation by the Law Commissions in the summer of 2014, and the provisions on late payment were withdrawn before the Bill came before the Special Public Bill Committee.[90] However, the Government supported the policy behind the late payment provisions, and took the opportunity to include the relevant clauses in the Enterprise Bill introduced in 2015, which received Royal Assent as the Enterprise Act 2016 on 4 May 2016.

Aids to interpretation: Explanatory Notes and papers by the Law Commissions

1.24 Parts of the Insurance Act contain drafting which is (perhaps deliberately) ambiguous. Obvious examples include the 'reasonable search' and 'senior management' in section 4, a 'term defining the risk as a whole' in section 11(1), the meaning of the test in section 11(3), and what is a 'reasonable time' in which to pay a claim under section 13A(1).[91] This difficulty is compounded by the absence of decided cases under the Insurance Act.[92] There are, however, a large number of thoroughly researched Law Commission papers which are bound to be of considerable utility in understanding the Act and how it is intended to operate. There are also the Explanatory Notes, which are more limited. A comprehensive treatment of the principles of statutory interpretation is beyond the scope of this book, and the reader should consult specialist works on that subject.[93] However, given the particular relevance of the status of Explanatory Notes and Law Commission papers, this matter is discussed below.

1.25 The task confronting a court when construing any statute is to determine Parliament's intention, which is to be ascertained from the words of the statute. Explanatory Notes and Law Commission papers are not directly admissible in construing the words of a statute.[94] However, it does not follow that these sources are irrelevant. They are likely to have 'considerable influence' on the meaning of the Act,[95] or at the very least the proper approach to construction is likely to be informed by what the Law Commissions were attempting to achieve.[96]

1.26 Reports of the Law Commissions may be referred to in order to discern the mischief which Parliament intended to address and the policy behind a given statute.[97] In *Black-Clawson*, Viscount Dilhorne asked: 'what more accurate source of information both as to the law at the time and as to the evil or defect which the Act was intended to remedy can be imagined than … the reports of the Law Commission?'[98] In *Yaxley v Gotts,* Law Commission papers were referred to as 'invaluable guides to

89 July 2014 Report, p.357 (cl.14).

90 HL Paper 81, pp.52, 68 and 123–124.

91 For further examples of those parts of the Act which are likely to be difficult, see the evidence of Lord Mance to the Special Public Bills Committee at HL Paper 81, pp.55–60.

92 See fn.8 above.

93 Oliver Jones & Francis A.R. Bennion, *Bennion on Statutory Interpretation* 6th edn (LexisNexis, London, 2013); Daniel Greenberg, *Craies on Legislation* 11th edn (Sweet & Maxwell, London, 2016).

94 *Arnould*, supp. to 18th edn, para.1.1–03.

95 Sir Bernard Rix, 'Conclusion General reflections on the law reform' in Clarke & Soyer 2016, 110.

96 *Arnould*, supp. to 18th edn, para.1.2–02.

97 *Black-Clawson International Ltd. v Papierwerke Waldhof-Aschaffenburg A.G.* [1975] AC 591, 622–623 (Viscount Dilhorne).

98 *Black-Clawson International Ltd. v Papierwerke Waldhof-Aschaffenburg A.G.* [1975] AC 591, 622–623 (Viscount Dilhorne).

the old law and to the problems which constituted the "mischief"'[99] For this reason, Clarke LJ said that where 'a statute has been enacted as a result of the recommendations of the Law Commission, it is, as I see it, both appropriate and permissible for the court to consider those recommendations in order to help to identify both the mischief which the Act is designed to cure and the public policy underlying it ... although ... they cannot be conclusive as to how a particular provision should be construed ...'[100]

1.27 The utility of Law Commission papers is not limited to identifying the nature of the mischief, however. Where, as in the case of the Insurance Act, there is a report by the Law Commission attaching a draft Bill (i.e. the July 2014 Report) the courts are entitled to compare the provisions of the draft Bill with those of the Act, and if there is no material difference in their language, the court may legitimately conclude that Parliament accepted the recommendation of the Law Commission and intended to implement it.[101] As Viscount Dilhorne said in *Black-Clawson*, where a committee or the Law Commissions publish a report and draft Bill which is enacted without alteration:

> it can safely be assumed that it was Parliament's intention to do what the committee recommended and to achieve the object the committee had in mind. Then, in my view the recommendations of the committee and their observations on their draft Bill may form a valuable aid to construction which the courts should not be inhibited from taking into account.

That observation applies to much of the Insurance Act, although it is not a mirror image of the draft Bill attached to the Law Commissions July 2014 Report.[102] That Report is, therefore, likely to be of particular utility in interpreting the Insurance Act, and extensive reference is made to it throughout this book.

1.28 As for Explanatory Notes, these are an admissible aid to construction insofar as they cast light on the objective setting and contextual scene of the statute, and the mischief at which it is aimed.[103] However, as Lord Steyn said in *R. (on the application of Westminster City Council) v National Asylum Support Service*, it is:

> impermissible ... to treat the wishes and desires of the Government about the scope of the statutory language as reflecting the will of Parliament. The aims of the Government in respect of the meaning of clauses as revealed in explanatory notes cannot be attributed to Parliament. The object is to see what is the intention expressed by the words enacted.[104]

---

99 *Yaxley v Gotts* [2000] Ch 162, 176 (Robert Walker LJ).

100 Ibid., 182 (Clarke LJ).

101 *Black-Clawson International Ltd. v Papierwerke Waldhof-Aschaffenburg A.G.* [1975] AC 591, 622–623. (Viscount Dilhorne).

102 The exceptions are Insurance Act 2015, s.4(4), s.4(8)(a) and s.11, the provisions relating to damages for late payment, and the provisions amending the Third Parties (Rights Against Insurers) Act 2010.

103 *Flora v Wakom* [2007] 1 WLR 482, [15]–[17] (Brooke LJ).

104 [2002] 1 WLR 2956, [6].

CHAPTER 2

Application of the Act

22 Application etc. of Parts 2 to 5

(1) Part 2 (and section 21) and section 14 apply only in relation to—

a. contracts of insurance entered into after the end of the relevant period, and
b. variations, agreed after the end of the relevant period, to contracts of insurance entered into at any time.

(2) Parts 3 and 4 of this Act apply only in relation to contracts of insurance entered into after the end of the relevant period, and variations to such contracts.

(3) In subsections (1) and (2) "the relevant period" means the period of 18 months beginning with the day on which this Act is passed.

(4) Unless the contrary intention appears, references in Parts 2 to 5 to something being done by or in relation to the insurer or the insured include its being done by or in relation to that person's agent.

23 Extent, commencement and short title

(1) This Act extends to England and Wales, Scotland and Northern Ireland, except for

a. section 21(4), which does not extend to Northern Ireland; and
b. section 21(5), which extends to Northern Ireland only.

(2) This Act (apart from Part 6 and this section) comes into force at the end of the period of 18 months beginning with the day on which it is passed.

(3) In Part 6—

a. section 19 comes into force at the end of the period of two months beginning with the day on which this Act is passed; and
b. section 20 and Schedule 2 come into force on the day appointed under section 21(2) of the Third Parties (Rights against Insurers) Act 2010 for the coming into force of that Act.

(4) This section comes into force on the day on which this Act is passed.

(5) This Act may be cited as the Insurance Act 2015.

Commencement: when did the Act come into force?

2.1 The Act came into force on 12 August 2016, which was 18 months after the date of Royal Assent on 12 February 2015,[1] subject to four exceptions described below. The following Parts therefore came into force on 12 August 2016: Part 2 (the duty of fair presentation), Part 3 (Warranties and Other Terms), Part 4 (Fraudulent Claims) and Part 5 (Good Faith and Contracting out). Consequently, and subject to the four exceptions below, any contract of insurance entered into on or after 12 August 2016 which is

1 Insurance Act 2015, s.23(2).

governed by the laws of the United Kingdom[2] will be governed by the Act. 'Contract of insurance' is not defined in the Insurance Act (or the Marine Insurance Act), and the meaning of that phrase will continue to be governed by the common law.[3]

2.2 There are four exceptions to the commencement date of 12 August 2016. Firstly, section 23 (which governs the extent and commencement of the Act) came into force on 12 February 2015, being the day the Act was passed (as is customary).[4] Secondly, section 19 came into force on 12 April 2016, being two months after the date of Royal Assent.[5] Section 19 amends the Third Parties (Rights Against Insurers) Act 2010, and in particular the powers of the Secretary of State to alter the meaning of a 'relevant person' in that statute. Thirdly, section 20 and Schedule 2 came into force on 1 August 2016, which was the day appointed under section 21(2) of the Third Parties (Rights Against Insurers) Act 2010.[6] Section 20 and Schedule 2 amend the Third Parties (Rights Against Insurers) Act 2010 in relation to the insured persons to whom the Act applies.[7] Finally, and of particular pertinence, section 13A of the Act came into force on 4 May 2017. Section 13A was introduced into the Act through Part 5 of the Enterprise Act 2016.[8] As a result, there will be implied into every insurance contract a duty on the part of the insurer to pay all sums due in respect of a claim within a reasonable time, failing which the insured may have a remedy in damages for loss suffered as a result of the late payment.[9] Being a late addition to the Act, section 13A came into force a year after the Enterprise Act 2016 received Royal Assent.[10] The table below summarises the dates when the various parts of the Act came into force.

2.3 It has been explained that the Act came into force on 12 August 2016, subject to the exceptions above. The Act therefore applies to all contracts of insurance entered into on or after 12 August 2016.[11] For example, if one insurer in a subscription market agreed to underwrite a risk on 11 August 2016, and four additional underwriters agreed to underwrite the same risk on 12 August 2016, the former contract would be governed by the old law, whereas the latter four contracts would be governed by the Act. It would follow (for example) that the duty owed to the first insurer at placing would be the old duty of utmost good faith, whereas the other four insurers would be owed the duty of fair presentation. If either duty was breached, the remedies available would differ.[12] Similarly, if the contracts contained a warranty with which the

---

2 That is to say the laws of either England and Wales, Scotland or Northern Ireland. Technically, there is of course no such thing as United Kingdom Law, and the phrase is used herein as shorthand for the laws of each of the constituent parts of the United Kingdom of Great Britain and Northern Ireland.

3 Law Com No 353, 2.5. See John Birds, Ben Lynch, Simon Milnes, *MacGillivray on Insurance Law* 13th edn (Sweet & Maxwell, London, 2015) (hereafter *MacGillivray* 2015), 1–001.

4 Insurance Act 2015, s.23(4).

5 Insurance Act 2015, s.23(3)(a).

6 Third Parties (Right Against Insurers) Act 2010 (Commencement) Order 2016, SI 2016/550, art.2: 'The Third Parties (Rights Against Insurers) Act 2010, so far as not already in force, comes into force on 1st August 2016.'

7 The Third Parties (Right Against Insurers) Act 2010 is beyond the scope of this work, and specialist texts on that subject should be consulted.

8 Enterprise Act 2016, ss.28–30.

9 See Chapter 10.

10 Insurance Act 2015, s.23(2).

11 Ibid.

12 See Chapter 5.

Table 2.1 Dates of coming into force of the Act

Part or section of Act	*Date in force*
Section 23 (commencement and extent of the Act)	12 February 2015[1]
Section 19 (meaning of 'relevant person' in Third Parties (Rights Against Insurers) Act 2010)	12 April 2016[2]
Section 20 and Schedule 2 (amending the insured persons to whom the Third Parties (Rights Against Insurers) Act 2010 applies)	1 August 2016[3]
Section 13A (late payment of insurance claims)	4 May 2017[4]
Remainder of the Act	12 August 2016[5]

1. Insurance Act 2015, s.23(4).
2. Insurance Act 2015, s.23(3)(a).
3. Third Parties (Right Against Insurers) Act 2010 (Commencement) Order 2016, SI 2016/550, art.2: 'The Third Parties (Rights against Insurers) Act 2010, so far as not already in force, comes into force on 1st August 2016.'
4. Enterprise Act 2016, s.44(3).
5. Insurance Act 2015, s.23(2).

insured failed to comply, the first insurer's liability would be permanently discharged,[13] whereas the liability of the other four insurers would be suspended unless and until the breach of warranty was remedied.[14]

2.4 The position is different for contractual variations: it is not the case that every part of the Act will apply to every contractual variation concluded on or after 12 August 2016. Part 2 of the Act (i.e. the duty of fair presentation, remedies for its breach, and the law on knowledge for the purposes of the duty) applies to any variation to a contract concluded on or after 12 August 2016, regardless of when the actual contract was concluded.[15] Before the Act, where the insured wished to vary the terms of the original contract so that the insurer took on additional risk, the insured would owe a duty to disclose all known circumstances that were material to the variation, and to desist from making any material misrepresentation in respect of the variation.[16] The position is analogous under the Act: if the insured seeks to vary a contract so that the insurer takes on additional risk, it will owe the duty of fair presentation in respect of that risk. That will be the case regardless of when the original contract was concluded (whether before or after 12 August 2016). Accordingly, it is possible that one could have a contractual variation in respect of which the insured must fulfil the duty of fair presentation, even though the original contract was concluded before 12 August 2016, at which time the insured owed the duty of utmost good faith. For example, a marine policy insuring a vessel was concluded on 1 January 2016, and on 1 September 2016 the insured asked the insurer to agree to cover the vessel whilst it was outside the territorial limits of the policy, which the insurer agreed to do in return for additional premium. The insured would owe the duty of fair presentation before that variation to

13 Marine Insurance Act 1906, s.33(3).

14 Insurance Act 2015, s.10: see Chapter 6.

15 Insurance Act 2015, s.22(1)(b): 'Part 2 … [applies] only in relation to … variations, agreed after the end of the relevant period, to contracts entered into at any time.'

16 *Black King Shipping Corporation* v *Massie (The Litsion Pride)* [1985] 1 Lloyd's Rep 437 [511]; *Iron Trades Mutual Insurance v Companhia de Seguros Imperio* (1992) 1 Re LR 213, [224].

the contract was entered into. If the insured failed to fulfil the duty, the insurer might be entitled to the proportionate remedies in Schedule 1.[17] However, if the insured breached the duty of utmost good faith which it owed before the original contract was concluded (which was before the Act came into force), the insurer's only remedy would be avoidance.

2.5 The position differs when it comes to the application of Parts 3 and 4 of the Act to contractual variations. Parts 3 and 4 govern warranties and other terms, and fraudulent claims respectively. Both of those Parts apply to any contract of insurance concluded on or after 12 August 2016, and also to any variation to a contract of insurance, if the contract was concluded on or after 12 August 2016.[18] However, Parts 3 and 4 do not apply to contractual variations if the contract was concluded before 12 August 2016.[19] Where a contract of insurance was entered into on 1 January 2016, and was then varied through the addition of a warranty on 13 August 2016, that warranty would not be subject to the Act, because the contract was concluded before 12 August 2016. However, in those circumstances the insured would owe the duty of fair presentation in respect of the variation, notwithstanding the original contract was concluded before 12 August 2016.[20]

Insurance, reinsurance and retrocession

2.6 Although the point is not made expressly in the Act, it will apply to all contracts of insurance, reinsurance and retrocession. Contracts of reinsurance and retrocession are treated as contracts of insurance at common law.[21] In such contracts, the party purchasing the insurance (the insurer or the reinsurer) is the 'insured' for the purposes of the Act, and the party providing the insurance (the reinsurer or the retrocessionaire) is the 'insurer'.[22]

When is a contract 'entered into'?

2.7 It is important to understand when a contract of insurance (or variation) was 'entered into'[23], since only then may one ascertain whether or not it is governed by the Act. A contract is 'entered into' at the moment of agreement between the insured and the insurer. In the Lloyd's Market, that is likely in most cases to be the moment when the underwriter scratches a slip or Market Reform Contract[24] accepting a proportion

17 See Chapter 5.

18 Insurance Act 2015, s.22(2).

19 Insurance Act 2015, s.22(2). That is because Parts 3 and 4 of the Act 'apply only in relation to contracts of insurance entered into after the end of the relevant period, and *variations to such contracts*.' In other words, Parts 3 and 4 do not apply to variations to contracts concluded *before* 12 August 2016. See Explanatory Notes to the Insurance Act 2015, para.149.

20 Insurance Act 2015, s.22(1)(b).

21 *Delver, Assignee of Bunn v Barnes* (1807) 1 Taunt 48, 127 ER 748.

22 Explanatory Notes to the Insurance Act 2015, para.36.

23 Taking the words in Insurance Act 2015 s.22(1)(a). s.22(1)(b) refers to variations 'agreed', which has a materially identical meaning to 'entered into'.

24 The Market Reform Contract (or MRC) replaced a standardised London Market slip with effect from 1 July 2007, and its use has been mandatory as regards most Lloyd's business (and accordingly has been widely adopted in the London market generally) since 1 November 2007. The MRC is designed to be

of the risk, which creates a binding contract between the parties.[25] It should be noted that the date when a contract of insurance is entered into is not necessarily the same as the inception date; indeed, the two are often distinct, and should not be confused. The inception date is the time when the insurer begins to run the risk insured, which is usually later than the date when the parties enter into the contract.

2.8 There are other more complicated cases, however. This is particularly true of open cover insurance and treaty reinsurance, where there may be uncertainty over when a contract is entered into (and therefore whether it is governed by the Act, or not). Some of the possibilities are summarised below.

2.9 In obligatory/obligatory (oblig/oblig) contracts, floating policies and treaty reinsurance, the insured must cede certain risks and the insurer must take them. The contract is therefore entered into on a specific date, and subsequent declarations of risks by the insured do not give rise to new contracts.[26] Therefore, if an oblig/oblig open cover is concluded before 12 August 2016, but risks are ceded to the open cover after that date, the contract will nonetheless be governed by the old law. That would remain the case even if the open cover remained afoot for many years after 12 August 2016, provided the original contract was concluded before that date.

2.10 An oblig/oblig contract is to be contrasted with facultative/obligatory (fac/oblig) contracts, under which the insured has a choice as to which risks it cedes, but the insurer must take all of the risks ceded. It is as though the insurer has made a standing offer to the insured to take such business as might be ceded to him at the insured's option. In such a case, the cession of each risk by way of a declaration by the insured gives rise to an individual contract.[27] Therefore, if a fac/oblig open cover is concluded before 12 August 2016, but risks are ceded after that date, the contract governing the individual cession will be governed by the Act. However, at the time of each declaration, the insured will not owe the (new) duty of fair presentation to the insurer, because in a fac/oblig contract, no fresh duty of disclosure is owed at the time of each declaration, essentially because the insurer has no choice but to take the risks declared.[28]

2.11 Finally, there is the facultative/facultative contract, under which the insured has a choice as to whether to cede risks, and the insurer has a choice as to whether to take them.[29] As with fac/oblig contracts above, this is a contract for insurance under which the cession of each risk produces a fresh contract, meaning that cessions which post-date 12 August 2016 will be governed by the Act, even if the original contract was concluded before this date.

2.12 A further scenario worth considering is the contract of insurance which exists for a long period of time, such as the long-tail contracts commonly seen in

---

used both as a placing document (in substitution for the traditional slip) and as the final contract of insurance. In accordance with the Contract Certainty Code of Practice issued by the London Market Group (www.londonmarketgroup.co.uk), the MRC is intended to include all the terms of the contract between the insurer and the insured. See Julian Burling, *Lloyd's: Law and Practice* (Informa, London, 2013), paras 11.4, 11.5.

25 *General Reinsurance Corp. v Forsakringsaktiebolaget Fennia Patria* [1983] QB 856 (CA), [1983] 2 Lloyd's Rep 287.

26 For example, *The Beursgracht,* [2001] EWCA Civ 2051, [2002] 1 Lloyd's Rep 574 [21] (Tuckey LJ).

27 *Glencore International AG v Alpina Insurance Company Limited (No 2)* [2004] EWHC 66 (Comm), [2004] 1 Lloyd's Rep 567.

28 *Citadel Insurance Co v Atlantic Insurance Co SA* [1982] 2 Lloyd's Rep 543 (CA) [548] (Kerr LJ).

29 As in *Berger and Light Diffusers Pty Ltd v Pollock* [1973] 2 Lloyd's Rep 442 (Com Ct).

life insurance. In such a case, if the contract is concluded before 12 August 2016, but not renewed for (say) 10 years, it will remain subject to the old law. If, however, the contract is renewed at some point after 12 August 2016, a new contract will have been concluded, which will be subject to the Act.

Is the contract governed by UK law?

2.13 The Insurance Act will apply to any contract of insurance (including reinsurance and retrocession) which is governed by the laws of the constituent parts of the United Kingdom; namely the laws of England and Wales, Scotland or Northern Ireland. In the majority of cases, a contract of insurance will contain a jurisdiction clause which ought to state in clear terms the applicable law governing the contract (indeed, this is now a requirement for all policies underwritten at Lloyd's[30]). If there is no jurisdiction clause, a contract of insurance that was placed in London, or which contains a London arbitration or English High Court jurisdiction clause, is likely to be governed by English law.[31] However, the question of applicable law may be a complicated one which is beyond the scope of this work.[32]

Extent: where does the Act apply?

2.14 The Act will apply to the whole of the United Kingdom; that is, under the laws of England and Wales, Scotland and Northern Ireland. The only exception is the consequential provision in section 21(4), which does not extend to Northern Ireland, and section 21(5), which extends only to Northern Ireland. This reflects distinctions between the Road Traffic Act 1988 (the relevant parts of which apply in England and Wales, and Scotland) and the Road Traffic (Northern Ireland) Order 1981, which applies only in Northern Ireland.

---

30 Contract Certainty Code of Practice; Lloyd's Performance Management Directorate Market Bulletin Y4821.

31 However, as regards risks situated within European Economic Area States, in respect of insurance contracts entered into after 17 December 2009, the applicable law is to be determined under Regulation 593/2008 (commonly referred to as the Rome I Regulation). Although a detailed analysis of the application of the Rome I Regulation is beyond the scope of this work, it should be noted that unless the risk is a Large Risk or is a contract of reinsurance, in general a choice of law clause in the contract of insurance will not bind the insured unless the choice is of the law of the Member State in which the risk is situated at the time the contract is concluded (which will apply in the absence of a choice of law) or is the law of the place of habitual residence of the insured: *MacGillivray* 2015, para.13–074. 'Large Risks' are defined in art.5(d) of Council Directive 73/239/EEC, as amended by art.5 of Directive 88/357/EEC, and art.2 of Directive 90/618/EEC. In summary, large risks are risks of the following types: (a) aircraft; (b) ships; (c) goods in transit; (d) aircraft liability and liability for ships; (e) credit and suretyship risks which relate to business carried on by the policyholder; and (f) vehicle, fire, property, motor vehicle liability, general liability or miscellaneous financial loss risks where the policyholder carries on a business which satisfies certain conditions as to balance sheet total, net turnover and number of employees: *MacGillivray*, 2015, Ch.13, fn.205.

32 See *MacGillivray*, 2015, Ch.13; and for detailed coverage of the conflict of laws, see Lord Collins and others, *Dicey, Morris & Collins on the Conflict of Laws*, 15th edn (Sweet & Maxwell, London, 2016) and, Adrian Briggs, *Civil Jurisdiction and Judgments*, 6th edn (Informa, London, 2015).

Application to consumer vs. non-consumer insurance

2.15 Different Parts of the Act will apply to 'consumer' and/or 'non-consumer' insurance, as illustrated in Table 2.2 below.

2.16 It is therefore necessary to understand the difference between consumer and non-consumer insurance contracts. A 'consumer insurance contract' is one where 'the insured is an individual who enters into the contract wholly or mainly for purposes unrelated to that individual's business, trade or profession'.[33] It has been said that if the insured is anything other than a natural person (or persons), such as a company, trust or corporation, the policy cannot be a consumer insurance contract.[34] If the insured is a natural person or persons, whether he or she is a consumer depends upon the individual's subjective motivation for entering into the contract of insurance. For example, an individual insures his car intending to use it primarily for personal reasons, but occasionally for work. Provided his intention is that the car will be put mainly to personal use, it will be a consumer insurance contract.[35] It does not matter if the insured intends occasionally to use the car for business purposes, since the definition of consumer insurance specifically provides for mixed use insurance.[36] Provided the intended use is primarily for purposes outside the business, trade or profession, it will be a consumer insurance contract. However, if the insured intends to use the insured car primarily for a taxi service, it would be a non-consumer insurance contract. If, at the time the insurance was entered into, the insured contemplated that the car would be used mainly for personal reasons, but during the policy term he began to use the car mainly in connection with his business, it will nonetheless be a non-consumer

Table 2.2 Application of the Act to consumer/non-consumer insurance

Part	*Relevance*	*Application*
2	Duty of fair presentation; knowledge of insured & insurer; remedies for breach of the duty.	Non-consumer insurance only[1]
3	Warranties and terms not relevant to the loss	Consumer and non-consumer insurance
4	Fraudulent claims and late payment damages	Consumer and non-consumer insurance
5	Good faith and contracting out	Consumer and non-consumer insurance[2]
6	Amendment of the Third Parties (Rights Against Insurers) Act 2010	Consumer and non-consumer insurance
7	General provisions	Consumer and non-consumer insurance

1. For the equivalent law in consumer insurance, see Consumer Insurance (Disclosure and Representations) Act 2012.
2. Different rules on contracting out apply to consumer and non-consumer insurance; see Chapter 8.

33 Consumer Insurance (Disclosure and Representations) Act 2012, s.1. This definition applies under s.1 of the Act.
34 Explanatory Notes to the Consumer Insurance (Disclosure and Representations) Act 2012, para.18.
35 Ibid., para.18; see also Law Com No 319, [5.17]–[5.18].
36 Law Com No 319, [5.17]–[5.18].

insurance contract, since the relevant consideration is the policyholder's purpose at the time the insurance contract is concluded.[37] However, if at the time of renewal the insured intends to continue using the car primarily in connection with his business trade or profession, it will be a non-consumer contract.

2.17 The subjective intention of the insured might not be determinative of whether a policy is consumer or non-consumer insurance in every case, and in certain cases an objective assessment of the purpose of the insurance will be necessary. For example, an insured buys property insurance for a building which comprises a shop with a flat above it. The insured's subjective belief is that the insurance is primarily for purposes unrelated to his business running the shop, but if the flat is over the shop and the insured buys one policy in respect of both, that is likely to be non-consumer insurance, when one considers the objective purpose of the insurance. That is because the insurance would not in those circumstances be mainly for purposes unrelated to the insured's business, trade or profession.

2.18 The phrase 'business, trade or profession' is intended to be interpreted widely.[38] It will capture insurance taken out in connection with an individual's job, but the phrase extends more widely than this. For example, the Law Commissions have indicated that where an individual lets a property commercially and takes out insurance for it, that will be non-consumer insurance, even if commercial letting is not the insured's main job.[39] Presumably, that is because the insurance is taken out in connection with the insured's 'business' or, perhaps, 'trade', namely commercial letting. The Law Commissions have also indicated that in their view, an individual who takes out insurance to protect his income in the event of illness or disability would be considered a consumer, regardless of whether the income was gained through employment or self-employment.[40] Presumably, that is because the insured's purpose was to protect his income, and that purpose is arguably unrelated to the insured's business, trade or profession. It has also been said that if an individual were to insure an employee's health, this would normally be for business purposes.[41] That will probably be correct in most cases, but not where (for example) somebody insures the health of his personal butler, which is presumably for purposes unconnected to his business, trade or profession.

2.19 In distinguishing between consumer and non-consumer contracts of insurance, the Law Commissions have indicated that the courts may have regard to relevant case law in other areas.[42] In *Standard Bank London Ltd v Apostolakis (No 1)* a married couple resident in Greece entered into a foreign exchange agreement with a UK bank involving considerable sums of money (up to US$7 million). The bank later closed several of the transactions, allegedly causing loss to the couple. The couple argued that their contracts were consumer contracts for the purposes of the Unfair Terms in Consumer Contracts Regulations 1999, which defined a consumer as 'any natural person who … is acting for purposes which are outside his trade, business

37 Law Com No 319, 5.12. This is consistent with the definition in section 1 of the 2012 Act, which refers to a contract where the 'insured is an individual who *enters into* the contract wholly or mainly for' non-business purposes.

38 Explanatory Notes to the Insurance Bill, para.A.4, cit. Law Com No 319, p.147.

39 Law Com No 319, 5.18.

40 Ibid.

41 Law Com No 319, 5.18.

42 Consumer Insurance Law: Pre-Contract Disclosure and Misrepresentation (Law Com No 319), 5.16.

or profession'. The couple in question were a civil engineer and a lawyer. Longmore J held 'it is certainly not part of a person's trade as a civil engineer or a lawyer (as Mr and Mrs Apostolakis respectively were) to enter into foreign exchange contracts. The only question is whether Mr and Mrs Apostolakis were engaging in the trade of foreign exchange contracts as such. I do not consider that they were. They were disposing of income which they had available'.[43] The large scale of their transactions was not a determining factor.[44] The contract was therefore a consumer contract.

2.20 Comparisons with the definition of a consumer contract in other areas must be treated with some caution, however. Under the Act, a consumer insurance contract may qualify as such notwithstanding it is taken out partly for business purposes. That was a deliberate decision on the part of the Law Commissions, since it reflects the reality of mixed-use policies.[45] Provided the insurance is 'wholly or mainly' for purposes unrelated to the business, trade or profession, it is a consumer contract.[46] Contrastingly, the definition in the Unfair Terms in Consumer Contracts Regulations 1999, which was considered in *Apostolakis*,[47] does not provide expressly for mixed-use contracts. The same is true of the FCA definition of a consumer,[48] which follows the definition used in the EU Directive on Distance Marketing of Consumer Financial Services,[49] and a range of EU consumer directives, including directives on unfair terms and consumer sales.[50] The definition is also similar to that used in the Brussels Convention on Jurisdiction.[51] The Law Commissions considered these formulations, but decided to insert the words 'wholly or mainly' into the definition of a consumer insurance contract, lest a policyholder be deprived of the protection afforded to consumers merely because the insurance had some peripheral business use.[52] For example, a person taking out home insurance where there was a room in the house occasionally used as an office should nonetheless be treated as a consumer.[53]

2.21 Any insurance contract which is not a consumer contract will be a non-consumer contract.[54]

---

43 *Standard Bank London Ltd v Apostolakis* [2002] CLC 933 (Com Ct) 936–937 (Longmore J).

44 Ibid.

45 Law Com No 319, 5.17–5.18.

46 Consumer Insurance (Disclosure and Representations) Act 2012, s.1. This definition applies under Insurance Act 2015, s.1.

47 See para.2.19 above.

48 ICOBS Rule 2.1.1(3) defines a consumer as a natural person who is acting for purposes that are 'outside his trade or profession'.

49 Directive 2002/65/EC of 23 September 2002 concerning the distance marketing of consumer financial services and amending Council Directive 90/619/EEC and Directives 97/7/EC and 98/27/EC [2002] OJ L 271/16, art.2(d).

50 For example, directives on Doorstep Selling (Council Directive 85/577/EEC of 20 December 1985 to protect the consumer in respect of contracts negotiated away from business premises [1985] OJ L 372/31); Distance Selling (Directive 97/7/EC of 20 May 1997 on the protection of consumers in respect of distance contracts [1997] OJ L 144/19) and Consumer Sales (Directive 1999/44/EC of 25 May 1999 on certain aspects of the sale of consumer goods and associated guarantees [1999] L171/12) use a similar approach, though there are some minor variations in the words used.

51 Brussels Convention on Jurisdiction and Enforcement of Judgments in Civil and Commercial Matters 1968 [1972] OJ 299/32, art.13: 'a purpose which can be regarded as being outside his trade or profession'. See also Civil Jurisdiction and Judgments Act 1982, sch.8, rule 3(1).

52 Law Com No 319, 5.8–5.12.

53 Law Com No 319, 5.17.

54 Insurance Act 2015, s.1: '"non-consumer insurance contract" means a contract of insurance that is not a consumer insurance contract.'

CHAPTER 3

The duty of fair presentation

3 The duty of fair presentation

(1) Before a contract of insurance is entered into, the insured must make to the insurer a fair presentation of the risk.

(2) The duty imposed by subsection (1) is referred to in this Act as 'the duty of fair presentation'.

(3) A fair presentation of the risk is one –

- (a) which makes the disclosure required by subsection (4),
- (b) which makes that disclosure in a manner which would be reasonably clear and accessible to a prudent insurer, and
- (c) in which every material representation as to a matter of fact is substantially correct, and very material representation as to a matter of expectation or belief is made in good faith.

(4) The disclosure required is as follows, except as provided in subsection (5) –

- (a) disclosure of every material circumstance which the insured knows or ought to know, or
- (b) failing that, disclosure which gives the insurer sufficient information to put a prudent insurer on notice that it needs to make further enquiries for the purpose of revealing those material circumstances.

(5) In the absence of enquiry, subsection (4) does not require the insured to disclose a circumstance if –

- (a) it diminishes the risk,
- (b) the insurer knows it,
- (c) the insurer ought to know it,
- (d) the insurer is presumed to know it, or
- (e) it is something as to which the insurer waives information.

(6) Sections 4 to 6 make further provision about the knowledge of the insured and of the insurer, and section 7 contains supplementary provision.

The pre-contractual duties

3.1 As confirmed in Lord Mansfield's judgment in *Carter v Boehm*[1] 250 years ago, a contract of insurance is one of the utmost good faith. As a consequence, English law has imposed on the insured duties of disclosure consisting of an obligation to disclose, and not to misrepresent, to the underwriter all circumstances material to the risk to be underwritten prior to the underwriter entering into the insurance contract. These principles were codified in sections 17 to 20 of the Marine Insurance Act 1906.

1 (1766) 3 Burr. 1905, 97 ER 1162.

3.2 Following the Consumer Insurance (Disclosure and Representations) Act 2012 (CIDRA), a consumer buying insurance is under no such duty to disclose in respect of contracts entered into on or after 6 April 2013 (sections 2(1) and 12(2) CIDRA). The consumer's only duty is to take reasonable care not to make a misrepresentation of a material circumstance to the insurer (section 2(2) CIDRA). A consumer for these purposes is 'an individual who enters into the contract wholly or mainly for purposes unrelated to the individual's trade, business or profession' and the contract which they enter into is a 'consumer insurance contract' (section 1 CIDRA). All other contracts are non-consumer insurance contracts (section 1 Insurance Act). For example, if Ms Jones buys property insurance for her flat, it will be consumer insurance, but if she buys property insurance for her shop, it will be non-consumer insurance. If her flat is over the shop and she buys one policy in respect of both, that is likely to be non-consumer insurance (see paragraphs 2.16–2.20).

3.3 Section 3 of the Insurance Act preserves the insured's duties of disclosure for non-consumer insurance contracts and defines them as a duty of fair presentation. Although the Law Reform Committee's 1957 Report, the Law Commission's 1980 Report, and the Law Commissions' 2007 Joint Consultation Paper considered and proposed revisions to the duties, the Law Commissions' 2012 Joint Consultation Paper proposed that the duty of fair presentation should be set out in the legislation based on principles drawn from the case law (paragraph 2.30 of the 2012 Consultation Paper). This was confirmed in the Law Commissions' Notes accompanying the first draft clauses of the Insurance Bill in January 2014: 'We have therefore adopted an evolutionary approach, building on the current case law.'[2] That is largely reflected in section 3 with one subtle change from the prior case law that may have a significant impact in practice, being the insurer's obligation to ask questions if put on notice that disclosure is not complete.

3.4 The Insurance Act does, however, make major departures from the prior case law and the provisions of the Marine Insurance Act 1906 in its definition of what is to be treated as the insured's and the insurer's knowledge for the purposes of disclosure. The remedies for breach of the insured's duties of disclosure are also changed significantly by the Insurance Act. These topics are the subject of separate chapters.

Who owes the duty of fair presentation?

3.5 The duty of fair presentation is owed by the insured to the insurer. The insured means the party to the contract of insurance that is subsequently entered into (section 1 Insurance Act). As the Law Commissions acknowledged in paragraphs 7.14 and 7.15 of their July 2014 Report, 'one party may enter into a contract on behalf of others', and that who 'the insured' is, or are, will be 'a question of construction of the

2 Para.2.10 'Reforming Insurance Contract Law: Initial Draft Clauses', The Law Commissions, January 2014.

particular contract'. In a Note posted to the Law Commissions' website on 6 October 2014,[3] it was said:

> The legal structure of an insurance arrangement providing cover for multiple parties is determined by several factors, including the wording of the contract, the intention of the parties and the nature of the various parties' interests.
>
> We wish to preserve the flexibility provided by this fact-specific analysis, given the wide variety of arrangements which engage these issues. We are particularly keen to avoid formulating a statutory rule which would inappropriately constrain the outcome. Where there is a single policy which provides cover for other entities or individuals who are not parties to the contract, the existing wording of the [Insurance] Bill gives sufficient flexibility to require disclosure of material circumstances relating to those entities or individuals where that is appropriate.
>
> In the non-consumer insurance scenario, if insurers wish a particular analysis to apply, or a particular outcome to be achieved, this should be made clear in the contract (in accordance with the transparency requirements in clause 16 of the Bill).[4]

3.6 Where multiple persons are insured under the same policy, the question of which of them is an 'insured' for the purposes of the Insurance Act is an important one, as each 'insured' will owe its own duty of fair presentation. If the insurance is composite so that each insured has a separate interest in the subject matter of the insurance, an insured who is in breach of its duty of fair presentation will not impair the validity of the insurance for a co-insured who is not in breach.[5] However, where the policy is joint (so that the interests of the parties covered by the policy are the same[6]), breach of the duty of fair presentation by any one insured will entitle the insurer to its remedies for breach as against all the insureds. That may also be the case if one of the insureds acts as an agent for all the other insureds when entering into a composite insurance, as the other insureds will be fixed with any non-disclosure or misrepresentation by the agent insured.

3.7 In their July 2014 Report, the Law Commissions relied on the case of *New Hampshire Insurance Co Ltd v MGN Ltd*[7] to illustrate the point that a parent company may arrange insurance on behalf of all group or subsidiary companies, who are then parties to a composite policy.[8] In *New Hampshire Insurance Co Ltd v MGN Ltd*, the insured was described as 'The Maxwell Group of Companies' and the task of the court was to determine which companies were included in that description, each of which would be an insured under the policy. This is to be contrasted with a policy in which the policyholder is stated to be a company, but the policy extends cover to other persons, who may be subsidiary or associated companies of the policyholder, or directors or employees of the group, or joint venturers. There is no rule of construction that the policyholder in those circumstances is acting as agent for those other persons in entering into the policy, although that may be the case, and those other persons may be

3 'The Duty of Fair Presentation under the Insurance Bill: How does it affect Insurance taken out for Multiple Parties?'.

4 Ibid., paras 1.42–1.44.

5 *New Hampshire Insurance Co Ltd v MGN Ltd* [1997] LRLR 24 (CA).

6 *General Accident Fire & and Life Assurance Corp Ltd v Midland Bank Ltd* [1940] 2 KB 388 (CA), 404–406 (Sir Wilfrid Greene MR); *MacGillivray*, 2015, para.1-202.

7 Ibid., *New Hampshire Insurance Co Ltd v MGN Ltd* [1997] LRLR 24 (CA).

8 July 2014 Report, para.7.16.

entitled to ratify the policyholder's inclusion of them as parties to the contract where there was no actual authority at the time of contracting.[9] In *Sumitomo Bank Ltd v Banque Bruxelles Lambert*,[10] Langley J said:

> It is a well known concept that policies of insurance may be granted to one party as insured but for the benefit of others so that in the event a claim has to be made the insured may recover for the interests of those others and hold any recovery on trust for them.[11]

The cases in this area of law concern contracts that pre-date the coming into force of the Contracts (Rights of Third Parties) Act 1999 and turn on whether or not the policyholder could be said to have been acting as an agent or trustee for the other persons when entering into the policy. It is suggested that the more natural construction now would be that those other persons are beneficiaries of the policy, and therefore not 'insureds' for the purposes of the Insurance Act, but who would be entitled to enforce the policy as against the insurer in reliance on the Contracts (Rights of Third Parties) Act 1999.[12] The existence of persons for whom cover is provided by the contract of insurance, but who are not parties to the contract, is recognised in sections 4(5), 4(7) and 13(1)(b) of the Insurance Act.

3.8 As the duty of fair presentation is one owed by those persons who are parties to the contract of insurance, but not by those who are beneficiaries of the insurance but not parties to the contract, the categorisation of those who are insured by a policy providing cover to multiple persons is important. Although arguable, it is doubtful whether a third-party beneficiary owes any duty of fair presentation to the insurer under the Contracts (Rights of Third Parties) Act 1999, although the contrary was suggested in an Appendix to its Note posted to the Law Commissions' website on 6 October 2014.[13] The position taken by the Law Commissions in their July 2014 Report was:

> We are not recommending any change to the law in this area, and the courts will continue to construe contracts as they do now.[14]

3.9 The Explanatory Notes to the Insurance Act state at paragraph 42:

> In some situations, one party may enter into a contract on behalf of others. Who is 'the insured' in such cases is, and will continue to be, determined by reference to the particular contract.

3.10 By way of example, a holding company buys general liability insurance that provides insurance to insureds that are defined to include the holding company's

---

9 See for example, *National Oilwell (UK) Ltd v Davy Offshore Ltd* [1993] 2 Lloyd's Rep 582 (Com Ct); *O'Kane v Jones (The Martin P)* [2003] EWHC 2470 (Comm), [2004] 1 Lloyd's Rep 389 concerning the insurance of an undisclosed principal.

10 *Sumitomo Bank Ltd v Banque Bruxelles Lambert SA* [1997] 1 Lloyd's Rep 487 (Com Ct).

11 Ibid., 495. See also *Williams v Baltic Insurance Association of London Ltd* [1924] 2 KB 282 (KB).

12 The requirement in the 1999 Act that the contract should purport to confer a benefit on the third party is readily satisfied where the insurer agrees with the policyholder to insure the third party: see Robert Merkin, *Colinvaux's Law of Insurance*, 11th edn (Sweet & Maxwell, London, 2016), para.15-023.

13 'The Duty of Fair Presentation under the Insurance Bill: How does it affect Insurance taken out for Multiple Parties?' It was said in the Note that a defence of breach of duty of fair presentation might be available to the insurer under s.3(4) Contracts (Rights of Third Parties) Act 1999 but s.7(4) of that Act provides that a third party shall not be treated as a party to a contract for the purposes of any other Act, which would include the Insurance Act.

14 July 2014 Report, para.7.18.

subsidiaries, joint venturers, directors, officers and employees. The holding company is clearly the entity that enters into the contract of insurance with the insurer and accordingly owes a duty of fair presentation under section 3 Insurance Act. Unless it is recorded in the contract, or there is evidence that the holding company has entered into the contract of insurance as agent for the persons defined as insureds, it is very doubtful that those persons are parties to the contract of insurance, and indeed it would be remarkable if each employee of a large organisation owed a duty of fair presentation to the insurer in these circumstances. The authors suggest that the preferable analysis is that the holding company is the insured for the purposes of the Insurance Act and that all the other persons are third-party beneficiaries of the contract of insurance.

3.11 Under section 19 of the Marine Insurance Act 1906, the insured's agent (typically, and perhaps exclusively,[15] the placing broker) was under a separate duty to disclose material circumstances to the insurer. Breach of that duty entitled the insurer to avoid the contract of insurance as against the insured, but did not give rise to a separate claim in damages against the broker.[16] Section 19 has been repealed by the Insurance Act,[17] and although the placing broker's knowledge remains relevant to disclosure, it is because it is treated as the insured's knowledge (see paragraphs 4.10 and 4.11 below), and not because the insured's agent is under an independent duty to make a fair presentation of the risk. The Law Commissions had considered imposing a separate duty on the broker to the insurer but decided not to proceed with such a radical reform.[18]

3.12 Although the contract of insurance remains one of utmost good faith as modified by CIDRA and the Insurance Act,[19] section 14(1) of the Insurance Act abolishes any rule of law permitting a party to a contract of insurance to avoid the contract on the ground that utmost good faith has not been observed by the other party. As a consequence, although the insurer is probably still under a duty to disclose material information to the insured as it was under the previous law,[20] the insured has no remedy under the Insurance Act for breach of that duty. The insured's remedies for any misrepresentation by the insurer in respect of the making of the contract of insurance will be those available under the Misrepresentation Act 1967 (see paragraphs 5.28 and 5.29 below), or in deceit if deliberate.[21]

Duty of disclosure

3.13 The first limb of the duty of fair presentation is the duty of the insured to make disclosure to the insurer of every material circumstance which the insured knows or ought to know, in a manner which would be reasonably clear and accessible to a prudent insurer.[22]

15 See *PCW Syndicates v PCW Reinsurers* [1996] 1 Lloyd's Rep 241 (CA) 258 (Saville LJ).
16 *HIH Casualty and General Ins Ltd v Chase Manhattan Bank* [2003] 4 Lloyd's Rep 230 (Com Ct).
17 Insurance Act, s.21(2).
18 See para.7.46 of the Law Commissions' 2012 Joint Consultation Paper.
19 Insurance Act 2015, s.14(2).
20 See *Banque Financiere de la Cité SA v Westgate Insurance Co Ltd* [1991] 2 AC 249 (HL).
21 *Derry v Peek* (1889) LR 14 App Cas 337 (HL).
22 Insurance Act 2015, ss.3(3)(a) and 3(4)(a).

3.14 The term 'circumstance' is defined to include any communication made to, or information received by, the insured.[23] This replicates the now repealed section 18(5) of the Marine Insurance Act 1906. The definition is not exhaustive: for example, a decision by the insured to manufacture a dangerous chemical at its plant is likely to be a material circumstance to be disclosed to the insurer, even though it is not the subject of a communication made to, or information received by, the insured. Not every material communication received by the insured will however be disclosable: the duty to disclose depends on whether the insured knew or ought to have known of the communication and its content, and knowledge is subject to the test set out in section 4 of the Insurance Act (see Chapter 4 below).

3.15 A circumstance will be 'material', and therefore disclosable, if it would influence the judgment of a prudent insurer in determining whether to take the risk and, if so, on what terms.[24] This is very similar to the test set out in sections 18(2) and 20(2) Marine Insurance Act 1906, and deliberately so. Although at various times those charged with insurance law reform have proposed changing the test so that materiality is to be determined by reference to that which a prudent policyholder would consider relevant,[25] the Law Commissions eventually came to the view that 'a "reasonable insured" test would introduce a new, unknown and untested concept in the law'[26] and that the existing test should be retained, albeit with some clarification in the legislation.[27]

3.16 The clarification as to what is material is contained in two sub-sections in the Insurance Act. Firstly, the decision of the House of Lords in *Pan Atlantic Insurance Co Ltd v Pine Top Insurance Co Ltd*[28] that before an underwriter could avoid a contract for non-disclosure of a material circumstance, he had to show that he had actually been induced by the non-disclosure to enter into the policy on the relevant terms, has been enacted in section 8(1) of the Act.

3.17 The second clarification of materiality takes the form of examples of things which may be material listed in section 7(4) of the Act which the Law Commissions say they derived from existing case law.[29] Taking each in turn:

---

23 Insurance Act 2015, s.7(2).

24 Insurance Act 2015, s.7(3). It would appear that the decision of the House of Lords in *Pan Atlantic Insurance Co Ltd v Pine Top Insurance Co Ltd* [1995] 1 AC 501 (HL) that, to be material, it is not necessary that the circumstance should have a decisive effect on the prudent insurer's acceptance of the risk or on the amount of premium demanded, will continue to apply.

25 In the Fifth Report of the Law Reform Committee, January 1957, a distinguished committee chaired by Lord Justice Jenkins and including Parker LJ, Devlin J and Diplock J, recommended that for the purposes of any contract of insurance other than marine insurance, no fact should be deemed material unless it would have been considered material by a reasonable insured (para.14, Law Reform Committee (1957) Cmnd 62). The Law Commission recommended in its 1980 Report that a fact should be disclosed to an insurer 'if it is one which a reasonable man in the position of the applicant would disclose to his insurers, having regard to the nature and extent of the insurance cover which is sought and the circumstances in which it is sought' (para.10.9(c)). The BILA 2012 Report preferred a test 'whether a reasonable insured would have considered the undisclosed matter to be material to a prudent insurer' (para.17.2). In its June 2007 Joint Consultation, the Law Commissions proposed replacing the current test by a 'reasonable insured' test, meaning 'what a reasonable insured in the circumstances would think was relevant to the insurer' (para.5.83).

26 Para.4.71, Law Commissions' 2012 Joint Consultation Paper.

27 Ibid., paras 5.78 and 5.79.

28 *Pan Atlantic Insurance Co Ltd v Pine Top Insurance Co Ltd* [1995] 1 AC 501 (HL).

29 July 2014 Report, paras 7.26–7.28.

(i) **Section 7(4)(a): special or unusual facts relating to the risk**. In cases where the insured has argued that the insurer has waived its failure to disclose material information, the courts have found that the insurer is not put on enquiry about the existence of unusual or special facts which increase the risk.[30] The Insurance Act effectively codifies these earlier decisions.

(ii) **Section 7(4)(b): any particular concerns which led the insured to seek insurance cover for the risk**. The Law Commissions justify this example by reference to the judgment of Potter J in *Aiken v Stewart Wrightson Members Agency Ltd*,[31] which was a case concerned with the duty of care owed by a Lloyd's managing agent to syndicate members when arranging reinsurance on behalf of the syndicate.[32] The underlying dispute between the reinsurers and the syndicate was subject to arbitration and the issues are described in Potter J's judgment. The reinsurers successfully avoided the reinsurance in reliance on material misrepresentations and non-disclosure of particular facts, including the description of a long-tail account as short-tail and the treatment of certain block reserves as IBNR reserves. The reinsurers did not allege that there was a failure by the syndicate to disclose particular concerns, although the judge found that those concerns should have led the managing agents to take more care in their presentation of the risk to reinsurers. If concerns are based on facts, then those facts are disclosable to the extent they are material.[33] Likewise, 'opinions reasonably entertained by the assured or a third party, which are material must be disclosed'.[34] In contrast, in *Carter v Boehm*,[35] Lord Mansfield said that concern on the part of the governor of the insured fort about a possible attack by the French was 'mere speculation of the governor's from the general state of the war' and therefore not a matter for disclosure to the insurer.[36] It would be a change to the law to require an insured to disclose its concerns if those concerns are not grounded in fact, but matters of conjecture. This does not appear to have been the intention of the Law Commissions. If the insured expresses a concern to the insurer that is one of expectation or belief and that is material to the risk to be underwritten, then that representation must be one made in good faith: section 3(3)(c) Insurance Act.

(iii) **Section 7(4)(c): anything which those concerned with the class of insurance and field of activity in question would generally understand as being something that should be dealt with in a fair presentation of risks of the type in question**. This

30 *CTI v Oceanus Mutual Underwriting Association (Bermuda) Ltd* [1984] 1 Lloyd's Rep 476 (CA) 498 (Kerr LJ); *Marc Rich & Co AG v Portman* [1997] 1 Lloyd's Rep 225 (CA) 234 (Leggatt LJ) ('It is obvious that a presentation cannot be fair if unusual facts are not disclosed') and the cases cited at paras 5.31–5.33 of the Law Commissions' Joint Consultation and Discussion Paper on 'Insurance Contract Law: The Business Insured's Duty of Disclosure and the Law of Warranties', June 2012.

31 [1995] 2 Lloyd's Rep 618 (Com Ct).

32 See paras 5.34–5.36 of Law Commissions' 2012 Joint Consultation Paper.

33 See for example, *Fraser Shipping Ltd v Colton (The Shakir III)* [1997] 1 Lloyd's Rep 586 (Com Ct) where the insurer was entitled to avoid an endorsement to the policy for non-disclosure of port and weather conditions, not the insured's concerns about those conditions.

34 Peter MacDonald Eggers, Simon Picken, Patrick Foss, *Good Faith and Insurance Contracts*, 3rd edn (Lloyd's List, London, 2010) (hereafter MacDonald Eggers, Picken & Foss, 2010), para.7.61.

35 (1766) 3 Burr 1905, 97 ER 1162.

36 Ibid., 1168.

example appears to be based on a number of matters which the courts have assumed should be disclosed as a matter of course. They include existing loss experience,[37] criminal convictions of directors or senior staff,[38] and insolvency associated with the insured.[39] The Law Commissions suggested in their July 2014 Report that insurers, brokers and policyholder bodies should work together to develop guidance and protocols for classes of business setting out what a standard presentation of the risk should include.[40] This does not appear to have happened in practice.

Duty not to misrepresent

3.18 Disclosure by the insured will often take the form of representations. The duty of fair presentation requires that every material representation as to a matter of fact be substantially correct, and that every material representation as to a matter of expectation or belief be made in good faith.[41]

3.19 In the first draft of the Insurance Bill dated 16 January 2014, the Law Commissions proposed that a presentation would be fair if any material representations as to something the insured knows or ought to know were substantially correct. This would have resulted in a significant change to the existing law and made insurance contracts subject to less exacting rules than other commercial contracts under which all material statements of fact must be true.[42] After representations were made by the Lloyd's Market Association (LMA) and the International Underwriting Association (IUA), the Commissions reverted to the language of section 20 Marine Insurance Act 1906, and so the case law applicable to that section will continue to be relevant.

3.20 The test of materiality is the same as that applied to disclosure, so the misrepresentation must be as to a circumstance that a prudent insurer would want to take into account in determining whether to take the risk and, if so, on what terms.

3.21 If the representation is one of fact, it must be substantially correct. Section 7(5) Insurance Act provides that a representation is 'substantially correct' if a prudent insurer would not consider the difference between what is represented and what is actually correct to be material. This concept is taken from section 20(4) Marine Insurance Act 1906,[43] and is reflected in cases such as *Commonwealth Insurance Co of Vancouver v Groupe Sprinks SA*,[44] *Avon Insurance plc v Swire Fraser Ltd*,[45] and *ERC Frankona Reinsurance v American National Insurance Co*.[46] As Andrew Smith J observed in the latter case, 'the question of materiality is inextricable from the question whether the

37 Paras 5.15–5.24 of the Law Commissions' 2012 Joint Consultation Paper.
38 Ibid., para.5.26.
39 Ibid., paras 5.27 and 5.28.
40 July 2014 Report, paras 7.29–7.31.
41 Insurance Act 2015, s.3(3)(c).
42 Hugh Beale (ed.), *Chitty on Contracts* 32nd edn (Sweet & Maxwell, London, 2015), para.76.
43 Marine Insurance Act 1906, s.20(4) provides that a representation of fact will be substantially correct 'if the difference between what is represented and what is actually correct would not be considered material by a prudent insurer'.
44 [1983] 1 Lloyd's Rep 67 (Com Ct).
45 [2000] Lloyd's Rep IR 535 (Com Ct).
46 [2006] Lloyd's Rep IR 157 (Com Ct).

representation was false'. A string of errors in the insured's presentation of the risk may not amount to a breach of the duty of fair presentation if, overall, they would not affect the judgment of a prudent insurer. Conversely, misrepresentation of an important fact may breach the duty of fair presentation even if it is part of a substantial presentation that is otherwise accurate and complete.

3.22 If the representation is one of expectation or belief, section 3(3)(c) of the Insurance Act requires that it be made in good faith, which tracks the requirement in section 20(5) Marine Insurance Act 1906. The requirement that the representation be made in good faith essentially means that it must be made honestly so that it is false only if the insured did not believe it to be true. Where the representor is a corporation, there may be some doubt about whose belief is relevant. The leading case under the old law, *Economides v Commercial Union Assurance Co Plc*[47] concerned the representation of the belief of an individual. In *Highlands Insurance Co v Continental Insurance Co*[48] it was held that a representation of belief made by a professional person carried with it a representation that there were reasonable grounds for the belief (so that there would be a misrepresentation where there were no such grounds) but it is doubtful that this is still the law after *Economides*.[49] The absence of reasonable grounds for the belief may be a relevant factor in determining whether the representor honestly believed his expectation or belief.[50] The scheme in the Insurance Act for determining the insured's knowledge[51] applies to the duty of disclosure, but not to misrepresentations. The beliefs of the individual(s) making the representation on behalf of a corporation will be relevant to whether it is made honestly; it may also be the case that the beliefs of those individual(s) who are the 'directing mind and will' of the corporation will be relevant, particularly if they differ from the beliefs represented to the insurer as being those of the corporation.

3.23 There is uncertainty in the old law about whether the honesty of the belief held by the representor may be impugned if he deliberately closes his eyes to information that may change that belief. MacDonald Eggers et al. suggest that such conduct may be in breach of the insured's duty of good faith,[52] although the Insurance Act provides no remedy for breach of that duty. Section 6(1) Insurance Act states that for the purposes of sections 3 to 5 of the Act (which would therefore include section 3(3)(c)), 'references to an individual's knowledge include not only actual knowledge, but also matters which the individual suspected, and of which the individual would have had knowledge but for deliberately refraining from confirming them or enquiring about them'. Since an expectation or belief is something which is only capable of being held by an individual, the authors suggest that it would be appropriate to apply section 6(1) when determining whether an expectation or belief was honestly held for the purposes of section 3(3)(c) of the Act.

---

47 [1997] 3 All ER 636 (CA).

48 [1987] 1 Lloyd's Rep 109 (Com Ct).

49 See *Sirius International Insurance Corporation v Oriental Assurance Corporation* [1999] Lloyd's Rep IR 343 (QB); *Kamidian v Holt* [2008] EWHC 1483 (Comm), [2009] Lloyd's Rep IR 24.

50 *Economides v Commercial Assurance Co Plc* [1997] 3 All ER 636 (CA) 645 (Brown LJ).

51 Insurance Act 2015, s.4.

52 MacDonald Eggers, Picken & Foss, 2010, para.7.49.

Non-disclosure and misrepresentation

3.24 In their July 2014 Report, the Law Commissions said that 'there is often little practical difference between a non-disclosure and a misrepresentation'.[53] Reference was made to a comment by Lord Mustill in *Pan Atlantic Insurance Co Ltd v Pine Top Insurance Co Ltd*[54] that in practice the difference between the two is 'often imperceptible'. There is, however, one critical difference which takes on greater importance with the focus of the Insurance Act on the need for the insurer to ask questions of the insured about material circumstances at the time of placing, because questions will elicit representations. Non-disclosure depends on the insured's knowledge, and what the Act treats as the insured's knowledge (as to which, see paragraphs 4.2–4.34 below). The insured cannot breach its duty of fair presentation by a non-disclosure if it does not know, and is not deemed to know, the circumstance which has not been disclosed. Contrastingly, a misrepresentation does not depend on knowledge, but rather on whether or not the representation that has been made is true.

3.25 This distinction is illustrated by an example which the Law Commissions give in paragraph 7.53 of their July 2014 Report. They suppose that the insurer asks whether any of the insured's employees have criminal convictions and the insured answers no. In fact, one member of staff has a conviction for theft. The Law Commissions suggest that this would be a breach of the duty of fair presentation if a senior manager or insurance buyer knew about the conviction, or if the insured should have known about the conviction by carrying out a reasonable search. The authors suggest this analysis is wrong as there is nothing in the insured's answer to the insurer's question that ties the response to the insured's knowledge. The representation that there are no criminal convictions is not true. If the conviction for theft is a material circumstance, the insured will have breached its duty of fair presentation, whether or not it was aware of the employee's criminal conviction.

Timing and content of presentation

3.26 The insured is under the duty to make a fair presentation of the risk before the contract is entered into,[55] which in most cases means up to the time when the insurer agrees to underwrite the risk (although there may be occasions when the insured accepts an offer by the insurer to provide the insurance).[56] This reflects the old law as codified in section 18 Marine Insurance Act 1906, although section19(b) of the 1906 Act did appear to recognise that if the insurance was being

53 July 2014 Report, para.7.47.

54 [1995] 1 AC 501 (HL).

55 Insurance Act 2015, s.3(1).

56 Marine Insurance Act 1906, s.21 provides that a contract of marine insurance is deemed to be concluded when the proposal of the insured is accepted by the insurer 'whether the policy be then issued or not'. The scratching by the underwriter of the slip, or Market Reform Contract, is generally the time that the contract between the insured and that underwriter (on behalf of the insurer) is concluded. *Morrison v The Universal Marine Insurance Company* (1872–73) LR 8 Ex 197, 199 (Honyman J); *General Reinsurance Corporation v Forsakringsaktiebolaget Fennia Patria* [1983] QB 856 (CA) 866 (Kerr LJ).

arranged by an agent (typically a broker), there may be situations in which a material circumstance had come to the insured's knowledge too late to be communicated to the agent for the purposes of disclosure to the insurer.[57] In *CTI v Oceanus*[58] Kerr and Parker LJJ appeared to be of the view that section 19(b) might excuse non-disclosure if the relevant information came to the broker too late (although that was not the position on the facts of that case), and this is supported by Hardy Ivamy[59] and MacDonald Eggers.[60] The Law Commissions thought that section 19(b) of the 1906 Act appeared to add little to an insurer's existing remedies for non-disclosure and recommended its repeal.[61] There is accordingly nothing in the Insurance Act that would excuse non-disclosure by the insured of a material circumstance as a consequence of its being impossible, or possibly impracticable, for the insured to communicate recently acquired material information to the broker prior to the insurer underwriting the risk. Although in the modern era of rapid communication, this may be of less concern than it was at the beginning of the twentieth century, where there is a chain of producing and placing brokers, delay in passing material information recently acquired by the insured down that chain to the insurer is a real possibility.

3.27 Section 7(1) of the Insurance Act recognises that the process of arranging a contract of insurance may involve more than one communication between the insured and the insurer. It provides that a fair presentation need not be contained in only one document or oral presentation. The Law Commissions expected that, as a consequence of the new legislation, insurers would ask more questions as part of the underwriting process[62] and this will mean that the insured, or its broker, may have to make enquiries and return to the insurers with the answers to those enquiries. Whether or not the presentation is a fair one will depend on the overall content of the information provided and representations made.

3.28 Section 7(6) of the Insurance Act provides that any representation made by the insured may be withdrawn or corrected before the contract of insurance is entered into, which reflects the previous law in section 20(6) Marine Insurance Act 1906. Although it is unlikely that an insurer could establish that it had relied on a misrepresentation if that misrepresentation had been withdrawn prior to the insurer entering into the contract, section 7(6) reinforces the Law Commissions' view that the underwriting process should be one of dialogue in which mistakes of presentation may be made, but which are capable of being corrected, provided that is done before the insurance is underwritten.

---

57 Marine Insurance Act 1906, s.19(b): 'Subject to the provisions of the preceding section as to circumstances which need not be disclosed, where an insurance is effected for the assured by an agent, the agent must disclose to the insurer – ...(b) Every material circumstance which the assured is bound to disclose, unless it comes to his knowledge too late to communicate it to the agent.'

58 [1984] 1 Lloyd's Rep 476 (CA).

59 E.R. Hardy Ivamy, *Chalmers' Marine Insurance Act 1906*, 10th edn (Butterworths, London, 1993), pp.32, 33.

60 MacDonald Eggers, Picken and Foss, 2010, paras 8.87–8.89, 13.77.

61 July 2014 Report, para.9.10 and Recommendation 11.

62 July 2014 Report, paras 5.21, 6.6 and 6.7, and para.72 of the Explanatory Notes: 'The Act is intended to recognise that the insurer may need to ask questions about the information in the initial presentation in order to draw out the information it requires to make the underwriting decision.'

Disclosure that is reasonably clear and accessible

3.29 Section 3(3)(b) of the Insurance Act requires a fair presentation of the risk to be one which makes disclosure of every material circumstance 'in a manner which would be reasonably clear and accessible to a prudent insurer'. If this requirement is not satisfied, there will have been a breach of the insured's duty of fair presentation. The Law Commissions said in their July 2014 Report that the current law permitted 'policyholders to overwhelm the insurer with a large amount of undigested information', which was 'neither efficient nor effective'.[63] The purpose of the section is to combat so-called 'data dumps' where the insurer is presented with a large amount of information with no indication of what is relevant, and also cryptic or oblique presentations made in the hope that the insurer will not make enquiries.[64]

3.30 Stephenson LJ in *CTI v Oceanus*[65] said that an underwriter 'can expect to be given a fair summary and can assume that placing files which he has an opportunity of examining contain nothing exceptional or unusual; for a summary which excludes such matters is not a fair summary'.[66] Reflecting this view, the Law Commissions suggest at paragraph 7.44 of their July 2014 Report that:

> a large volume of data would not be objectionable if it were organised appropriately and presented to the underwriter in a form which would allow it to navigate to what is important. Equally, it would be acceptable if it were accompanied by an overview highlighting material points, provided that the summary is 'fair and accurate'.[67]

It appears from guides issued by policyholder and broker organisations that these suggestions have been taken on board, so the section is likely to have an impact on the quality of presentations made by or on behalf of insureds.[68]

3.31 The requirement that to be fair, a presentation must be clear and accessible, is likely to give rise to issues of waiver by the insurer. Section 3(5) of the Insurance Act excuses the insured from the duty to disclose a circumstance if it is something as to which the insurer waives information. If the insurer is presented with a large amount of information which is not indexed and is not accompanied by an overview, but proceeds to underwrite the risk anyway, can it later complain that the presentation was unfair because it was not clear and accessible? Probably not, although under the old law, the courts were reluctant to find that where the insured had breached its duty of disclosure, that breach had been impliedly waived by the insurer.[69] The introduction in the Insurance Act of a positive obligation on the insurer to ask questions if

---

63 July 2014 Report, para.7.42.

64 July 2014 Report, para.7.46.

65 [1984] 1 Lloyd's Rep 476 (CA).

66 Ibid., 529.

67 *Garnat Trading & Shipping (Singapore) Pte Ltd v Baominh Insurance Corp* [2010] EWHC 2578 (Comm), [2011] 1 Lloyd's Rep 589.

68 Association of Insurance and Risk Managers in Industry and Commerce (AIRMIC), *Insurance Act 2015 A guide to fair presentation* (AIRMIC 2016) 14, 15; British Insurance Brokers' Association (BIBA), *Insurance Act 2015: An Introductory Guide* (BIBA 2016) 6.

69 *Commonwealth Insurance Co of Vancouver v Groupe Sprinks SA* [1983] 1 Lloyd's Rep 67 (Com Ct); *Iron Trades Mutual Insurance Co Ltd v Companhia de Seguros Imperio* (1992) 1 Re LR 213 (Com Ct); *CTI v Oceanus Mutual Underwriting Association (Bermuda) Ltd* [1984] 1 Lloyd's Rep 476 (CA); *Axa Versicherung AG v Arab Insurance Group* [2015] EWHC 1939 (Comm); [2016] Lloyd's Rep IR 1, affd [2017] EWCA Civ 96 (CA). See also the cases referred to in paras 3.32 and 3.33 below concerning the asking of questions.

the insured's presentation prompts it to do so (and a 'data dump' is likely to prompt questions) may change that approach (see paragraphs 3.33–3.37 below). Would it make any difference if the insurer complained at the time that the presentation was a 'data dump' and/or stated that it would underwrite the risk but without waiving the insured's duty to make a reasonably clear and accessible presentation of the risk? Possibly, although the insurer's decision to proceed with the underwriting of the risk might influence the court's view as to whether the presentation was in fact clear and accessible to a prudent underwriter.

3.32 Because of the issues of waiver, section 3(3)(b) is likely to have most application where the presentation is not overly long, or has an overview highlighting material points, but where a critical piece of information is buried in a footnote, or similar. The information has been disclosed, but is it clear and accessible? If a prudent insurer would have overlooked the footnote, there is clearly a risk that the presentation would not be a fair one because it is not 'clear and accessible'.

Disclosure putting the insurer on notice

3.33 The insured may have failed to disclose every material circumstance which it knows or ought to know and yet not be in breach of its duty of fair presentation, provided it has made sufficient disclosure to put a prudent insurer on notice that it needs to make enquiries. The enquiries that the insurer is prompted to make must be in respect of the material circumstances that the insured has omitted to disclose.[70] Under the previous law, where the insured made a fair presentation of the risk in, say, a summary form, and that was considered to have put the underwriter on enquiry that there may be other matters relevant to the risk, the underwriter's failure to ask questions about those other matters could be relied on as a waiver of the insured's failure to make disclosure of those matters.[71] Rix LJ's dissenting judgment in *WISE (Underwriting Agency) Ltd v Grupo Nacional Provincial SA*[72] suggested that there could be waiver by the insurer even if the initial presentation was not fair, and this is the approach that has been followed in the Insurance Act.

3.34 The other difference between the previous law and section 3(4)(b) Insurance Act is that prior to the Act, the failure by the insurer to ask questions was treated as a waiver of the insured's duty to disclose and so was deployed as a defence by the insured to the insurer's avoidance of the policy for non-disclosure.[73] Under the new provision, the presentation is a fair presentation even if the insured fails to make full disclosure, provided the insured has disclosed enough to put a reasonable insurer on notice to make further enquiries. It will therefore fall on the insurer in the first instance to establish that there was a breach of the duty of fair presentation by the insured in (a) failing to disclose material circumstances, and (b) failing to provide sufficient information to put a reasonable insurer on notice that it needed to make enquiries. If the insurer asks

70 Insurance Act 2015, s.3(4)(b).

71 *CTI v Oceanus Mutual Underwriting Association (Bermuda) Ltd* [1984] 1 Lloyd's Rep 476 (CA) 511–512 (Parker LJ); *WISE (Underwriting Agency) Ltd v Grupo Nacional Provincial SA* [2004] EWCA Civ 962, [2004] 2 Lloyd's Rep 483 [107]–[108] (Longmore LJ).

72 Ibid., paras 46, 60, 62, 64 and 66.

73 *Synergy Health v CGU Insurance* [2011] Lloyd's Rep IR 500 [172]–[175] (Flaux J).

questions and the insured responds with material misrepresentations, then the insured will have breached its duty of fair presentation. If the insurer is prompted by the insured's presentation to make enquiries, but receives no response, or an inadequate response, to those enquiries, yet still underwrites the risk, then the insured's presentation may well have been fair, because it did enough to put the insurer on notice to ask questions.

3.35 By way of illustration of the way in which section 3(4)(b) Insurance Act may operate, a financial institution crime insurance proposal form refers to the fact that the institution in question is 'under investigation by the FCA'. It so happens that the investigation relates to a suspected fraud by the management (which is a material circumstance for disclosure). The institution's disclosure may nonetheless satisfy the duty of fair presentation, since it begs an obvious question which the insurer should ask, namely: 'under investigation for what?'

3.36 The Insurance Act is not clear as to the consequences if the insured deliberately withholds information from its presentation to the insurer, perhaps in the expectation that if the insurer considers the information to be material, it will ask for it. Does the presentation satisfy the insured's duty of fair presentation if it put the insurer on notice that it needed to make enquiries, but the insurer did not do so? There are various possible responses:

(i) It may be said that the insured has breached its duty of fair presentation by failing to make disclosure in a manner which would be reasonably clear and accessible to a prudent insurer: see section 3(3)(b) Insurance Act and paragraphs 3.29 to 3.32 above. However, if the presentation has prompted the need to make enquiries, it may nonetheless be fair; alternatively, the insurer may have waived the failure to make a clear and accessible presentation.

(ii) The insurance contract remains one of utmost good faith,[74] although the remedy of avoidance for breach of that duty has been abolished.[75] The Law Commissions suggested at paragraph 30.23(1) of their July 2014 Report that both parties are expected to act in good faith in exchanging information, and that if the insured deliberately withheld information from the insurer in the hope that the latter would not ask questions, that would be a breach of the insured's duty of fair presentation. The difficulty with this approach is that under the previous law, the duty of utmost good faith required the disclosure of all material information known to the insured and did not differentiate between non-disclosure that was intentional, negligent, or entirely innocent (because, for example, the insured was deemed to know the relevant information, but did not actually know it: see *Proudfoot v Montefiore*[76]), except that fraud on the part of the insured precluded the recovery of its premium from the insurer if the policy was avoided for deliberate breach of the duty of good faith.[77] Why should breach of the duty of utmost good faith taint the insured's presentation if it is done knowingly, but not if it is done negligently or innocently?

74 Insurance Act 2015, s.14.
75 Insurance Act 2015, s.14(1).
76 (1866–67) LR 2 QB 511.
77 Marine Insurance Act 1906, s.84(3).

(iii) It is an old rule of law that fraud unravels all. Once fraud is proved, 'it vitiates judgments, contracts and all transactions whatsoever'.[78] As Lord Blackburn said in *Brownlie v Campbell*:[79]

> where there is a duty or an obligation to speak, and a man in breach of that duty or obligation holds his tongue and does not speak, and does not say the thing he was bound to say, if that was done with the intention of inducing the other party to act upon the belief that the reason he did not speak was because he had nothing to say, I should be inclined myself to hold that that was fraud also.[80]

It is this rule that should prevent the insured (or its agent) from being able deliberately to withhold material information from the insurer and then arguing that the presentation was fair because the insurer failed to ask questions prompted by the presentation. A party cannot contract out of its liability for fraud,[81] and there is no reason to think that the Insurance Act intended such a result.

3.37 The Law Commissions considered that the change to the law introduced by section 3(4)(b), although not on its face substantial, was an important element of its approach to tackling the problems that it identified with the old law in Chapter 5 of its July 2014 Report. They were particularly concerned about what was perceived to be 'underwriting at claims stage', in other words the acceptance by an insurer of a poor presentation when underwriting the risk, but then asking questions about whether there had been full disclosure only once a claim arose.[82] Section 3(4)(b) is 'intended to ensure that insurers are engaged in the disclosure and presentation process'.[83]

What must be disclosed?

3.38 The insured's duty of fair presentation concerns the disclosure of 'material circumstances'.[84] This expression derives from the previous law, and in particular section 18(1) Marine Insurance Act 1906, and was intentionally taken from that statute.[85] The existing case law as to what constitutes a 'circumstance' will accordingly continue to apply.

3.39 A 'circumstance' for the purposes of disclosure under the previous law, and accordingly now under the Insurance Act, means a fact. An opinion or a belief may constitute a 'fact' if it is sufficiently well-grounded,[86] even though the opinion may

78 *Lazarus Estates Ltd v Beasley* [1956] 1 QB 702 (CA) 712 (Denning LJ), cited by *HIH Casualty and General Ins Ltd v Chase Manhattan Bank* [2003] UKHL 6, [2003] Lloyd's Rep IR 230 [15] (Lord Bingham).

79 (1880) 5 App Cas 925 (HL) 950 (Lord Blackburn).

80 Cited with approval by *HIH Casualty and General Ins Ltd v Chase Manhattan Bank* [2003] 4UKHL 6, [2003] Lloyd's Rep IR 230 [72] (Lord Hoffmann).

81 'A party cannot be allowed to benefit from his own fraud or from the fraud of his alter ego. So if an exclusion clause on its true construction purports to cover such fraud, it cannot, on public policy grounds, be permitted to have that effect.' *HIH Casualty and General Ins Ltd v Chase Manhattan Bank* [2003] 4 UKHL 6, [2003] Lloyd's Rep IR 230 [121] (Lord Scott).

82 July 2014 Report, para.5.37.

83 July 2014 Report, para.7.38.

84 Insurance Act 2015, s.3(4).

85 July 2014 Report, para.7.25.

86 *Edgington v Fitzmaurice* (1885) 29 Ch D 459 (CA).

turn out to be wrong.[87] Disclosure of the facts on which the opinion or belief is based is likely to be a safer way of proceeding, and may obviate the need to disclose the insured's opinion or belief as to what those facts mean (see paragraph 3.17(ii) above).[88] A rumour may also constitute a fact. In *Brotherton v Aseguradora Colseguros SA*,[89] the Court of Appeal held that media reports about fraud at the insured bank were disclosable whether or not they were true. As Mance LJ suggested in that case, loose or idle rumours may be immaterial and therefore not disclosable, but rumours of more substance may be disclosable, even if ultimately untrue.[90]

3.40 Under section 18(3)(d) Marine Insurance Act 1906, an insured did not have to disclose any circumstance which it was superfluous to disclose because of an express or implied warranty in the policy. For example, if the burglar alarm on the insured's premises was not working, the insured did not have to disclose that fact if the policy contained a warranty that there would be a working burglar alarm on the premises at all times. Such disclosure was regarded as superfluous, because the insurer was protected by the warranty in any event. With the change in the nature of warranties in the Insurance Act to suspensory conditions (see Chapter 6 below), circumstances which are the subject matter of warranties in the policy might now be disclosable, hence section 18(3)(d) is omitted from the Marine Insurance Act.[91] It is likely in most cases that circumstances forming the subject matter of warranties in the policy are likely to be material matters to be disclosed.

Matters not required to be disclosed

3.41 As with the previous law (section 18(3) Marine Insurance Act 1906), there are certain circumstances that the law does not require the insured to disclose. They are set out in section 3(5) Insurance Act:

- **Section 3(5)(a): a circumstance that diminishes the risk**. The insured's presentation will be fair if it omits material facts, provided those facts would reduce the risk to be underwritten.[92] Whether or not the non-disclosed circumstances diminish the risk will be a matter for expert evidence from a prudent insurer.[93]
- **Section 3(5)(b): the insurer knows the relevant circumstance**. What an insurer knows is the subject of paragraphs 4.37–4.38 below.
- **Section 3(5)(c): the insurer ought to know the relevant circumstance**. What an insurer ought to know is the subject of paragraphs 4.39–4.47 below.
- **Section 3(5)(d): the insurer is presumed to know the relevant circumstance**. What an insurer is presumed to know is the subject of paragraphs 4.48–4.55 below.

---

87 *Shirley v Wilkinson* (1781) 3 Doug KB 41, 99 ER 529.

88 *General Accident Fire & Life Assurance Corporation Ltd v Campbell* (1925) 21 Ll L Rep 151 (KB).

89 *Brotherton v Aseguradora Colseguros SA (No 2)* [2003] EWCA Civ 705, [2003] Lloyd's Rep IR 746 (CA).

90 Ibid., [28].

91 Insurance Act 2015, s.21(2).

92 *Carter v Boehm* (1766) 3 Burr 1905, 97 ER 1162; *Pawson v Watson* (1778) 2 Cowp 785, 98 ER 1361.

93 *Inversiones Manria SA v Sphere Drake Insurance Co (The Dora)* [1989] 1 Lloyd's Rep 69 (Com Ct) [89]–[90] (Phillips J).

- **Section 3(5)(e): it is something as to which the insurer waives information**. Apart from circumstances in which the insurer has expressly stated that it does not require information from the insured in respect of particular matter(s), which may be reflected in a term in the insurance contract, it is likely that most cases of waiver will now fall within Section 3(4)(b) of the Insurance Act where the insurer is put on notice by the insured's presentation that it needs to make enquiries.[94] Issues of waiver may also arise in relation to a presentation that is not clear and accessible (see paragraphs 3.29–3.32 above).

94 See paras 3.33–3.37 above.

CHAPTER 4

Knowledge

Knowledge of the insured

4 Knowledge of insured

(1) This section provides for what an insured knows or ought to know for the purposes of section 3(4)(a).

(2) An insured who is an individual knows only –

(a) what is known to the individual, and

(b) what is known to one or more of the individuals who are responsible for the insured's insurance.

(3) An insured who is not an individual knows only what is known to one or more of the individuals who are –

(a) part of the insured's senior management, or

(b) responsible for the insured's insurance.

(4) An insured is not by virtue of subsection (2)(b) or (3)(b) taken to know confidential information known to an individual if –

(a) the individual is, or is an employee of, the insured's agent; and

(b) the information was acquired by the insured's agent (or by an employee of that agent) through a business relationship with a person who is not connected with the contract of insurance.

(5) For the purposes of subsection (4) the persons connected with a contract of insurance are –

(a) the insured and any other persons for whom cover is provided by the contract, and

(b) if the contract re-insures risks covered by another contract, the persons who are (by virtue of this subsection) connected with that other contract.

(6) Whether an individual or not, an insured ought to know what should reasonably have been revealed by a reasonable search of information available to the insured (whether the search is conducted by making enquiries or by any other means).

(7) In subsection (6) "information" includes information held within the insured's organisation or by any other person (such as the insured's agent or a person for whom cover is provided by the contract of insurance).

(8) For the purposes of this section –

(a) "employee", in relation to the insured's agent, includes any individual working for the agent, whatever the capacity in which the individual acts,

(b) an individual is responsible for the insured's insurance if the individual participates on behalf of the insured in the process of procuring the insured's insurance (whether the individual does so as the insured's employee or agent, as an employee of the insured's agent or in any other capacity), and

(c) "senior management" means those individuals who play significant roles in the making of decisions about how the insured's activities are to be managed or organised.

4.1 The insured's duty of fair presentation under section 3 Insurance Act gives rise to questions of knowledge, both on the part of the insured for the purposes of disclosure, and on the part of the insurer for the purposes of determining what the insured does not have to disclose. These questions arose under the old law and were the subject of case law and sections 18 and 19 Marine Insurance Act 1906. The principles of that old law have been made largely redundant by sections 4 and 5 Insurance Act, which introduce a new regime for the purposes of assessing what is known by an insured and by an insurer, such that they know 'only' those matters that are set out in the sections. These sections contain new concepts which may give rise to some uncertainty until the courts have had the opportunity to consider how they are to be applied to particular cases. The Explanatory Notes suggest that future interpretation of some of the provisions 'is likely to be guided by existing case law'.[1]

4.2 The insured is under an obligation to disclose every material circumstance that he, she or it 'knows or ought to know' (sections 3(3)(a) and 3(4)(a) Insurance Act). What an insured knows or ought to know is provided for in section 4 of the Act which defines exhaustively what is to be treated as the insured's knowledge for the purposes of satisfying its duty of disclosure. The old statutory law in sections 18 and 19 Marine Insurance Act 1906 is repealed,[2] as is any rule of law to the same effect.[3]

4.3 Where the insured is an individual (and not a consumer: see paragraphs 2.16–2.20 and 3.2 above), he or she knows only what that individual actually knows, and what is known by those individuals who are responsible for the insured's insurance (section 4(2) Insurance Act). As has been pointed out by the authors of *Arnould's Law of Marine Insurance and Average*, this in itself represents a significant change in that an individual is treated as knowing something which others knew,[4] although under section 18 Marine Insurance Act 1906 the individual insured would be deemed to know that which in the ordinary course of business he or she ought to know. The individual insured will also be deemed to know what should have been revealed by a reasonable search:[5] see paragraphs 4.20–4.30 below. An individual's actual knowledge ought not to include matters which the individual once knew, but had forgotten at the time of making the presentation to the insurer, although issues might arise about 'wilful blindness' where the individual deliberately avoids refreshing his/her memory: see section 6(1) Insurance Act, paragraphs 4.58–4.60 below, and paragraph 7.100 MacDonald Eggers et al.[6] It may also be necessary to assess whether the insured's exposure to the material information was at a time when it was likely to be relevant to the purchasing of the insurance.[7] For example, if an insured nightclub owner is

1 Explanatory Notes to the Insurance Act 2015, para.57.

2 Insurance Act 2015, s.21(2).

3 Insurance Act 2015, s.21(3).

4 Jonathan Gilman and others, *Arnould's Law of Marine Insurance and Average*, 1st supp., 18th edn (Sweet & Maxwell, London, 2016) (hereafter *Arnould*, supp. to 18th edn), para.1.2-30.

5 Insurance Act 2015, s.4(6).

6 Peter MacDonald Eggers, Simon Picken and Patrick Foss, *Good Faith and Insurance Contracts*, 3rd edn (Informa, London, 2010) (hereafter MacDonald Eggers, Picken & Foss, 2010).

7 See *London General Insurance Co Ltd v General Marine Underwriters Association Ltd* [1920] 3 KB 23, (1920) 3 Ll l Rep 199 in the context of what is actually known by a reinsurance underwriter.

informed by the police of threats by vandals to burn down local nightclubs at the time he is renewing the property insurance for the premises, that knowledge is likely to be disclosable. However, if the owner may have heard about such threats in a casual conversation nine months before renewal, that may not constitute his knowledge for the purposes of disclosure at renewal unless it can be shown that he had it clearly in mind.

4.4 If the insured is not an individual, its knowledge will be determined by what is known by certain individuals[8] and what would have been revealed by a reasonable search.[9] A general partnership constituted in accordance with the Partnership Act 1890 does not have a separate legal personality for most purposes and its knowledge may accordingly be that of its individual partners to be assessed in accordance with section 4(2) Insurance Act. In *Ackman & Scher v Policyholders Protection Board*,[10] Lord Mustill expressed the view that as a matter of English law, 'a policy of insurance taken out by a partnership in respect of its liabilities is in theory a bundle of contracts between the insurer and the individual partners'. Companies, charitable trusts, public authorities, statutory bodies and limited liability partnerships are not individuals and the knowledge of those entities will be determined by sections 4(3) and (6). The relevant individuals fall into two categories:

- those individuals who are part of the insured's senior management (section 4(3)(a) Insurance Act);
- those individuals who are responsible for the insured's insurance (section 4(3)(b) Insurance Act).

Knowledge of senior management

4.5 For the purposes of section 4 Insurance Act, 'senior management' is defined as 'those individuals who play significant roles in the making of decisions about how the insured's activities are to be managed or organised'.[11] In their July 2014 Report, the Law Commissions said at paragraph 8.55:

> The definition would include (and be more or less limited to) board members or their equivalent in a non-corporate organisation. It is not generally intended to capture, for example, regional or middle managers. It replicates the common law 'directing mind and will' test, but without its broader extensions.

4.6 In paragraph 8.59 of their July 2014 Report, the Law Commissions gave examples of who they thought would constitute 'senior management' across a range of different kinds of entities. In each case, it is clear that the Law Commissions thought that 'senior management' would be limited to those in board or equivalent positions. They thought that knowledge of managers below that level 'should generally be caught by the "reasonable search" requirement' (as to which see paragraphs 4.20–4.30 below).[12]

8 Insurance Act 2015, s.4(3).
9 Insurance Act 2015, s.4(6).
10 [1994] 1 Lloyd's Rep 121 (HL), 129.
11 Insurance Act 2015, s.4(8)(c).
12 July 2014 Report, para.8.60.

4.7 Under the old law, knowledge of natural persons was attributed to a corporate insured either by way of agency or by the doctrine of imputation associated with the 'directing mind and will' of the company.[13] While this would include the company's board of directors, it might also include 'those who are sufficiently concerned with the operation of the company and the activity at hand, whether it be the operation of the interest insured, the placing of the insurance or the making of a claim'.[14]

4.8 The narrowness of the Law Commissions' interpretation of what was then clause 4(6)(c) of the Insurance Bill was reflected in HM Treasury's Explanatory Notes accompanying the Bill. It was raised as a matter of concern by members of the Special Public Bill Committee of the House of Lords at the proceedings of the Committee on 15 December 2014. Amendments were moved to broaden the definition to make it clear that it included those involved in the actual managing or organising of the whole or a substantial part of the activities of the insured.[15] There was concern in particular that in larger organisations, executives below board level often had more relevant knowledge of the insured's operations for the purposes of its insurance cover than members of the board, particularly non-executive members of the board. In response to that criticism, the Government agreed to review its Explanatory Notes and the final version of those Notes issued on 12 February 2015 contained the following statements:

> 54. Section 4(8)(c) defines 'senior management'. It captures those individuals who play significant roles in the making of decisions about how the insured's activities are to be managed or organised. In a corporate context, this is likely to include members of the board of directors but may extend beyond this, depending on the structure and management arrangements of the insured.
> 55. Because the knowledge of the senior management and those individuals responsible for the insurance is directly imputed to the insured for the purposes of the duty of fair presentation, those categories of person are expected to be construed relatively narrowly, but are capable of being applied flexibly. The knowledge of those individuals who do not fall within the category of senior management, yet who perform management roles or otherwise possess relevant information or knowledge about the risk to be insured, may be captured by the 'reasonable search' referred to in section 4(6).

4.9 Unfortunately, the Explanatory Notes have tended to muddy rather than clarify the scope of the definition of 'senior management'. Lord Mance suggested when giving evidence to the Special Public Bill Committee that the statutory wording was perfectly acceptable, but that the encrustation of the July 2014 Report and Explanatory Notes would give rise to arguments.[16] Since the knowledge of those who are part of senior management stands as the knowledge of the insured for the purposes of disclosure,

13 MacDonald Eggers, Picken and Foss, 2010.

14 Ibid., para 7.101; *Manifest Shipping Co Ltd v Uni-Polaris Insurance Co Ltd: The Star Sea* [1977] 1 Lloyd's Rep 360; *Red Sea Tankers Ltd v Papachristidis: The Hellespont Ardent* [1997] 2 Lloyd's Rep 547, 594–597 (Mance J).

15 House of Lords Special Public Bill Committee, *Insurance Bill* (HL), *House of Lords Papers* (2014–15, HL 81), 116.

16 House of Lords Special Public Bill Committee, *Insurance Bill* (HL), *House of Lords Papers* (2014–15, HL 81), 55–56. Oral Evidence taken before the Special Public Bill Committee on 9 December 2014.

knowing who is within, and who is without, the definition is important. For reasons explored in paragraphs 4.29–4.30 below, a reasonable search may not necessarily reveal the knowledge of those outside the defined term, in which case material information may not be disclosed, but the presentation of the risk will be a fair one. Reflecting the concern of insurers and insureds alike about this uncertainty, the LMA and AIRMIC have recommended that the insured and the insurer should agree in the insurance contract who is part of the insured's senior management.[17] The LMA has suggested a Model Clause as follows:

Insurance Act 2015 – definition of 'senior management'
Under Section 4(3)(a) of the Insurance Act 2015, the Insured must disclose all material circumstances known to (amongst others) its 'senior management'. For these purposes, the 'senior management' shall include the persons occupying the positions listed below (or their equivalents):
{Insert relevant positions: e.g. head of operations}[18]

Knowledge of those responsible for the insured's insurance

4.10 Under sections 4(2)(b) and 4(3)(b) Insurance Act, both the individual insured and the corporate insured will be deemed to know that which is known by those individuals who are responsible for the insured's insurance. Section 4(8)(b) defines such an individual as one who 'participates on behalf of the insured in the process of procuring the insured's insurance'. The definition makes it clear that the capacity in which the individual participates in that process does not matter: 'whether the individual does so as the insured's employee or agent, as an employee of the insured's agent or in any other capacity'. Section 4(8)(a) defines an 'employee' of the insured's agent (usually the broker) for these purposes as including any individual working for the agent 'in whatever capacity the individual acts'. At the proceedings of the Special Public Bill Committee on 15 December 2014, Baroness Noakes asked whether this definition would mean that if a professional adviser were working for an agent, the knowledge of that professional adviser would in effect be treated as that of the agent. Lord Newby, the responsible Treasury Minister, responded that the definition would not cover an external adviser 'because they would not fall under the definition of "employee"'.[19]

4.11 The Explanatory Notes state that the definition in section 4(8)(b) is expected to catch the insured's risk manager and any employee of the insured who assists in the collection of data or negotiates the terms of the insurance; it will also include the individual broker who places the insurance with the insurer,[20] but it would not include the broking firm as that would not be an individual.[21] The breadth of the definition may encompass a number of individuals acting in different capacities in the process of procuring the insured's insurance. For example, it will include individuals involved

17 The LMA recommended this in its *Guidance to Suite of LMA Model Clauses* (LMA March 2016), and AIRMIC in its *Insurance Act 2015: A guide to fair presentation* (AIRMIC 2016) 9.

18 LMA Model Clause 9120, 16 March 2016.

19 Transcript of Proceedings of Committee Stage of the Special Public Bill Committee on 15 December 2014, p.113.

20 Explanatory Notes to the Insurance Act 2015, para.53.

21 Confirmed by the Law Commissions at para.8.65 of the July 2014 Report.

in arranging the insurance at each of the broking firms involved in a chain of brokers placing insurance for the insured, and not just the placing broker. If the insured's legal department is involved in handling claims against the insured, the knowledge of individuals in the legal department involved in the compilation of claims data for the purposes of preparing the presentation of the risk to insurers is likely to be treated as the insured's knowledge. As regards the response of Lord Newby to Baroness Noakes' question (see paragraph 4.10 above), if the insured or the broker engaged an external adviser, for example a lawyer, to negotiate the terms of the policy with the insurer, it is likely that the knowledge of that adviser would be treated as the knowledge of the insured as he or she would have been involved in the process of procuring the insurance. AIRMIC has recommended that insureds should 'seek to agree a specific and brief list of individuals who are "responsible for the insured's insurance" with the broker and insurer, to contain the actual knowledge that must be disclosed'.[22]

Confidential information

4.12 Information known to the insured (or deemed to be known if the insured is not an individual) may be confidential. Confidential information can be any non-public information expressly or impliedly imparted in confidence.[23] It will include information which the insured has agreed with a third party is held subject to a duty of confidentiality, for example information received during the course of arbitration proceedings. Once the information is readily available to the public it ceases to be confidential.[24] In *Carter v Boehm*,[25] Lord Mansfield said that information held by the governor of the insured fort about the weaknesses of the fort's defences was information that the insurer knew the governor could not disclose 'consistent with his duty'.[26] The insurer did not press for disclosure of that information and by proceeding to underwrite the risk, he effectively waived its disclosure. The authors suggest that confidentiality is not a bar to disclosure (unless the insured is subject to a statutory duty of confidentiality, particularly under the Official Secrets Act 1989[27]), but if the insurer knows that the insured has withheld information because it is confidential, failing to press for disclosure of the information, or to ask questions about it, will probably amount to waiver by the insurer of the insured's duty to disclose that information.[28]

4.13 The Insurance Act has a special scheme for dealing with confidential information held by an individual who is the insured's agent, or is an employee of the insured's agent (in sections 4(4) and (5) of the Act). The insured's agent to arrange its insurance is usually a broker, and it is the particular difficulties faced by brokers in dealing

22 AIRMIC, *Insurance Act 2015: A guide to fair presentation* (AIRMIC 2016), 11.

23 Peter G. Watts (ed.), *Bowstead and Reynolds on Agency*, 20th edn (Sweet & Maxwell, London, 2016) (hereafter *Bowstead and Reynolds* 20th edn), para.6-077.

24 *Bowstead and Reynolds* 20th edn, para.6-077.

25 (1766) 3 Burr 1905, 97 ER 1162.

26 Ibid., p.1167.

27 MacDonald Eggers, Picken & Foss, 2010, para.8.83.

28 Insurance Act 2015, s.3(5)(e), paras 3.32–3.35. MacDonald Eggers, Picken & Foss, 2010, paras 8.80 and 8.81.

with confidential information that the Act seeks to address. The Law Commissions described the problem in paragraph 9.41 of their July 2014 Report:

> An agent may receive information relevant to the risk from other clients. The large brokers, for example, receive advance notice of claims from many thousands of customers, and this may alert them to risks within whole industries.

4.14 Section 4(4)(b) provides that where the insured's agent acquires confidential information through a business relationship with a person who is not connected with the contract of insurance, then such knowledge of that agent (if it is an individual), or the knowledge of an individual who is an employee of the agent,[29] is not to be treated as knowledge of the insured, and so would not be disclosable to the insurer. Section 4(5) defines what is meant by a person who is connected with the contract of insurance and is considered in paragraph 4.19 below. The exception gives rise to the following issues:

- What is meant by 'confidential information'?
- What is a 'business relationship'?
- What should the individual broker do if he or she has material information that is not disclosable?

What is meant by 'confidential information'?

4.15 The Law Commissions initially proposed that any information received by the broker from another client should not be imputed to the insured.[30] In their July 2014 Report, the Law Commissions said that they had developed their thinking and identified the key issue as being not the capacity in which information was acquired, but whether it was confidential to other clients.[31] This approach is reflected in the Insurance Act. However, the Law Commissions did not consider what was meant by 'confidential' in these circumstances. Is it sufficient for the individual broker to say that the person giving him the information asked him to keep it confidential, or that the broker thought it was confidential information? Must the individual broker, or his employer, be under a legal duty to keep the information confidential? The authors consider that the test of confidentiality should be an objective one and that the broker, or his employer, should be under a legal duty to maintain confidentiality in the information if it is not to be disclosed to the insurer, whether that duty arises out of the legal relationship between the broker and the provider of the information (usually that of principal and agent where the provider is the broker's client[32]), or out of a specific undertaking of confidentiality provided by the broker. Whether the test is objective or subjective may be critical in determining the status of the information. If the information is not confidential, but the broker believes it is and does not disclose it to the insurer, the insured may have breached its duty of fair presentation if the information is material. If the broker does not believe that the information is confidential, but objectively it is, and the broker

29 Insurance Act 2015, s.4(4)(a).

30 Para.7.74 of the Law Commissions' Joint Consultation and Discussion Paper on 'Insurance Contract Law: The Business Insured's Duty of Disclosure and the Law of Warranties', June 2012.

31 July 2014 Report, para.9.43.

32 An agent is under a fiduciary duty not to use confidential information acquired during the course of the agency to acquire a secret profit: *Bowstead & Reynolds*, 20th edn, para.6-075.

discloses it to the insurer, the insured may have a claim against the broker for any detriment that the insured may suffer (such as additional premium or the imposition of an exclusion) as a consequence of the information being wrongly disclosed.

4.16 A relatively simple example illustrates the difficulties that this issue may present. It is taken from one of the examples used by the Law Commissions at paragraph 9.45 of its July 2014 Report. Assume that the individual broker acts for a manufacturer of medical implants which provides claims information to the broker for the purposes of renewing its liability insurance. The information discloses notifications concerning injuries allegedly caused by the off-label use of one of its products by a chain of clinics. The individual broker also arranges the liability insurance for the chain of clinics, which is apparently unaware of the claim notifications. Should the broker disclose the notifications to (a) the chain of clinics and/or (b) the chain's insurers when renewing the chain's insurance with them? As the broker probably falls into that category of agents who, like estate agents and accountants, are not under a duty to disclose knowledge acquired from one principal to another,[33] and as the information about the claims is likely to be confidential, the authors' view is that it probably ought not to be disclosed to the clinic or its insurers.

What is a 'business relationship'?

4.17 The exception for confidential information applies only to information that is acquired through a 'business relationship'. Information that the individual broker receives 'in confidence' from a neighbour would not fall within the exception, unless it was received in the course of a business relationship. Would confidential information received by the individual broker from an underwriter for whom the broker does not act be information acquired through a 'business relationship' if the broker places business with that underwriter? Is it necessary for the provider of the information to be at an organisation that has a client relationship with the broker's organisation, or does any sort of contractual relationship suffice? The authors suggest that a requirement that the broker should be under a legal duty to preserve the confidentiality of the relevant information for section 4(4) Insurance Act to apply may avoid some of these difficulties (see paragraph 4.15 above).

What should the individual broker do if he or she has material information that is not disclosable?

4.18 In light of the difficulties discussed in paragraphs 4.15–4.17 above, where the individual broker is in receipt of material information from another client that may be confidential, the safest course would be to check with that client whether there is any objection to the information being shared with the client for whom the broker is to procure insurance. If the other client refuses to provide that consent, unless objectively the information is confidential, the individual broker should probably cease to be involved in arranging insurance for the first client. Even if the information is confidential, the individual broker may find himself in difficulties if he knowingly withholds that information from the underwriter (if the information is material): see paragraph 3.36 above on the consequences

33 *Harlequin Property (SVG) Limited & Another v Wilkins Kennedy* [2016] 3188 EWHC (TCC) [492]–[495] (Coulson J).

of deliberately withholding material information on placing. Knowledge under the Insurance Act focuses on the knowledge of the individual broker, so unless the individual broker disseminates the potentially confidential information within his firm, a replacement broker will not be fixed with knowledge of that information.

Who is a person connected with the insurance?

4.19 Confidential information received by the individual broker is not protected from disclosure if it is received from a person who is 'connected with' the contract of insurance that the broker is seeking to procure. Section 4(5) Insurance Act defines what is meant by a person connected with the contract of insurance. It includes the insured and any other persons who are beneficiaries of the insurance, although they may not be parties to the contract of insurance (see paragraphs 3.6–3.10 above). It also includes persons who are connected with an insurance contract (in the sense that they are insured by that contract or are beneficiaries of it) that is to be reinsured by a reinsurance contract that the broker is arranging. This latter provision is intended to deal with the situation where the broker receives information in confidence from the original insureds which is material to a contract of reinsurance (typically a facultative reinsurance) that the broker is procuring for the insurers of the original insurance.[34]

Knowledge revealed by a reasonable search

4.20 In addition to what particular individuals know, under section 4(6) Insurance Act, the insured is deemed to know 'what should reasonably have been revealed by a reasonable search of information available to the insured (whether the search is conducted by making enquiries or by any other means)'. The Law Commissions were of the view that this positive duty on an insured to seek out information was supported by existing case law,[35] but the cases relied on would not appear to support that proposition insofar as the duty is 'to take positive steps to collate relevant information for the purposes of making a fair presentation'.[36] The authors of *Arnould*[37] suggest that under the old law, what an insured ought to know for the purposes of disclosure should be subject to the same test as that applied to what an insurer ought to know, and that the test accordingly involved an objective element as to what a reasonable, prudent insured in that class of insureds in the ordinary course of business ought to know.[38] This view found favour with the Law Commissions and was relied on in support of the introduction of the concept of a 'reasonable search'.[39] It is not a view shared by *MacGillivray*[40] or MacDonald Eggers et al.[41]

34 See for example the case of *General Accident Fire and Life Assurance Corp Ltd v Peter William Tanter (The Zephyr)* [1984] 1 Lloyd's Rep 58 (Com Ct), affd [1985] 2 Lloyd's Rep 529 (CA).

35 July 2014 Report, para.8.81.

36 July 2014 Report, para.8.80.

37 *Arnould*, 18th edn.

38 Ibid., paras 16–37 to 16–48, by reference to s.18(3)(b) Marine Insurance Act.

39 July 2014 Report, para.8.83. The basis for this view appears to be criticised in *Arnould*, 18th edn at fn.74 to para.1.2-37.

40 John Birds, Ben Lynch, Simon Milnes, *MacGillivray on Insurance Law*, 13th edn (Sweet & Maxwell, London, 2015), para.17-014.

41 MacDonald Eggers, Picken & Foss, paras 7.122 and 7.123.

4.21 The Law Commissions relied on three cases to support the proposition that insurance buyers have a positive duty to seek out information about their organisation for the purposes of arranging their insurance:[42]

- *Inversiones Manria SA v Sphere Drake Insurance Co Plc* (*The Dora*)[43]
- *Aiken v Stewart Wrightson Members Agency Ltd* (*Aiken*)[44]
- *London General Insurance Co Ltd v General Marine Underwriters Association Ltd* (*London General*)[45]

4.22 The relevant issue in *The Dora* concerned the insured's failure to disclose to insurers the fact that the skipper of the insured yacht had a criminal record. The insured did not know that fact, but Phillips J held that the insured's agent, the manager of the vessel, ought in the ordinary course of business to have known of that fact because he should have carried out checks on the skipper's character. The insured was deemed to know that which its agent in the ordinary course of business ought to have known under section 18(1) Marine Insurance Act 1906. This decision turned on what the insured's manager ought to have discovered in the ordinary course of business; there was no suggestion that for the purposes of arranging its insurance, the insured (or its manager) should have conducted a search for material information, and no consideration of what a reasonable search in the circumstances of that case should reasonably have revealed.[46]

4.23 In *Aiken*, the relevant duty to search for information for the purposes of arranging the syndicate's reinsurances was one owed by the syndicate's managing agent to the syndicate members.[47] It was not suggested that this was a duty owed to the reinsurers, and consideration of whether or not such a duty existed was not relevant to the issues to be determined by the court.

4.24 *London General* is another case concerning what the (re)insured ought to know in the ordinary course of business. In that case, the reinsured's underwriting agency had received information about a loss of an insured vessel but had failed through neglect to pass that information on to its broker who was arranging facultative reinsurance of the same risk. Bailhache J and the Court of Appeal held that, in the ordinary course of business, the underwriting agency was or ought to have been aware of the casualty, and that accordingly the reinsurer was entitled to avoid the reinsurance for non-disclosure of that material fact. Again, there was no suggestion that the reinsured or its agents were under an obligation to conduct a search for material information; the agent had received the material information but had failed to act on it.

4.25 The authors suggest that these three cases do not support the view that, under the old law, insureds were under a duty to conduct a reasonable search of information, and they are of limited assistance in determining what the scope of the duty introduced by section 4(6) Insurance Act should be. The only case to have addressed the

42 July 2014 Report, para.8.81 and fn.40.

43 [1989] 1 Lloyd's Rep 69 (Com Ct).

44 [1995] 2 Lloyd's Rep 618 (Com Ct).

45 [1920] 3 Ll L Rep 199 (Com Ct), affd 4 Ll L Rep 382 (CA).

46 For example, would it have been reasonable to expect a search carried out by the insured to have included asking the yacht manager whether he had carried out character checks on the skipper? Or making enquiries about the character of the skipper?

47 [1995] 2 Lloyd's Rep 618 (Com Ct), 643

issue directly[48] found that under the previous law there was no such duty. *Australia & New Zealand Bank, Ltd v Colonial & Eagle Wharves, Ltd; Boag (Third Party)*[49] concerned the non-disclosure by the insured of the fact that its warehouse manager had been releasing cargo without production of bills of lading. McNair J held that the insured did not know, and was not deemed to know, of the warehouse manager's negligence. As regards the suggestion that a reasonable search would have uncovered the manager's conduct, and therefore the insured should be taken to know of it, McNair J said:[50]

> … the submission that the board of the defendant company ought to have known the material facts because they would have known them if they had made such inquiries as to their system as a reasonable, prudent board of such company in the ordinary course of business would have made, in my judgment fails both in law and on the facts. I have been referred to no authority to suggest that the board of a company proposing to insure owe any duty to carry out a detailed investigation as to the manner in which the company's operations are performed, and I know of no principle in law which leads to that result. If a company is proposing to insure wages in transit, I cannot believe that they owe a duty to the insurers to find out exactly how the weekly wages are in fact carried from the bank to their premises, though clearly they must not deliberately close their eyes to defects in the system and must disclose any suspicions or misgivings they may have. To impose such an obligation upon the proposer is tantamount to holding that insurers only insure persons who conduct their business prudently, whereas it is a commonplace that one of the purposes of insurance is to cover yourself against your own negligence or the negligence of your servants.

4.26 Rather than being derived from existing case law, the concept of a 'reasonable search' appears to be based on what the Law Commissions considered would be part of 'good insurance placement processes'.[51] The evidence given by Paul Hopkin, Technical Director of AIRMIC, to the Special Public Bill Committee of the House of Lords on 9 December 2014 describes the guidance that AIRMIC was already providing to its members about the gathering of information for disclosure to insurers:[52]

> As has been said, we publish guidance for our members, drawing on their experience and best practice to produce consolidated advice. I have brought along some samples to show the weight of the reports that we produce. One report was specifically about disclosure of material facts and information in business insurance. This guidance, which we produced three or four years ago, drew on my own experience as an insurance buyer for a large multinational plc with a turnover of about £2 billion. The guidance refers to and sets out a suggested process which many insurance buyers follow and identifies roles for: a responsible person who, in a large organisation, will typically be the insurance manager; a series of knowledgeable people who have relevant information and know the material facts to be disclosed; and an authorised person who will sign off on the submission. Technically, within a large organisation where there is an insurance manager, that manager will undertake the reasonable search that has been described and contact all the people within the organisation whom the responsible person – the insurance buyer – knows, or has reason to believe, has the knowledge required

48 See also *Simner v New India Assurance Co* [1995] LRLR 240 (Com Ct) 253–255 (HHJ Diamond).
49 [1960] 2 Lloyd's Rep 241 (Com Ct).
50 Ibid., 252.
51 July 2014 Report, para.8.78.
52 House of Lords Special Public Bill Committee, *Insurance Bill (HL), House of Lords Papers* (2014–15, HL 81), 61.

to develop the submission to the insurance market. The reasonable search will consist of contact with all the knowledgeable people in the organisation and then consolidation of that information into a market report. That represents a reasonable process for the discovery of that information.

4.27 Some assistance is given in the Insurance Act about the scope of the search by the insured. In section 4(7), information that is the subject of the search is defined to include 'information held within the insured's organisation or by any other person (such as the insured's agent or a person for whom cover is provided by the contract of insurance)'. There is accordingly no limit, other than one of reasonableness, as to the persons who may need to be asked to provide relevant information. In spite of this, the identification of particular types of person (i.e. '[someone within] the insured's organisation', 'the insured's agent' and 'a person for whom cover is provided by the contract of insurance'[53]) in the definition suggests that at least those persons should be considered. The Law Commissions recognised that what is available to the insured is necessarily a matter of fact in the circumstances of the case.[54] They said that 'in some circumstances, the insured should also make enquiries of outside advisors such as brokers/agents, lawyers, technical advisors and suppliers who may know about matters that are relevant to the insurer'.[55] The Explanatory Notes say that the scope of the phrase 'information held ... by any other person' is intended to be flexible.[56]

4.28 The identification of information held within the insured's organisation as a target for search raises the question of what constitutes that organisation: is it limited to the insured itself or does it include the group of which the insured may be a part? If the other members of the group are beneficiaries of the cover (so that cover is provided for them by the contract of insurance), then one would expect that a search of the information held by those group members would be conducted in any event. There may, however, be circumstances in which group members are not covered by the insurance, but where it will be important for the insured to know whether it is expected to make enquiries of those members as part of its search. A good example would be that of a group captive insurance company seeking to arrange reinsurance. It will have received information from its insureds, being the other members of the group of which it is a part, as part of the process of insuring those risks, but the information that it has received may be out of date, or be limited because the insured's duty of disclosure is limited under the law applicable to the insurance contract issued by the captive insurer. Would a reasonable search by the captive insurer include conducting enquiries of its insureds (as members of its organisation) for relevant and current information? To address this uncertainty, the LMA has produced the following Model Clause for insurance contracts:

Insurance Act 2015 – Definition of 'insured's organisation'
Under Section 4 of the Insurance Act 2015, the Insured ought to know what should reasonably have been revealed by a reasonable search of information available to it, which includes

53 That is, a person who is a beneficiary of the cover but not a party to the contract of insurance, and therefore an 'insured': see para.3.7.

54 July 2014 Report, para.8.88.

55 July 2014 Report, para.8.90.

56 Explanatory Notes to the Insurance Act 2015, para.56.

(under Section 4(7)) information held within the 'insured's organisation'. For these purposes only, the 'insured's organisation' shall include:
{List relevant entities within the Insured}[57]

4.29 The Explanatory Notes state that section 4(6) Insurance Act 'largely codifies principles derived from some case law' (citing *Aiken*).[58] For the reasons given above, section 4(6) actually introduces a new concept into English insurance law and with one or two exceptions, cases decided under the old law are unlikely to be of much assistance in the application of the new test. A number of aspects are worth noting:

(i) Although the Law Commissions describe section 4(4) as introducing a statutory duty to take positive steps to collate relevant information,[59] the insured is under no duty to carry out a search. If it chooses not to search for information and it transpires that material information was not disclosed at the time the contract of insurance was entered into, it will be for the insurer to establish that relevant individuals were aware of the information (see paragraphs 4.3 and 4.4 above) or that a reasonable search by the insured should have revealed that information.

(ii) The purpose of the search is to reveal material information. Material information is that which would influence the judgement of a prudent insurer in determining whether to take the risk and on what terms (section 7(3) Insurance Act and see paragraphs 3.15–3.17 above). Proposal or application forms produced by the insurer will be a guide as to what information is likely to be relevant. The lay insured (i.e. one not in the insurance industry) may also expect to be guided by its insurance brokers, who are insurance professionals, as to what is likely to be material.

(iii) In conveyancing, a statement that a vendor is not aware of a defect in title carries with it the implied representation that he has taken reasonable steps to ascertain whether any exist (see *William Sindall plc v Cambridgeshire County Council*[60]). 'This may require him, in the first instance, to examine his title deeds and other records, inspect the property and obtain legal advice. If there is anything to put him on inquiry as to the existence of a defect, he may have to pursue the matter further by questioning others or examining their documents' (*per* Hoffmann LJ in *William Sindall plc v Cambridgeshire County Council*[61]). This may be some guide as to what a reasonable search for material information should entail.

(iv) The rules governing the disclosure of documents in civil proceedings may also be relevant in that they require a party to conduct a 'reasonable search' for relevant documents. Part 31.7 Civil Procedure Rules 1998 provides as follows:

> (1) When giving standard disclosure, a party is required to make a reasonable search for documents falling within rule 31.6(b) or (c).

---

57 LMA Model Clause 9119 (16 March 2016).
58 Explanatory Notes to the Insurance Act 2015, para.56.
59 July 2014 Report, para.8.80.
60 [1994] WLR 1016 (CA).
61 Ibid., 1025.

(2) The factors relevant in deciding the reasonableness of a search include the following:
   (a) the number of documents involved;
   (b) the nature and complexity of the proceedings;
   (c) the ease and expense of retrieval of any particular document; and
   (d) the significance of any document which is likely to be located during the search.

(3) Where a party has not searched for a category or class of document on the grounds that to do so would be unreasonable, he must state this in his disclosure statement and identify the category or class of document.

The overriding principle of proportionality is relevant in determining the extent of the search. The Part 31 Practice Direction notes that it may be reasonable to decide not to search for documents coming into existence before some particular date, or to limit the search of documents to some particular place or places or to documents of a particular category: Practice Direction, Disclosure and Inspection, paragraphs 2 and 2A(4).

(v) The search may be conducted by making enquiries 'or by any other means' (section 4(6) Insurance Act). Information held in paper files, in electronic databases, or available online or through electronic media is all available to be searched and may be subject to disclosure.

(vi) The Law Commissions' view was that what amounts to a 'reasonable' search will depend on the particular set of facts, including the size, nature and complexity of the business to 'be judged objectively, by reference to a reasonable, prudent assured in that class'.[62] The insured will need to consider what information is likely to be material to the insurer's consideration of the risk it wants to insure, and where that information is likely to be found. It can then consider whether it would be reasonable to incur the time and expense in seeking to obtain that information having regard to the likelihood of there being material information to be produced by the sources identified, and the likely significance of that information.

(vii) The insured will only be taken to know that which 'should reasonably have been revealed' by its search (section 4(6) Insurance Act). This is directed primarily at circumstances in which the person who is asked for information could not reasonably be expected to provide it, for example where the person had been negligent and could not be expected to admit to that negligence: see paragraph 57 of the Explanatory Notes, citing *Australia & New Zealand Bank, Ltd v Colonial & Eagle Wharves, Ltd; Boag (Third Party)*[63] by way of example. Would it be reasonable to expect a person who had no legal duty to provide information to the insured, to respond to the insured's enquiries? The authors consider that whether or not the person was under a legal duty to respond to the insured's enquiries will be a factor to take into account when assessing whether the person should reasonably have been expected to provide the information, but it is not conclusive. The Law Commissions included suppliers in the categories of person who might be the subject of

62 July 2014 Report, para.8.83.
63 [1960] 2 Lloyd's Rep 241 (Com Ct).

a reasonable search and it is unlikely that a supplier would be under a legal obligation to respond to enquiries by the insured (see paragraph 4.27 above).

(viii) The 'reasonable search' concept introduces a standard of negligence into the insured's duty of fair presentation which was absent from the previous law (see paragraph 4.25 above). Will expert evidence now be required to establish what search a reasonable insured would be expected to carry out in the circumstances of the case, and what information would reasonably be expected to be revealed by that search?

4.30 The timing of the insured's search for information is relevant in two respects:

(i) Firstly, the duty to disclose material information is a continuing duty up to the date that the contract of insurance is entered into (see paragraph 3.25 above). Any search by the insured for information is likely to be concluded some time before the presentation of the risk to the insurer. If material information is received or is available to the insured after the search is completed, but before the risk is underwritten, and is not disclosed to the insurer, is the insured in breach of its duty of fair presentation? If the information was received by or known by an individual insured or an individual whose knowledge is treated as that of the insured (see paragraphs 4.3–4.11 above), there will have been a breach of the duty. If the information was received by any other individual, there will only have been a breach of the insured's duty if a reasonable search should reasonably have revealed that information. Whether the search that was conducted by the insured was reasonable will therefore depend on whether the timing of the search that was conducted was reasonable.

(ii) Secondly, the Law Commissions' July 2014 Report[64] and the Explanatory Notes[65] assume that the reasonable search is to be conducted for the purposes of the arranging of the insured's insurance. However, in the case of *The Dora*,[66] a case relied on by the Law Commissions in the formulation of the concept of a 'reasonable search', the insured was fixed with knowledge of the skipper's criminal conviction because, in the ordinary course of business, the insured's manager should have made enquiries at the time the skipper was recruited.[67] The enquiries that the manager should have made were not connected to the purchase of insurance by the insured. If the approach in *The Dora* is applied, the insured will be deemed to know anything which, in the course of the management of its business, it ought to have known about by making a reasonable search, including by making enquiries. If this reading of section 4(6) is correct (and there is nothing in the language of the Insurance Act to suggest it is not), the burden of disclosure on the insured is significant since it is required not only to conduct a reasonable search to reveal material information for the purposes of arranging its insurance, but must also act

64 Paras 8.77–8.81.

65 Para.56.

66 *Inversiones Manria SA v Sphere Drake Insurance Co Plc* [1989] 1 Lloyd's Rep 69 (Com Ct).

67 See paras 4.21 and 4.22 above.

reasonably in the conduct of its business when gathering information relevant to its business because it will be deemed to know that which it should have known had it acted reasonably.

Differences between the old and the new law

4.31 Under section 18(1) Marine Insurance Act 1906, the insured's constructive knowledge was qualified as being that which it ought to know 'in the ordinary course of business'. The cases were mainly concerned with what the insured was deemed to know as a consequence of its agents (so-called 'agents to know') being under a duty to inform it of relevant matters. In *Proudfoot v Montefiore*,[68] the insured's port agent knew that the insured's cargo had been damaged due to the vessel grounding but delayed communicating that information to the insured. In the meantime, the insured had arranged insurance for the cargo. The Court of Appeal held that the port agent ought to have communicated the fact that the cargo was damaged, in the ordinary course of his duty. Although the insured did not personally know of the loss of the cargo at the time of arranging the insurance, the insurer was entitled to avoid the policy for non-disclosure of the information that his agent should have passed to him. Cockburn CJ said:[69]

> By thus holding, we shall prevent the tendency to fraudulent concealment on the part of masters of vessels and agents at a distance, in matters on which they ought to communicate information to their principals, as also any tendency on the part of principals to encourage their servants and agents so to act.

4.32 Under the Insurance Act, imputation of knowledge to the insured by reference to what the insured ought in the ordinary course of business to know, is entirely replaced by the concept of information that should reasonably have been revealed by a 'reasonable search' of a potentially broad range of sources. The 'reasonable search' will, therefore, assume a position of importance. It seems probable that, in many cases, this alteration of the law could materially increase the insured's burden of disclosure, for the following reasons:

(i) Knowledge that should be revealed by a 'reasonable search' is probably a broader category than knowledge the insured ought to know 'in the ordinary course of business' (although this is far from certain, and remains to be seen). That is because the express language of the Act does not delimit the potential repositories of information which is to be subject to a reasonable search. The information does not need to be in the possession or control of the insured, and may include information held by the open-ended category of 'any other person' – not merely the insured's agent. The sole parameter is that of reasonableness. This means that the scale and scope of a reasonable search is likely to vary even within the same class of risk depending upon, for example, the sum insured, since it may well be reasonable to require a wider search where the sum insured is significantly greater.

68 (1866–67) LR 2 QB 511 (QB).
69 Ibid., 522.

(ii) The 'reasonable search' focuses on what should have been revealed by the insured's search. If it would not be reasonable for the insured to enquire of its agent whether it had anything material to disclose (because, for instance, it expected the agent to report anything material to it on a regular basis), then the insured will not be fixed with the agent's knowledge (cf *Proudfoot v Montefiore*, paragraph 4.31 above). The Law Commissions suggested at paragraph 8.87 of the July 2014 Report that the knowledge of an 'agent to know' may well be included in what the insured 'ought to know' and the authors of *Arnould* suggest that the concept will continue to be of relevance.[70] The view in *Colinvaux* is that the concept of 'agent to know' has been removed by the Insurance Act, which seemingly strengthens the position of the insured when compared to the old law.[71] Lord Mance expressed concern on this point when giving evidence to the Special Public Bill Committee.[72]

(iii) For example, a private bank takes out cyber insurance. Its external IT consultant knows about a latent virus in the bank's IT system, but does not tell anybody about it, and is not approached by the bank during the placing process. In those circumstances, it is possible that the insured 'ought to know' that the virus exists, if in the circumstances of the case the court considers that it should reasonably have made enquiries of the consultant. The fact that the consultant is neither an employee nor agent of the bank is irrelevant, because the information which is subject to the reasonable search may be 'held … by any other person'. The IT consultant would probably not have been an 'agent to know' under the old law.

(iv) Moreover, formerly the courts were able to consider the subjective characteristics of the insured in assessing what it ought to know 'in the ordinary course of business'. Thus, if the insured ran its business in an inefficient manner, it might not have been taken to have constructive knowledge of information which (by its inefficiency) it overlooked (contrary to the views of the Law Commissions and *Arnould*: see paragraphs 4.20–4.25 above). The rationale behind the old

---

70 *Arnould*, supp. to 18th edn, para.1.2-39.

71 Robert M. Merkin, *Colinvaux's Law of Insurance*, 11th edn (Sweet & Maxwell, London, 2016) (hereafter *Colinvaux*, 2016), para.7-046.

72 At p.56 of the Oral Evidence on 9 December 2014, where Lord Mance said:

> Cases like *Proudfoot v Montefiore*, and the cases in it, deal with situations where the insured would have absolutely no reason to inquire of the agent. The agent there had specific knowledge, which he ought to have disclosed, about the object to be insured – the ship or the goods – but deliberately concealed it from the insured to enable the insured to place the insurance while it was still possible to do so in ignorance. Not surprisingly, the agent's knowledge was deemed to be knowledge which the insured had and the insurance was voidable. It seems to me quite arguable that the current proposal would reverse that line of authority because, instead of the information of the 'agent to know' being imputed to the principal, you have no third category of imputed knowledge. Instead, you have the obligation of a reasonable search. Reasonable search is very sensible if you do not expect to have information already, but where you have an agent who is charged with responsibility for the subject matter of the insurance, you will, on the face of it, have no duty to search or inquire. I am not sure how the language works in that situation. Is the language saying that you have a duty to ask people whose duty it is to tell you without asking? In other words, do you have to go through a formality before every insurance of asking all your agents who are charged with the property or activity to be insured: 'Do you have information which you ought to have disclosed to me, pursuant to your ordinary duty?'. That seems a rather artificial interpretation of the concept of making a reasonable search. It may be what is intended, but I do not think it is clear.

law is that not every insured runs its business efficiently, and in certain cases the courts recognised this reality.[73] Under the Insurance Act, there is probably no such leniency, since the 'reasonable search' test appears to be purely objective, based upon what 'should' have been revealed by a 'reasonable search'. Accordingly, there may be no place for consideration of the subjective qualities of the insured, and its burden may therefore be increased, because it will be held to the (higher) standard of a *reasonable* insured. That is not to say that what amounts to a reasonable search should not take account of the characteristics of the insured's business (including its size and the sector in which it operates) but what is required of it should be measured against what is expected of businesses similarly situated. This may require expert evidence.

(v) For example, an insurance policy covers soybeans stored in a warehouse. The insured tells its insurer that the warehouse contains 20,000 tonnes of soybeans, whereas it actually contains almost double that amount, although the insured does not realise this, since the foreman does not keep an accurate record of the soybeans entering and leaving the warehouse. The insurer later seeks to avoid for breach of the duty of fair presentation on the basis that the insured failed to state accurately the quantity of soybeans in the warehouse. Under the old law, it is probable that the actual quantity of soybeans was not something the insured ought to have known in the ordinary course of business, since the law took account of the fact that not every insured ran its business in an efficient manner. However, under the Act it is likely that the actual quantity of soybeans should reasonably have been revealed by a reasonable search of information, and therefore failure to disclose the matter was a breach of the duty of fair presentation.

4.33 It is suggested in *Colinvaux* that what the insured ought to know for the purposes of disclosure under section 3 Insurance Act is not limited by section 4 to what should reasonably have been revealed by a reasonable search, and that the courts might follow authorities under section 18 Marine Insurance Act 1906 that treat the insured as knowing information that ought reasonably to have been obtained given the insured's state of knowledge of other facts.[74] This is unlikely to be the case. Section 21(2) Insurance Act omits section 18 Marine Insurance Act 1906 and section 21(3) abolishes any rule of law to the same effect as, *inter alia*, section 18. What the insured knows and ought to know for the purposes of making a fair presentation of the risk is accordingly confined to the provisions of section 4 Insurance Act, as supplemented by section 6 (see paragraphs 4.58–4.60 below).

4.34 In view of the potential increase in the insured's burden of disclosure, not to mention the uncertainties surrounding the concept of the 'reasonable search', and what it should entail, it is expected that insureds and brokers will seek to agree with their insurers general guidelines on what constitutes a reasonable search. It is also possible that they will seek to agree wordings under which the parameters of the reasonable search are set out in the contract itself, to avoid subsequent disputes on this

73 *Australia & New Zealand Bank, Ltd v Colonial & Eagle Wharves, Ltd; Boag (Third Party)* [1960] 2 Lloyd's Rep 241 (Com Ct), and see para.4.25 above.

74 *Colinvaux*, 2016, para.7-055.

point. An agreement by the insurer that the insured has conducted a reasonable search is likely to be binding on the insurer absent fraud on the part of the insured.

Knowledge of the insurer

5 Knowledge of insurer

(1) For the purposes of section 3(5)(b), an insurer knows something only if it is known to one or more of the individuals who participate on behalf of the insurer in the decision whether to take the risk, and if so on what terms (whether the individual does so as the insurer's employee or agent, as an employee of the insurer's agent or in any other capacity).

(2) For the purposes of section 3(5)(c), an insurer ought to know something only if –

(a) an employee or agent of the insurer knows it, and ought reasonably to have passed on the relevant information to an individual mentioned in subsection (1), or

(b) the relevant information is held by the insurer and is readily available to an individual mentioned in subsection (1).

(3) For the purposes of section 3(5)(d), an insurer is presumed to know –

(a) things which are common knowledge, and

(b) things which an insurer offering insurance of the class in question to insureds in the field of activity in question would reasonably be expected to know in the ordinary course of business.

4.35 If the insured has failed to disclose a material circumstance as part of its duty to make a fair presentation of the risk, it may be relieved of the consequences of that non-disclosure if the insurer knows, or is treated as knowing, the non-disclosed circumstance (sections 3(4) and (5)(b)–(d) Insurance Act). The insurer's knowledge, or deemed knowledge, of the true position would not excuse the misrepresentation by the insured of a material fact, expectation or belief (the insured would still be in breach of its duty of fair presentation under section 3(3)(c) of the Act), although the extent to which the underwriter could establish that he or she had relied on the misrepresentation in those circumstances would be relevant to the availability of a remedy for the misrepresentation (under section 8(1) Insurance Act – see paragraphs 5.3–5.5 below). This reflects the position under the old law where the insurer's knowledge only relieved the insured of a breach of the duty of disclosure and not of the consequences of a misrepresentation: section 18(3)(b) Marine Insurance Act applied 'absent enquiry', as does section 3(5) Insurance Act.[75] The insured is not required to disclose a material circumstance if:

- the insurer knows the relevant circumstance (section 3(5)(b));
- the insurer ought to know the relevant circumstance (section 3(5)(c));
- the insurer is presumed to know the relevant circumstance (section 3(5)(d)).

4.36 The Explanatory Notes say that these provisions are based on the exceptions in section 18(3) Marine Insurance Act[76] and the case law interpreting them.[77]

75 See para.8.5 of the Law Commissions' Joint Consultation and Discussion Paper on 'Insurance Contract Law: The Business Insured's Duty of Disclosure and the Law of Warranties', CP3, June 2012.

76 Marine Insurance Act 1906, s.18(3)(b) provides that the following circumstances need not be disclosed: 'Any circumstance which is known or presumed to be known to the insurer. The insurer is presumed to know matters of common notoriety or knowledge, and matters which an insurer in the ordinary course of business, as such, ought to know.'

77 Explanatory Notes to the Insurance Act 2015, para.60.

What the insurer knows

4.37 Section 5(1) Insurance Act sets out what an insurer knows for the purposes of section 3(5)(b): the insurer knows only what is known to the individuals who participate on behalf of the insurer in the decision to take the risk, and if so on what terms. If the insurer were an individual (say, a Lloyd's Name), that individual's knowledge would not be relevant unless he or she was involved in the underwriting of the risk. The same would apply to the knowledge of senior management, including directors, of a corporate insurer. The basis on which an insurer 'knows' something is accordingly different from that on which an insured 'knows' something (see paragraphs 4.3 and 4.4 above) and as the Law Commissions acknowledge, the basis of imputation is narrower than under the previous law.[78]

4.38 Section 5(1) makes it clear that the capacity in which an individual participates in the decision to take the risk and on what terms is irrelevant: 'whether the individual does so as the insurer's employee or agent, as an employee of the insurer's agent or in any other capacity'. It is suggested that, as with the old law, whether the knowledge of a junior employee is imputed to the insurer will depend on the tasks and responsibilities delegated to that employee. In *Evans v Employers Mutual*,[79] a case relied on by the Law Commissions to support this provision,[80] the knowledge of a clerk to whom the review of claim and proposal forms had been delegated was imputed to the insurer. The Law Commissions suggest that the individual whose knowledge is to count as the knowledge of the insurer must have played a 'meaningful role in the underwriting decision',[81] although the particular task delegated to the individual will also be relevant. For example, the knowledge of the clerk in *Evans v Employers Mutual*[82] was imputed to the insurer because he had been asked to compare the claim and proposal forms and there was a material discrepancy between the two forms which the clerk should have told his manager about. There may be a different outcome if, for example, the clerk knew that the insured was in financial difficulty but did not pass that information on to the underwriter. Would that information be treated as the insurer's knowledge if the clerk was not asked to consider that point?[83]

What the insurer ought to know

4.39 In addition to the actual knowledge of those individuals participating in the underwriting of the risk, the insurer will also be treated as knowing something which is available to, but not known by, those individuals in two circumstances:

- an employee or agent of the insurer has the relevant knowledge and ought to have passed it on to those individuals (section 5(2)(a) Insurance Act);
- the relevant information is held by the insurer and is readily available to those individuals (section 5(2)(b) Insurance Act).

78 July 2014 Report, para.10.38.
79 [1936] 1 KB 505 (CA).
80 July 2014 Report, para.10.37.
81 July 2014 Report, para.10.40.
82 [1936] 1 KB 505 (CA).
83 See *Malhi v Abbey Life* Insurance Co [1996] LRLR 237 (CA).

4.40 The first category of deemed knowledge reflects the old law concerning what is known by a so-called 'agent to know'. For example, in *Joel v Law Union*,[84] the insurer was deemed to know that which a doctor commissioned to examine a prospective policyholder knew because the doctor was regarded as an agent of the insurer who ought to have passed the relevant information to his principal. The same principle was applied in cases such as *Proudfoot v Montefiore*[85] and *London General Insurance Co Ltd v General Marine Underwriters Association Ltd*[86] when considering imputation to the insured of knowledge held by the insured's agent or employee. If the agent or employee participates in the underwriting of the risk, his or her knowledge will be treated as the insurer's knowledge under section 5(1) Insurance Act (see paragraph 4.38 above). Section 5(2)(a) concerns employees or agents who are not involved in underwriting, but who ought to pass on what they know to the underwriting team. The Explanatory Notes identify the insurer's claims department, or surveyors or medical experts retained for the purposes of assessing the risk, as falling into this category.[87] Whether in any given situation, a claims department 'ought' to have passed information on to the underwriter will depend on the circumstances, including whether claims information would be passed on as a matter of normal practice, and whether the claims department was aware, or should have been aware, that the relevant risk was in the course of being underwritten.[88]

4.41 The second category of deemed knowledge, being information held by the insurer and 'readily available' to those individuals participating in the underwriting, was apparently derived by the Law Commissions' consideration of the Court of Appeal judgments in *Malhi v Abbey Life*[89] and *The Grecia Express*,[90] which they took to suggest that insurers would not be expected to consult their records in the ordinary course of underwriting a risk, and would accordingly not be deemed to know what was in those records.[91] In the first draft of the Insurance Bill published by the Law Commissions in January 2014, the equivalent clause provided that the insurer would know something if the relevant information was readily available to the individuals participating in the underwriting of the risk. The LMA, among others, pointed out that this might capture information available to the underwriter were he or she to conduct an internet search for information relating to the risk to be insured, and the Law Commissions accepted that the provision had been drafted too widely.[92] In the version of the Bill appended to the July 2014 Report, the relevant information was restricted to that 'held by the insurer'. Information available on the internet is not 'held' by a person having access to the internet. Consequently, an underwriter is not expected to carry out an internet search 'at the Box' and the insurer is accordingly not fixed with knowledge of what that search would have revealed had it been carried

84 [1908] 2 KB 863 (CA).
85 (1866–67) LR 2 QB 511 (QB).
86 (1920) 3 Ll L Rep 199 (Com Ct), affd (1920) 4 Ll L Rep 382 (CA).
87 Explanatory Notes to the Insurance Act 2015, para.63.
88 See *Malhi v Abbey Life* Assurance Co [1996] LRLR 237 (CA).
89 [1996] LRLR 237 (CA).
90 [2002] EWCH 203 (Comm), [2002] 2 Lloyd's Rep 88.
91 July 2014 Report, paras 10.22–10.27.
92 July 2014 Report, para.10.54.

out. However, the same reasoning may not apply to information on (for example) the insurer's own intranet system, or on databases to which it subscribes.

4.42 In one sense, information on a subscription database is not 'held by' the insurer any more than information on the internet – because it is 'held by' the provider of the resource. For example, the Lloyd's Marine Intelligence Unit Seasearcher database contains information which, although accessible to its subscribers, is 'held by' the Lloyd's MIU itself. However, it might be argued that such information is nonetheless 'held by' the insurer, in the sense that during the currency of its subscription it has the right and ability immediately to access the information on the database, in a way that ordinary members of the public cannot do.

4.43 In *Malhi v Abbey Life*,[93] the Court of Appeal held that the provision of information to an insurer in a context other than for the underwriting of the particular risk in question:

> does not necessarily afford to that company knowledge sufficient to found waiver by election: whether it does afford such knowledge depends on the circumstances of its receipt and how it is dealt with thereafter. In particular, information will not give rise to such knowledge unless it is received by a person authorized and able to appreciate its significance.[94]

In the same vein, in *The Grecia Express*[95] Coleman J said that '[t]he proposer for insurance is thus not entitled to assume that the underwriter will carry in his mind previous casualties of vessels not insured by him and be in a position to relate that information to the new risk proposed'.[96] In *London General Insurance Co Ltd v General Marine Underwriters Association Ltd*,[97] Bailhache J and the Court of Appeal held that an insurer was not expected to carry in his mind information that was of no interest to him at the time it was obtained, and did not suggest that the insurer would be fixed with knowledge of information merely because it was readily available to him.

4.44 By way of contrast, there are cases applying the old law in which the courts considered that the insurer might be fixed with knowledge of material information if it had the means of checking the position. In *Brine v Featherstone*[98] the insurer was not entitled to avoid the policy for misrepresentation as to the position of the insured vessel when the underwriter could have established where she was by looking in Lloyd's List (with Mansfield CJ suggesting that the insurer was negligent for not so doing). In *Foley v Tabor*[99] Erle CJ said:

> The material fact must have been known to the assured, and unknown to the insurer. As to the latter point, actual knowledge is not essential if the insurer had the means of knowing the fact, and it was within his knowledge. If, for example, he knew that he could learn the exact cargo at Lloyd's, and chose not to ascertain it knowing or believing it would contain iron, it was *within* his knowledge.[100]

---

93 [1996] LRLR 237 (CA).

94 Ibid., *per* Rose LJ at 242, col.1.

95 [2002] EWCH 203 (Comm), [2002] 2 Lloyd's Rep 88.

96 Ibid., at 136, col.1.

97 (1920) 3 Ll L Rep 199 (Com Ct), affd (1920) 4 Ll L Rep 382 (CA).

98 (1813) 4 Taunt 869, 128 ER 574.

99 (1861) 2 F&F 663, 175 ER 1231.

100 Ibid., at 1235, emphasis in the original. This decision may be an example of the insurer having 'blind eye' knowledge: see paras 4.58– 4.60.

4.45 In MacDonald Eggers et al. it is suggested that under the old law, insurers may be fixed with knowledge of information that is available in the insurance marketplace, that is accessible to the insurer, and that may be presumed to be consulted by the insurer when rating the risk.[101] It was held in *Morrison v The Universal Marine Insurance Company*[102] that underwriters are not presumed to know the contents of Lloyd's List. In *Sea Glory Maritime Co v Al Sagr National Insurance Co (The 'M/V Nancy')*,[103] Blair J said that he did not think it correct to say that electronic databases should be treated as equivalent to information in hard copy such as newspapers because online information is available to be called up when required by conducting a search.[104] In that case, three online databases contained some or all of the information allegedly not disclosed by the insured, but the insurer did not subscribe to the database that contained the most clearly expressed information. Blair J did not have to decide in that case whether the insurer was deemed to know what was in that database (since the insurer had not established inducement in any event), but said that it would be a question to be determined in light of all the relevant circumstances concerning the placement of the risk.[105]

4.46 According to paragraph 64 of the Explanatory Notes, the intention of section 5(2)(b) is to require the relevant underwriter to make a reasonable effort to search such information as is available to him or her within the insurer's organisation, giving the insurer's electronic records as an example. As knowledge within this sub-section is likely to be in issue where the underwriter has not conducted a search, or has not found the relevant information, what was actually in the insurer's records at the time and whether it was 'readily available' will have to be ascertained.

4.47 What information is likely to qualify as being 'readily available', for these purposes? That is a question of fact. Where an insurer has written cover for an insured over a number of years, information about it, and its claims history, is likely to qualify as 'readily available'. However, if the claims history is not in fact available to the participating underwriter, because (for example) it is stored on a separate database to which the underwriter has no access, it is unlikely to be 'readily available' for these purposes.

What the insurer is presumed to know

4.48 Section 5(3) sets out two categories of information which the insurer is presumed to know, and therefore cannot complain that the insured has failed to disclose:

- things which are common knowledge (section 5(3)(a)), and
- things which an insurer offering insurance of the class in question to insureds in the field of activity in question would reasonably be expected to know in the ordinary course of business (section 5(3)(b)).

4.49 The reference to 'things which are common knowledge' is intended to replicate 'matters of common notoriety or knowledge' which the insurer was presumed to

101 MacDonald Eggers, Picken & Foss, 2010, paras 12.21, 12.22, 12.26 and 12.28.
102 (1872–73) LR 8 Ex 40, revd LR 8 Ex 197 (CA).
103 [2013] EWHC 2116 (Comm), [2014] 1 Lloyd's Rep 14.
104 Ibid., [173]–[174].
105 Ibid., [173]–[174] and *Arnould*, 18th edn, paras 16-181 and 16-194.

know under section 18(3)(b) Marine Insurance Act 1906. As the Explanatory Notes say, 'common notoriety' has not been retained because the meaning of 'notoriety' may have changed since 1906 from 'well known' to something suggesting an element of infamy.[106] Unlike sections 5(1) and (2), which impute knowledge to the insurer by reference to what is known or ought to be known by those individuals who participate in the decision to take the risk, presumed knowledge under section 5(3) is not limited to that which those individuals would be presumed to know. The test is accordingly entirely objective.

4.50 By way of example of matters that have been considered to be 'common knowledge', in *Carter v Boehm*,[107] Lord Mansfield said that the list of matters which the assured need not mention included:

> … general topics of speculation or every cause which may occasion natural perils, as the difficulty of the voyage, kind of seasons, probability of hurricanes, earthquakes etc.; or every cause which may occasion political perils, from the rupture of the States, from war, and the various operations of it, upon the probability of safety from the continuance and return of peace, or from the imbecility of the enemy.

4.51 Although the Law Commissions recognised that information available to the underwriting team for the purposes of section 5(2)(b) had to be 'held by the insurer' and be 'readily available', no such restrictions are placed on what may be treated as things which are common knowledge. The Law Commissions state that they do not intend any change in what is to be regarded as common knowledge but suggest it could be interpreted widely. They say that it may include matters on social media, giving an example of an entertainer's rumoured drug use reported in mainstream media as a matter of common knowledge.[108] If it is to be suggested by this that the mere fact that a matter is reported in the media (including social media) will be sufficient to establish that matter as common knowledge, this would not reflect the old law. In *Bates v Hewitt*[109] the fact that the insured vessel was previously a cruiser in the service of the Confederate States during the American Civil War was taken to be a matter of public notoriety, but the underwriter did not have this knowledge in mind at the time of underwriting. Even though the jury found that the underwriter could have recollected what he had previously known about the vessel by careful study of the placing memorandum, the court held that this was insufficient to excuse the insured's non-disclosure. It was necessary for the information to be present in the mind of the underwriter at the time of underwriting for it to be treated as the insurer's knowledge. The cases referred to in paragraph 4.41 above are to the same effect. If matters of common knowledge can be ascertained by a search of social media or news websites, then one is back in the realm of information available on the internet, which the Law Commissions accepted could not form part of the insurer's deemed knowledge for the purposes of section 5(2)(b) (see paragraph 4.41 above).[110]

---

106 Explanatory Notes to Insurance Act 2015, para.66.

107 (1766) 3 Burr 1905, 97 ER 1162.

108 July 2014 Report, paras 10.58 and 10.59.

109 (1867) LR 2 QB 595 (QB).

110 'Nearly two-thirds of adults in America now get news on social media and a fifth do so often, according to a recent survey by the Pew Research Centre, a polling outfit; the numbers continue to grow

4.52 The second category of what an insurer is presumed to know may shed some light on the scope of the 'common knowledge' which it is presumed to know under section 5(3)(a). In *Noble v Kennoway*,[111] Lord Mansfield said:

> Every under-writer is presumed to be acquainted with the practice of the trade he insures, and that whether it is established, or not. If he does not know it, he ought to inform himself. It is no matter if the usage has only been for a year.

4.53 Under section 18(3)(b) Marine Insurance Act 1906, the insurer was presumed to know 'matters which in the ordinary course of his business, as such, [it] ought to know.' The Law Commissions indicated in their June 2012 and July 2014 Reports that this was an appropriate standard 'though the concept could be expressed more clearly in the legislation'[112] and accordingly the previous case law will continue to be relevant. By way of example, in *Glencore International AG v Alpina Insurance Co. Ltd*,[113] Moore-Bick J said that a reasonable underwriter familiar with the business of oil trading would be expected to know of the whole range of circumstances that may arise in carrying on that kind of business.[114]

4.54 In expressing the concept more clearly, the Law Commissions did contemplate that this would introduce a change directed at the problem of so-called 'naïve capacity', which they described as inexperienced insurers entering into a new market, and underpricing the risk due to their lack of understanding, and then attempting to escape liability on the basis of non-disclosure.[115]

4.55 Section 5(3)(b) Insurance Act distinguishes between the class of business underwritten by the insurer and the insured's field of activity. The Explanatory Notes explain the distinction in paragraph 67:

> Many underwriters work by class of business (such as property or professional indemnity insurance) rather than by industry sector (such as oil and gas). An insurer ought to have some insight into the industry for which it is providing insurance, but this insight may reasonably be limited to matters relevant to the type of insurance provided.

Confidential information

4.56 The imputation of knowledge of confidential information to an insured insofar as such information is held by the insured's agent is covered by sections 4(4) and (5) Insurance Act (see paragraphs 4.12–4.19 above).

4.57 Recommendation 16 of the July 2014 Report[116] included a recommendation by the Law Commissions that references to an individual's knowledge should not include confidential information acquired by an agent through a business relationship with someone other than his principal, whether the insured or insurer. This recommendation was reflected in clause 6(3) of the Insurance Contracts Bill appended to

---

fast' *The Economist*, 10 September 2016, p.22. Is this a sufficient basis to establish a matter as 'common knowledge'? ('Yes, I'd lie to you' *The Economist*, 10 September 2016, p.22).

111 (1780) 2 Doug K B 511, 99 ER 326.

112 June 2012 Report, para.8.20.

113 [2003] EWHC 2792 (Comm), [2004] 1 Lloyd's Rep 111.

114 Ibid., [41].

115 July 2014 Report, para.10.61.

116 At 129.

the July 2014 Report, which provided that an insurer would not be deemed to know confidential information acquired by the insurer's agent through a business relationship with someone other than the insurer. This clause was not carried over into the Bill presented to Parliament in August 2014. Whether the insurer is fixed with knowledge of confidential information held by its agent will therefore depend on whether that agent 'ought reasonably to have passed on the relevant information' to an individual participating in the decision whether or not to take the risk (section 5(2) Insurance Act – see paragraphs 4.39 and 4.40 above) or whether the insurer would reasonably be expected to know the information in the ordinary course of business (section 5(3)(b) Insurance Act – see paragraphs 4.52–4.55 above).

Matters which are deemed to be known

4.58 Section 6(1) Insurance Act provides:

> For the purposes of sections 3 to 5, references to an individual's knowledge include not only actual knowledge, but also matters which the individual suspected, and of which the individual would have had knowledge but for deliberately refraining from confirming them or enquiring about them.

4.59 Apart from the specific categories of knowledge which the insured and the insurer are deemed to know by virtue of sections 4 and 5 Insurance Act, section 6(1) adds an additional category applicable to both insured and insurer, which is so-called 'blind-eye' knowledge. Lord Scott explained this concept in *Manifest Shipping Co v Uni-Polaris Insurance Co*[117] as follows, and section 6(1) follows this formulation:[118]

> 'Blind-eye' knowledge approximates to knowledge. Nelson at the battle of Copenhagen made a deliberate decision to place the telescope to his blind eye in order to avoid seeing what he knew he would see if he placed it to his good eye. It is, I think, common ground – and if it is not, it should be – that an imputation of blind-eye knowledge requires an amalgam of suspicion that certain facts may exist and a decision to refrain from taking any step to confirm their existence.

4.60 Since sections 4 and 5 Insurance Act are intended exhaustively to set out what will be treated as knowledge of the insured and the insurer for the purposes of the Act, it is not clear why section 6(1) also refers to section 3 (except possibly in relation to matters of expectation or belief for the purposes of section (3)(3)(c): see paragraph 3.23), but it is not thought that this is intended to extend the scope of knowledge beyond the categories set out in sections 4 and 5.

Matters which are deemed not to be known

4.61 It is a long-standing principle of English law that a principal will not be fixed with knowledge of a fraud being perpetrated against it by its own agent since, as a matter of common sense, the agent would not disclose to the principal that it was being defrauded: the so-called *Hampshire Land* exception.[119] The leading case applying this

117 [2001] UKHL 1, [2003] 1 AC 469 [112].
118 Explanatory Notes to the Insurance Act 2015, para.69.
119 *In re Hampshire Land Co* [1896] 2 Ch 743 (Ch).

principle in the context of the Marine Insurance Act 1906, and particularly sections 18 and 19, was *PCW Syndicates v PCW Reinsurers.*[120] In *Arab Bank PLC v Zurich Insurance Co*[121] Rix J applied the principle so as to exclude knowledge by the policyholder of a serious breach of duty by a director where the director's fraud was aimed at a third party:[122] the application of the principle to a fraud where the principal was only a 'secondary victim' was doubted by the Court of Appeal and House of Lords (by a majority) in *Stone & Rolls Ltd v Moore Stephens*[123] which is not an insurance case. In *Bilta (UK) Ltd v Nazir (No 2)*[124] Lord Sumption described the distinction between primary and secondary victimhood as elusive.[125]

4.62 In the first draft of the Insurance Bill produced by the Law Commissions, the *Hampshire Land* exception was not addressed, and accordingly may not have applied in determining what constituted the insured's and insurer's knowledge, since that knowledge would be determined 'only' by the provisions of the Bill. The omission was remedied in the version of the Bill that went to Parliament, and the principle has now been codified in section 6(2) Insurance Act:

> (2) Nothing in this Part affects the operation of any rule of law according to which knowledge of a fraud perpetrated by an individual ("F") either on the insured or on the insurer is not to be attributed to the insured or to the insurer (respectively), where –
> (a) if the fraud is on the insured, F is any of the individuals mentioned in section 4(2)(b) or (3), or
> (b) if the fraud is on the insurer, F is any of the individuals mentioned in section 5(1).

4.63 Section 6(2) focuses on the attribution of knowledge where a fraud has been perpetrated by a relevant individual on either the insured or the insurer. In its July 2014 Report, the Law Commissions acknowledged the different views expressed in *Arab Bank PLC v Zurich Insurance Co*[126] and *Stone & Rolls Ltd v Moore Stephens*,[127] and said that they wished to preserve the common law flexibility rather than recommending a defined rule.[128] The Explanatory Notes, however, take a different tack in making it clear that section 6(2) 'means that a company is not fixed with knowledge of a fraud practised *against it* by its agent or officer.'[129] It may accordingly be insufficient to prevent attribution of knowledge to the insured of a fraud by a member of senior management if the fraud was not directed at the insured, but rather at a third party, even if the senior manager was acting in serious breach of duty to the insured in perpetrating that fraud on the third party.

---

120 [1996] 1 Lloyd's Rep 241 (CA).
121 [1999] 1 Lloyd's Rep 262 (Com Ct).
122 The decision may turn on the fact that the insurance in question insured the policyholder in respect of liability for fraud by its directors, including the director who had defrauded third parties and who made the dishonest representation in the proposal form. It does not appear to have been acknowledged that the primary victim of fraud was the insurer who had underwritten the policy in reliance on a deliberately misleading proposal form signed by the dishonest director.
123 [2008] EWCA Civ 644, [2008] 2 Lloyd's Rep 319 [72]–[74] affd and [2009] UK HL 39, [2009] 1 AC 1391.
124 [2015] UCSC 23, [2016] AC 1.
125 Ibid., [93].
126 [1999] Lloyd's Rep 262 (Com Ct).
127 [2009] UKHL 39, [2009] 1 AC 1391.
128 July 2014 Report, paras 8.67–8.76.
129 Para.70, emphasis added.

CHAPTER 5

Remedies for breach of the duty of fair presentation

8 Remedies for breach

(1) The insurer has a remedy against the insured for a breach of the duty of fair presentation only if the insurer shows that, but for the breach, the insurer –
  (a) would not have entered into the contract of insurance at all, or
  (b) would have done so only on different terms.

(2) The remedies are set out in Schedule 1.

(3) A breach for which the insurer has a remedy against the insured is referred to in this Act as a "qualifying breach".

(4) A qualifying breach is either –
  (a) deliberate or reckless, or
  (b) neither deliberate nor reckless.

(5) A qualifying breach is deliberate or reckless if the insured –
  (a) knew that it was in breach of the duty of fair presentation, or
  (b) did not care whether or not it was in breach of that duty.

(6) It is for the insurer to show that a qualifying breach was deliberate or reckless.

Schedule 1

INSURERS' REMEDIES FOR QUALIFYING BREACHES
PART 1
CONTRACTS

General

1 This Part of this Schedule applies to qualifying breaches of the duty of fair presentation in relation to non-consumer insurance contracts (for (sic) variations to them, see Part 2).

Deliberate or reckless breaches

2 If a qualifying breach was deliberate or reckless, the insurer –
  (a) may avoid the contract and refuse all claims, and
  (b) need not return any of the premiums paid.

Other breaches

3 Paragraphs 4 to 6 apply if a qualifying breach was neither deliberate nor reckless.

4 If, in the absence of the qualifying breach, the insurer would not have entered into the contract on any terms, the insurer may avoid the contract and refuse all claims, but must in that event return the premiums paid.

5 If the insurer would have entered into the contract, but on different terms (other than terms relating to the premium), the contract is to be treated as if it had been entered into on those different terms if the insurer so requires.

6 (1) In addition, if the insurer would have entered into the contract (whether the terms relating to matters other than the premium would have been the same or different), but would have charged a higher premium, the insurer may reduce proportionately the amount to be paid on a claim.

(2) In sub-paragraph (1), "reduce proportionately" means that the insurer need pay on the claim only X% of what it would otherwise have been under an obligation to pay under the terms of the contract (or, if applicable, under the different terms provided for by virtue of paragraph 5), where –

$$X = \frac{\textit{Premium actually charged}}{\textit{Higher premium}} \times 100$$

PART 2
VARIATIONS

General

7 This Part of this Schedule applies to qualifying breaches of the duty of fair presentation in relation to variations to non-consumer insurance contracts.

Deliberate or reckless breaches

8 If a qualifying breach was deliberate or reckless, the insurer –
(a) may by notice to the insured treat the contract as having been terminated with effect from the time when the variation was made, and
(b) need not return any of the premiums paid.

Other breaches

9 (1) This paragraph applies if –
(a) a qualifying breach was neither deliberate nor reckless, and
(b) the total premium was increased or not changed as a result of the variation.
(2) If, in the absence of the qualifying breach, the insurer would not have agreed to the variation on any terms, the insurer may treat the contract as if the variation was never made, but must in that event return any extra premium paid.
(3) If sub-paragraph (2) does not apply –
(a) if the insurer would have agreed to the variation on different terms (other than the terms relating to the premium), the variation is to be treated as if it had been entered into on those different terms if the insurer so requires, and
(b) paragraph 11 also applies if (in the case of an increased premium) the insurer would have increased the premium by more than it did, or (in the case of any unchanged premium) the insurer would have increased the premium.

10 (1) This paragraph applies if –
(a) a qualifying breach was neither deliberate nor reckless, and
(b) the total premium was reduced as a result of the variation.
(2) If, in the absence of the qualifying breach, the insurer would not have agreed to the variation on any terms, the insurer may treat the contract as if the variation was never made, and paragraph 11 also applies.
(3) If sub-paragraph (2) does not apply –
(a) if the insurer would have agreed to the variation on different terms (other than terms relating to the premium), the variation is to be treated as if it had been entered into on those different terms if the insurer so requires, and
(b) paragraph 11 also applies if the insurer would have increased the premium, would not have reduced the premium, or would have reduced it by less than it did.

11 (1) If this paragraph applies, the insurer may reduce proportionately the amount to be paid on a claim arising out of events after the variation.
(2) In sub-paragraph (1) "reduce proportionately" means that the insurer need pay on the claim only Y% of what it would otherwise have been under an obligation to pay under the terms of the contract (whether on the original terms, or as varied, or under the different terms provided for by virtue of paragraph 9(3)(a) or 10(3)(a), as the case may be), where –

$$Y = \frac{\textit{Total premium actually charged}}{P} \times 100$$

(3) In the formula in sub-paragraph (2), "P" –
(a) in a paragraph 9(3)(b) case, is the total premium the insurer would have charged,
(b) in a paragraph 10(2) case, is the original premium,
(c) in a paragraph 10(3)(b) case, is the original premium if the insurer would not have changed it, and otherwise the increased or (as the case may be) reduced total premium the insurer would have charged.

PART 3
SUPPLEMENTARY

Relationship with section 84 of the Marine Insurance Act 1906

12 Section 84 of the Marine Insurance Act 1906 (return of premium for failure of consideration) is to be read subject to the provisions of this Schedule in relation to contracts of marine insurance which are non-consumer insurance contracts.

Remedies

5.1 One of the most sustained criticisms of the old law was that the insurer's remedy (and only remedy) for any material non-disclosure or misrepresentation by the insured on placing was avoidance of the insurance contract *ab initio*, irrespective of the seriousness of the insured's failure and whether it was deliberate, negligent or entirely innocent. The Law Commissions described the remedy as inflexible and failing to reflect normal compensatory principles and commercial reality.[1] The solution was to provide for proportionate remedies, which the Law Commissions thought worked well in other jurisdictions, and had been introduced for consumer insurance in the Consumer Insurance (Disclosure and Representations) Act 2012 (CIDRA 2012).[2] The proportionate remedies in CIDRA 2012 are largely carried into the Insurance Act.

5.2 One drawback with proportionate remedies for breach of the insured's duty of fair presentation is that it introduces uncertainty into an area where the remedies were previously reasonably clear, albeit harsh. In its 1980 Report on 'Insurance Law: Non-Disclosure and Breach of Warranty', The Law Commission considered a proposed EEC Directive whereby the remedy for breach of the duty of disclosure by the insured would entitle the insurer to 'provide only such cover as is in accordance with the ratio between the premium paid and the premium that the policyholder should have paid if he had declared the risk correctly'.[3] The Law Commission was of the view in 1980 that this requirement to determine the notional premium that would have been paid 'was impossible to do ... in any cogent or convincing manner'.[4] That remedy is now one of the proportionate remedies available to the insurer.

1 July 2014 Report, para.11.31.
2 July 2014 Report, para.11.33.
3 Para.4.4 Law Commission's 1980 Report. The BILA 2012 Report recommended the introduction of proportionate remedies for innocent or negligent non-disclosure or misrepresentation: para.17.3.4.
4 Ibid., para.4.17.

Inducement

5.3 The House of Lords made it clear in *Pan Atlantic Insurance Co Ltd v Pine Top Insurance Co. Ltd*[5] that in order to avoid a policy for non-disclosure or misrepresentation, it was necessary for the insurer to establish that it had relied on the insured's breach of its duty of good faith, meaning that, had the information given to the underwriter been complete and accurate, the insurer would not have underwritten the risk at all, or would only have done so on different (less favourable) terms. The requirement of reliance is kept in the Insurance Act in section 8(1) and accordingly the cases addressing inducement under the old law will continue to be relevant.

5.4 Under the old law, the question of how the insurer proved reliance arose in a number of cases, most notably where the insurer did not produce the actual underwriter to give evidence of inducement, or the underwriter may not have fully understood the risk he was underwriting.[6] Depending on the seriousness of the misrepresentation, the courts were willing to assume that there had been reliance, or there was a presumption or inference of reliance, unless the underwriter accepted the risk through his own inexperience or lack of care, rather than as the consequence of a misrepresentation.[7] In *AXA Versicherung AG v Arab Insurance Group*,[8] Males, J said that he did not think it was a rule of law that the presumption of inducement would only come into play if for good reason the insurer was unable to call the actual underwriter to give evidence, 'although no doubt it will be true as a matter of fact'.[9] In that case, Males J considered it relevant when considering the evidence of the underwriter as to inducement to take into account whether the non-disclosure or misrepresentation was deliberate or entirely innocent,[10] which was not relevant when considering remedies under the old law, such that 'avoidance for honest non-disclosure should be confined to plain cases' (*per* Staughton LJ in *Kausar v Eagle Star*[11]). Whether that approach will survive in the new world of proportionate remedies remains to be seen.

5.5 In *Marc Rich v Portman*,[12] Longmore J said that the question of inducement should be proved by reference to the actual risks underwritten and their immediate context, and not by reference to evidence of the underwriter's approach to the underwriting of other risks.[13] This has generally been the approach of judges and arbitrators when considering applications for disclosure of documents relating to similar risks underwritten by the same underwriter. As such evidence may now be relevant to the consideration of proportionate remedies (see paragraph 5.13 below), tribunals may no longer be so reluctant to consider what the actual underwriter did in similar circumstances.

---

5 [1995] 1 AC 501, [1994] 3 WLR 677.

6 See *St Paul Fire & Marine Insurance Co (UK) Ltd v McConnell Dowell Contractors Ltd* [1996] 1 All ER 96 (CA), [1995] 2 Lloyd's Rep 116; *Assicurazioni Generali SpA v Arab Insurance Group (BSC)* [2002] EWCA Civ 1642, [2002] Lloyd's Rep IR 131; and *Marc Rich v Portman* [1996] 1 Lloyd's Rep 430 (Com Ct).

7 See *Simner v New India Assurance Co. Ltd* [1995] LRLR 240 (QBD).

8 [2015] EWHC 1939 (Com Ct), [2016] Lloyd's Rep IR 1, affd [2017] EWCA Civ 96 (CA).

9 Ibid., [119].

10 Ibid., [121].

11 [2000] Lloyd's Rep IR 154 (CA).

12 [1996] 1 Lloyd's Rep 430 (Com Ct).

13 Ibid., 441.

Qualifying breach

5.6 If the insurer establishes that, but for the breach of the insured's duty of fair presentation, it would not have entered into the contract of insurance at all, or would only have done so on different (presumably more onerous) terms, then the insured's breach of duty is a 'qualifying breach'.[14] For the purposes of determining the insurer's remedies for the breach, a qualifying breach is either 'deliberate or reckless', or neither deliberate nor reckless.[15] A qualifying breach is deliberate or reckless if the insured (a) knew that it was in breach of duty, or (b) did not care whether or not it was in breach of duty.[16]

Deliberate or reckless breach

5.7 The burden of proving that the insured's breach was deliberate or reckless is on the insurer,[17] although the Law Commissions were keen to emphasise that establishing deliberate or reckless behaviour did not equate to proving fraud.[18] The Law Commissions identified the following kinds of behaviour as deliberate breaches of the insured's duty of fair presentation:[19]

(1) refraining from disclosing a circumstance that the insured knows to be material;
(2) making a 'data dump' in order to conceal information (see paragraphs 3.29–3.32 above);
(3) intentionally lying when making a material representation.

5.8 As regards recklessness, the Law Commissions thought this was best left to the courts to determine.[20] In the Explanatory Notes it is said that 'an insured will have acted recklessly if it "did not care" whether or not it was in breach of the duty', although acting carelessly will not be sufficient.[21]

5.9 It is not clear whether knowledge for the purposes of determining whether the insured deliberately breached its duty of fair presentation will be knowledge as determined by section 4 Insurance Act, or knowledge as determined at common law. Section 4(1) states that it provides for what an insured knows or ought to know for the purposes of section 3(4)(a), i.e. for the purposes of determining what the insured must disclose to the insurer at placing. If this is the test that applies for the purposes of section 8, then the knowledge of a corporate insured will be that of its senior management and those responsible for the insured's insurance (see paragraphs 4.5–4.11 above). This means that if the insured's broker knowingly withholds material

14 Insurance Act 2015, s.8(3).
15 Insurance Act 2015, s.8(4).
16 Insurance Act 2015, s.8(5).
17 Insurance Act 2015, s.8(6).
18 July 2014 Report, para.11.37; the authors of *Arnould* say with some force that a deliberate or reckless breach of duty is a fraudulent one, relying on Lord Herschell in *Derry v Peek* (1889) LR 14 App Cas 337 (HL), [374], *Arnould: Law of Marine Insurance and Average*, 1st supp., 18th edn (Sweet & Maxwell, London, 2016) (hereafter *Arnould*, supp. to 18th edn), para.1.2-66.
19 July 2014 Report, para.11.43.
20 July 2014 Report, paras 11.44–11.46.
21 Para.80, Explanatory Notes.

information from the insurer, there will have been a deliberate breach of the insured's duty for the purposes of section 8(5) Insurance Act, even though the insured's management was not aware that the information was material, and the corporate insured would not have been fixed with the broker's knowledge as a matter of common law (such that it knew it was in breach of its duty of fair presentation).

5.10 If the insured's qualifying breach of its duty of fair presentation is deliberate or reckless, the insurer's remedies are set out in paragraph 2 of Schedule 1 to the Insurance Act. If the insurer so elects, it may avoid the insurance contract *ab initio* and (as under the old law), refuse all claims and retain the premium. Under the old law, the insurer would also have been entitled to recover any claims already paid (applying the principle of *restitutio in integrum*),[22] and presumably this will also be the position under the new law. As under the old law, if the insurer affirms the insurance contract after it is aware of the qualifying breach, or otherwise acts in a manner inconsistent with its right to avoid the contract, it will lose its right to avoid, as avoidance is not automatic.[23] Discussion in cases concerned with the old law about whether the insurer must have acted in good faith to be entitled to avoid will presumably continue to apply, as the contract of insurance remains one of the utmost good faith.[24]

5.11 Avoidance is effective as against the insured in respect of a qualifying breach of that insured's duty of fair presentation. If a third-party beneficiary of the policy (see paragraphs 3.7 and 3.8 above) has failed to disclose material information, or made a material misrepresentation, the insurer's remedies will depend on whether the insured is deemed to know what the third party beneficiary knew (see paragraphs 4.20 to 4.30) or itself repeated or adopted the misrepresentation. In either case, the deliberate or reckless conduct of the third party beneficiary may not be attributable to the insured and accordingly the insurer may not have the right to avoid the contract.

5.12 If there are two or more insureds, and the policy is composite (see paragraph 3.6 above), the insurer may have a remedy of avoidance against one of the insureds for breach of that insured's duty of fair presentation, but not against any of the other insureds (applying the principles in *New Hampshire Insurance Co v MGN Ltd & Others*[25]).

Neither deliberate nor reckless breach

5.13 Where the qualifying breach by the insured is neither deliberate nor reckless, the remedies available to the insurer under Schedule 1 Insurance Act are proportionate, and depend upon what the insurer would have done in the absence of the breach. The actual underwriter, or the person to whom the actual underwriter reports if that person would have made the underwriting decision had a fair presentation of the risk

22 *Cornhill Insurance Company Ltd v L & B Assenheim* (1937) 58 Ll L Rep 27 (KB), [31].

23 *Mackender, Hill and White v Feldia AG, CH Brachfeld and Sons SA and Diamil SRL* [1996] 2 Lloyd's Rep 449 (CA), [457]–[459]; *Insurance Corp of the Channel Islands and Royal Insurance (UK) Ltd v The Royal Hotel Ltd* [1998] Lloyd's Rep IR 151 (Com Ct), [161].

24 See for example *Drake Insurance plc v Provident Insurance plc* [2003] EWCA Civ 1834, [2004] 1 Lloyd's Rep 268.

25 [1996] CLC 1692 (Com Ct).

been made,[26] will need to consider what he or she would have done had the material circumstances been disclosed, or the material misrepresentation not been made, at the time of underwriting. Underwriting guidelines or manuals will be taken into account in assessing the impact on the underwriter's decision had full and accurate disclosure of material facts been provided, for instance, as to the applicable premium if the insured's car accident was 'fault' or 'no fault' (*Drake Insurance plc v Provident Insurance plc*[27]). Notes made by the underwriter and the placing broker, any correspondence between them and others concerning the negotiation of the placing, and information entered on data systems, are also likely to be relevant.

5.14 The question inevitably arises whether the approach taken by the underwriter in relation to other, similar risks should also be considered. The courts have previously eschewed such evidence in determining whether the actual underwriter was induced by the non-disclosure or misrepresentation (see paragraph 5.5 above), but the proportionate remedies available under the Insurance Act require a more nuanced approach to what the underwriter would have done, so evidence of his or her conduct in relation to similar risks is likely to be relevant both to support and to undermine the underwriter's evidence.[28]

Avoidance

5.15 If the insurer can establish to the court's satisfaction that had the insured made a fair presentation, it would not have underwritten the risk on any terms, then the insurer's remedy for a qualifying breach of the duty will be that of avoidance of the contract of insurance *ab initio* (see paragraph 5.10) and the return of the premium. The recovery by the insurer, or the withholding from the premium to be returned, of claims paid prior to the insurer learning of the insured's breach would be the ordinary consequence of the application of the principle of *restitutio in integrum* (see paragraph 5.10), but it is not clear that this remedy is available under the Insurance Act. Paragraph 4 of Schedule 1 provides only that the insurer may avoid the contract and refuse all claims in these circumstances, but the authors suggest that the right to avoid carries with it the right to be placed in the same position that the insurer would have been in had the insured not breached its duty of fair presentation, and that accordingly the insurer should be entitled to recover any claims paid prior to knowledge of the breach.

5.16 Three issues arise in the context of the insurer's obligation to return premium to the insured if it elects to avoid the insurance contract because of the insured's qualifying breach:

- Must the insurer return the gross premium or only the net premium actually received (after deduction of the broker's commission)?

---

26 See *AXA Versicherung AG v Arab Insurance Group* [2015] EWHC 1939 (Com Ct), [2016] Lloyd's Rep IR 1, [152] (Males J) regarding the role of the actual underwriter's superior.

27 [2003] EWCA Civ 1834, [2004] 1 Lloyd's Rep 268 (CA).

28 The Law Commissions recognised the difficulties in some cases of establishing exactly what an insurer would have done had it known the information (para.9.32 of June 2012 Consultation Paper, and see *North Star Shipping v Sphere Drake Insurance plc* [2005] EWHC 665 (Com Ct), [2005] 2 Lloyd's Rep 76, [254] (Colman J)) and accepted that in some cases, the result would be imprecise (para.9.33 of June 2012 Consultation Paper).

- Must the insurer account for investment income or gain on the premium during the period it was held?
- If the insurance is composite with more than one insured, and avoidance is effected as against one insured only, how much premium is repayable and to whom?

5.17 The position concerning the insurer's obligation to repay premium gross or net of brokerage is complicated by the lack of clarity as to the status of insurance brokers' commission under English law. The broker is agent of the insured, but its commission is usually agreed between the broker and the insurer and recorded in the slip or Market Reform Contract. In these circumstances, the courts have characterised the commission as remuneration payable to the broker for introducing the risk to the insurer. Where the broker is being remunerated for services it is supplying to the insured by way of commission, a more logical analysis would be that the insured expects the broker to be remunerated for its services by way of the commission which is agreed with the insurer, and that remuneration is proper provided it is at a level which is usual for that kind of business in the market.[29] The insured pays the commission to the broker in circumstances where, as is usual, the broker receives the gross premium from the insured, deducts its brokerage, and pays on the net premium to the insurer. As the broker is the insured's agent, the insurer should only be liable to repay the net premium to the insured if it avoids the insurance contract *ab initio* since it will not actually, or as a matter of law, have received that part of the premium constituting the broker's commission.

5.18 It is usual for brokers to enter into Terms of Business Agreements (ToBA's) with insurers and managing agents governing the relationship between them when the former place insurance business with the latter. Clause 6.7 of the current forms of Risk Transfer and Non-Risk Transfer ToBA's issued by the LMA and IUA in May 2013 provides as follows (in the version used by Lloyd's managing agents):

> In the event of the cancellation or avoidance of a contract of insurance, where the Managing Agent is obliged by law, regulation, or the terms of the contract of insurance to repay gross premiums in respect of such contract of insurance, the Broker agrees to repay the relevant Commission (which shall not for the purpose of this clause include fees paid by the Insured). Such repayment shall, in the case of cancellation, be only in respect of Commission received by the Broker which is attributable to that part of the premium repaid. Unless otherwise obliged to by law, regulation or terms of the contract of insurance, the Managing Agent shall refund premiums net of Commission.

5.19 Although applying the principles of *restitutio in integrum*, it would be arguable that the insurer should account for any gain made on the premium; the Marine Insurance Act 1906 (in section 84(3)(a)) and the Insurance Act (in paragraph 4 of Schedule 1) only provide for the return of the premium, and the authors are not aware of any case in which the payment of interest or other gain earned on the premium has been considered.

5.20 If there are several insureds and the contract is only avoided as against one of them, it is necessary to determine how much of the premium paid for the insurance

29 *Great Western Insurance Company v Cunliffe* (1873–74) LR 9 Ch App 525; *Carvill America Inc v Camperdown UK Ltd* [2005] EWCA Civ 645, [2005] Lloyd's Rep IR 55; and *Absalom v TCRU Ltd* [2005] EWCA Civ 1586, [2006] 2 Lloyd's Rep 129.

is attributable to the insured against whom the policy is avoided. This is straightforward where the policy identifies how much premium is attributable to each insured, but less so where the sum payable is an unattributed lump sum. The courts have not addressed how this exercise should be carried out and no guidance is provided in the Insurance Act. *Pro rata* attribution of the premium received between the various insureds may not be fair if one of the insureds presents a much more significant risk (whether through the size of its business, its kind of business or its claims record) than the others. The Insurance Act requires the return of the premium on avoidance and if the premium is incapable of attribution between the different insureds, it may be that the insurer is obliged to return the entire premium to the insured against whom it has avoided, unless it can establish how much that insured actually contributed to the premium that was paid.

Varying the terms of the contract

5.21 Had the insured made a fair presentation of the risk, the insurer may say that it would have included a term in the insurance that was not included in the contract actually underwritten because of the failure to disclose material information, or would have deleted or amended a term. If the insurer's evidence as to what it would have done is accepted, then the contract will be treated as having the revised term *ab initio* pursuant to paragraph 5 of Schedule 1 of the Insurance Act, unless it is a term relating to premium (as to which see paragraph 5.25). Whether the revision has any consequence will depend on whether it has any effect on the coverage for a claim made under the policy. If the revision would have been the insertion of an exclusion, the issue will simply be one of determining whether the exclusion applies to the claim. If the revision would have been to impose stricter claims notification or handling terms, the consequences of the introduction of the new terms may be more difficult to assess if a claim has been handled in accordance with the original contract terms up to the time that the revision is ordered. At paragraph 11.67 of the July 2014 Report, the Law Commissions give three examples of terms that an insurer might want to include in a contract were a fair presentation of the risk made. Apart from exclusions, they are:

- warranties and other terms designed to reduce risks; and
- excesses.

One could add limits to the list. If the change is to insert a promissory warranty in the contract, as the insured would not have been aware of the warranty at any relevant time, it would be happenstance whether or not it complied with the new warranty. Even if it had been in a position to comply with the warranty, and would have been willing to comply with it, the effect of the revision may be to deprive the insured of cover for breach of warranty (subject to sections 10 and 11 of the Insurance Act – see Chapters 6 and 7 below). The Law Commissions considered this to be the appropriate outcome.[30] It is striking that an insured might lose cover as a consequence of failing to comply with a warranty of which it was not aware.

30 July 2014 Report, para.11.82.

5.22 By way of example, an insured factory owner stores highly flammable chemicals on the premises covered by the policy, but (without being deliberate or reckless) fails to disclose this matter to the insurer. Had it done so, the insurer would have imposed an exclusion on losses caused by fire damage arising in connection with the chemicals. The insurer will therefore have a remedy if such a term would have eliminated or reduced its liability under the contract. In certain cases, this could become somewhat complex. In the same example, the insurer might have imposed a warranty requiring the chemicals to be stored in a room fitted with sprinklers. Would compliance with such a warranty have prevented the loss? Or reduced its extent? Such questions might well require expert evidence, and may not be particularly straightforward.

5.23 The other notable effect of this remedy is that it might have an effect on losses which the insurer has already paid. That is because the remedy involves treating the contract 'as if it had been *entered into* on those different terms', thereby having a retrospective effect. If the insurer proves that it would have contracted on different terms which would have reduced or extinguished its liability for losses which pre-date the insurer's discovery of a breach of the duty of fair presentation, the insured will have to reimburse the insurer for those losses.

5.24 For example, an insured represents that its aircraft has been valued at $10 million, and the insurer agrees to insure it for that value. The aircraft is destroyed in a storm and the insurer pays the full limits of cover. The insurer subsequently discovers that the value of the aircraft on placing was $5 million, and successfully asserts that the insured was in breach of its duty of fair presentation. The underwriter establishes that had he been told the truth, the limit of insurance would have been $5 million. The insurer would be entitled to recover the $5 million overpaid to the insured, and there would be no obligation to give credit to the insured for the lower premium that the insurer would have charged for the lower limit of cover (as paragraph 5 of Schedule 1 applies to all terms except those relating to premium).

Proportionate reduction of the claim

5.25 In addition to, or rather than, varying the terms of the insurance contract, if the insurer's evidence is that it would have charged more premium had the insured made a fair presentation of the risk (and that evidence is accepted), then the insured's claim(s) under the policy will be reduced *pro rata* to the amount of additional premium that the insurer would have charged (paragraph 6, Schedule 1 of the Insurance Act). For example, if the insurer would have doubled the premium had it known the truth, then the insurer's liability for any claim(s) will be halved. The value of this remedy depends on whether or not there is one or more covered claims under the insurance contract. If there are no covered claims, the insurer is not entitled to require payment of the additional premium that it would have charged, and it will have no remedy under the Insurance Act for the insured's breach of duty. The Law Commissions considered that if the insurer's remedy was to have the right to recover the additional premium, rather than reduce any claim *pro rata* to the amount of that premium, that would undercompensate the insurer if the risk (that is, a claim) materialised.[31] Not

31 July 2014 Report, para.11.72.

having a remedy for underpayment of premium where there is no claim does however prejudice the insurer where, for example, there is persistent under-reporting of insured values over several renewals of the cover, as the insurer will never be in a position to recover the premium that it would have charged for earlier periods of insurance if the first claim is on a later period of insurance.

5.26 By way of example, the underwriter establishes that had the insured made a fair presentation of the risk, she would have charged premium 10% higher than that for which she underwrote the contract. Any claims on the policy would be reduced by 9.09%, and the insurer would probably be entitled to recoup from the insured 9.09% of any claims paid prior to discovery of the breach of the duty of fair presentation. (Although paragraph 6 of Schedule 1 refers to a reduction in the amount 'to be paid on a claim', the authors consider that the reduction should also apply to claims already paid as the increase in premium affects the contract *ab initio.*)

5.27 As with the insurer's right to avoid, where the insurance is composite and there is more than one insured, the remedies of varying the contract terms or reducing the value of claims are available only as regards the insured in breach of the duty of fair presentation. If it is difficult to allocate the premium paid between multiple insureds (see paragraph 5.20), calculating the percentage by which any claims presented by the insured in breach should be reduced may present difficulties.

Alternative remedies

5.28 The remedies in the Insurance Act for breach of the insured's duty of fair presentation are not exhaustive.[32] The Law Commissions recognised in their June 2012 Consultation Paper that in theory insurers might have a remedy for fraudulent misrepresentation[33] or for negligent misrepresentation under the Misrepresentation Act 1967.[34] The availability of alternative remedies was not referred to in the July 2014 Report or the Explanatory Notes. The Insurance Act does not expressly limit the remedies for breach of the duty of fair presentation to those set out in Schedule 1. Since, under the old law, the remedy for material non-disclosure or misrepresentation by the insured was avoidance *ab initio*,[35] and there was no remedy in damages for breach of the duty of good faith,[36] it is not surprising that there were few cases in which alternative remedies were considered. In *HIH Casualty and General Ins Ltd v Chase Manhattan Bank*[37] the House of Lords had to consider the insurers' remedies in a case where a waiver clause in the policy purported to restrict the insurers' remedy to avoid the policy for non-disclosure or misrepresentation. Lord Bingham said:[38]

> ... if the non-disclosure or misrepresentation were other than innocent, the insurer might have rights additional to that of avoidance: the right to damages given by section 2(1) of

32 The view is not accepted in Robert M. Merkin, *Colinvaux's Law of Insurance*, 11th edn (Sweet & Maxwell, London, 2016), para.7-196.
33 *Derry v Peek* (1889) 14 App Cas 337 (HL).
34 June 2012 Consultation Paper, para.2.53.
35 *Pan Atlantic v Pine Top* [1995] 1 AC 501, [1994] 3 WLR 677.
36 *Banque Financière de la Cité v Westgate Insurance* [1991] 2 AC 249.
37 [2003] UKHL 6, [2003] Lloyd's Rep IR 230.
38 Ibid., [5].

the Misrepresentation Act 1967 to the victim of a negligent misrepresentation; and the right to recover damages for deceit given by the common law to the victim of a fraudulent misrepresentation.

5.29 With the introduction in the Insurance Act of proportionate remedies for breach of the duty of fair presentation, the alternative remedy of damages for misrepresentation under the Misrepresentation Act 1967 could well become more important. Under section 2(1) of the 1967 Act, a party who makes a non-fraudulent misrepresentation will be liable in damages as if he were fraudulent unless he proves that he had reasonable grounds to believe that the facts represented were true, and believed that to be the position up to the time the contract was made. Thus, if the insured negligently misrepresents material information, and the insurer would have charged more premium had it known the true position, the insurer may be entitled to recover damages equivalent to the additional premium under the Misrepresentation Act 1967. This is not a remedy available to the insurer under the Insurance Act. It is also worth noting that the remedy is one in damages 'as if' the insured were fraudulent, which may broaden the recoverable damages beyond those foreseeable at the time of contracting, including consequential losses.[39]

Application to variations

5.30 Section 2(2) Insurance Act provides that Part 2 of the Act, which concerns the duty of fair presentation, applies in relation to variations of non-consumer contracts as it applies to conclusion of such contracts. The duty is one to make a fair presentation of changes in the risk relevant to the proposed variation.[40] There is no requirement for the insured to otherwise provide an update of circumstances material to the risk as a whole (unless that would have an impact on the insurer's assessment of the proposed variation). Variations to insurance contracts are usually effected by way of endorsements and will include such matters as the addition of insured assets, extensions of cover and the inclusion of additional insureds. Variations to an insurance contract are to be contrasted with arrangements by which the original insurance contract is cancelled and replaced by a new contract on new terms, in which case the insured's duty of fair presentation applies to the entire risk, and not just the changes in the risk.[41] It is suggested that this distinction was recognised under the old law[42] and is not changed by the Insurance Act.

---

39 Hugh Beale (ed.), *Chitty on Contracts*, 1st supp., 32nd edn (Sweet & Maxwell, London, 2016), para.7-078, *Royscot Trust Ltd v Rogerson* [1991] 2 QB 297 (CA), *Taberna Europe v Selskabet AF* [2016] EWCA Civ 1262.

40 Insurance Act 2015, s.2(2)(a).

41 John Birds, Ben Lynch, Simon Milnes, *MacGillivray on Insurance Law*, 1st supp., 13th edn (Sweet & Maxwell, London, 2016), para.17-026 and para.B2 of Appendix B to the July 2014 Report.

42 In the old case of *Lishman v The Northern Maritime Insurance Company* (1875) LR 10 CP 179, [182], Blackburn J (at 182) suggested that breach in the context of a variation vitiated the entire contract. However, in *The Mercandian Continent* [2001] EWCA Civ 1275, [2001] 2 Lloyd's Rep 563, [22(2)], Longmore LJ indicated that the right of avoidance would apply to the variation alone. This was also the approach of Potter LJ in *Fraser Shipping Ltd v Colton* [1997] 1 Lloyd's Rep 586 (Com Ct), [597] and is now the accepted position: see *AXA v Limit No 2* [2008] EWCA Civ 1231, [2009] Lloyd's Rep IR 396, [20] (Longmore LJ) and *AC Ward v Catlin (No 5)* [2009] EWHC 3122 (Com Ct), [2010] Lloyd's Rep IR 695, [195] (Flaux J).

5.31 The remedies in the Insurance Act for a qualifying breach of the insured's duty of fair presentation in respect of a variation to an insurance contract are set out in Part 2 of Schedule 1 to the Act. As with Part 1 of the Schedule, an important distinction is drawn between a breach that is deliberate or reckless and one that is not.[43] If the variation is procured by a deliberate or reckless breach of duty, then the insurer will be entitled to give notice to the insured treating the entire contract as having been terminated from the date the variation was made, and will be entitled to keep all premiums paid.[44] This goes further than the old law, where the insurer's remedy would only have been to avoid the variation,[45] and appears intended to penalise conduct on the part of the insured which is fraudulent, or bordering on fraudulent. Issues concerning the individuals whose knowledge will count as the insured's for these purposes are discussed in paragraph 5.9 above. If the insurer elects to give notice to terminate, it will remain liable in respect of any claim attaching to the insurance contract prior to the date of variation (and therefore termination).

5.32 If the insured's breach of the duty of fair presentation is neither deliberate nor reckless, paragraphs 9–11 of Schedule 1 provide that the remedies available to the insurer will depend on whether the premium for the insurance contract was increased or not changed as a result of the variation, or whether it was reduced. If the variation resulted in an increase or no change in the premium, then the remedies available to the insurer will be proportionate ones similar to those available in respect of new contracts.[46] The insurer will be obliged to return any extra premium paid in respect of the variation, if it can prove that it would not have agreed the variation on any terms and elects to avoid the variation (see paragraphs 5.15–5.20 above). If the insurer would have charged more premium had the presentation been fair, the amount to be paid in respect of any claim 'arising out of events after the variation'[47] must be reduced in proportion to the notional increase in premium over the total premium (not just any additional premium actually charged for the variation).[48]

5.33 The Law Commissions did not consider what would qualify as a claim 'arising out of events after the variation'. For the purposes of subsection 12(2)(a) and (3) Insurance Act concerning the termination of insurance cover after a fraudulent act, where the insurer may terminate the contract and avoid liability in respect of a 'relevant event', subsection 12(4) defines a 'relevant event' as being 'whatever gives rise to the insurer's liability under the contract' (see paragraph 9.7 below). Subsection 12(4) gives examples of a 'relevant event' as being the occurrence of a loss, the making of a claim, or the notification of a potential claim 'depending on how the contract is written'. In its July 2014 Report, the Law Commissions confirmed that they were intending to capture the event that triggers the insurer's liability under the contract.[49]

---

43 See para.5.6 above.
44 Insurance Act 2015, Sch.1,para.8.
45 See *AXA v Limit No 2* [2008] EWCA Civ 1231, [2009] Lloyd's Rep IR 396.
46 Insurance Act 2015, Sch.1,paras 9, 11.
47 Insurance Act 2015, Sch.1,para.11, subpara. (1).
48 Insurance Act 2015, Sch.1, para.11 subparas (2), (3)(a).
49 July 2014 Report, para.23.45.

5.34 Applying this approach to the meaning of a claim 'arising out of events after the variation' for the purposes of paragraph 11 of Schedule 1, it is suggested:

- The reference is to a claim on the insurance contract, not a claim against the insured.
- If the contract responds when the event giving rise to the loss occurs, then it is the date of the event which determines whether or not the claim arose prior to or after the variation.
- If the contract responds when a claim is first made against the insured in respect of an event giving rise to the loss, then it is the date when that claim is made which is the relevant event.
- Similarly, if the contract responds when notice is first given to the insurer either of a claim against the insured or of an event or circumstance giving rise to a loss, then it is the date of notice to the insurer that is the relevant event.

If the relevant event were to be the occurrence that has given rise to the loss, there would be no remedy for the insurer of a 'claims made' or 'occurrence notified' policy who underwrites a variation to the policy for a lower premium than he would otherwise have charged as a result of a misrepresentation, but then receives notice of a claim under the varied policy which triggers cover under that policy in respect of an event occurring prior to the variation.

5.35 If the variation resulted in a decrease in the premium charged, and the insured's breach was neither deliberate nor reckless, then the remedies available to the insurer will be proportionate ones similar to those available in respect of new contracts (see paragraphs 5.13–5.24 above). However, as the insurer agreed to a reduction in premium, if it would not have underwritten the variation on any terms, the insurer may treat the variation as having never been made, but appears to have no right to recover premium returned to the insured. Instead, any claim 'arising out of events after the variation' will be reduced by the proportion which the reduced premium bears to the original premium (paragraphs 10(2) and 11(b) of Schedule 1).

5.36 Where the insurer reduces the total premium in agreeing a variation, but would have charged more premium, or would not have decreased the premium by as much or at all, had a fair presentation been made in relation to the variation, paragraph 11 of Schedule 1 applies in relation to the calculation of the amount by which a claim 'arising out of events after the variation' should be reduced. The relevant formula is set out in paragraph 11(2), where Y is the percentage to be applied to reduce the claim:

$$Y = \frac{\textit{Total premium actually charged}}{P} \times 100$$

Under paragraph 11(3)(c), P is the premium that the insurer would have charged had there been no qualifying breach.

5.37 Paragraph 12 of Schedule 1 concerns the impact of the new remedies on section 84 Marine Insurance Act 1906. Section 84 provides for the return of premium to the insured in a number of different circumstances. Paragraph 12 provides that where there has been a qualifying breach of the insured's duty of fair presentation, Schedule 1 will govern the circumstances in which premium is returnable to the insured rather than section 84.

5.38 Section 8 Insurance Act does not address when the insurer must exercise its entitlement to remedies for any qualifying breach of the insured's duty of fair presentation. Under the old law, the insurer might lose its right to avoid the insurance contract for breach of the insured's duty of good faith by affirming the contract, or by waiving its right to avoid, after it had become aware of the insured's breach.[50] Since the remedies under section 8 and Schedule 1 are similarly elective, it is assumed that the old law concerning waiver and affirmation will continue to apply. As various remedies are now available to the insurer, it is assumed that once the insurer has asserted that there has been a breach of the insured's duty of fair presentation, it will not be necessary for the insurer to identify the remedy (or remedies) which it seeks for that breach within any particular period of time if it is not to lose the right to seek that remedy or remedies. What remedies are available to the insurer may only become clear once there has been a full investigation of the matters underlying the insured's breach of duty.

Example of the operation of remedies under the Act

5.39 Before the conclusion of a marine hull and machinery policy, the insured breaches the duty of fair presentation by failing to disclose that his superyacht is in dry dock undergoing an extensive refit, including potentially hazardous hot works (welding, for example). Subsequently, the yacht is severely damaged by an earthquake which unexpectedly occurs in the vicinity of the dry dock. The insured's breach was neither deliberate nor reckless.

5.40 The insurer attempts to avoid the policy, but it cannot prove that it would not have written the policy at all had there been a fair presentation, because the underwriter would have been and was generally willing to insure superyachts which were in dry dock undergoing a refit. Avoidance is consequently not possible.

5.41 The insurer therefore seeks to rewrite the contract so as to eliminate or reduce its liability. This, it may struggle to do. This is simply because, even if the underwriter had been told about the refit, it is not at all obvious that he would have imposed an exclusion for loss caused by earthquakes, or any other term which would enable the insurer to escape liability for such a loss. A more obvious course would be to impose an exclusion for fire damage, or terms relating to how the hot works should be conducted, none of which would be of any utility in these circumstances. In other words, the insurer may not be able to prove that, even if the risk had been fairly presented, it would have written cover in a way that would have excluded or reduced its liability for loss caused by earthquakes.

5.42 In those circumstances, the insurer would be left with the remedy of a proportionate reduction of the claim, but only it if can prove that it would have charged a higher premium for a yacht undergoing a major refit. Again, this may not be straightforward, since there may be an argument that a yacht in dry dock is in some respects at a lower risk than when sailing on the open sea, leading to (if anything) a reduction in premium.

---

50 *ICCI and Royal Insurance (UK) Ltd v The Royal Hotel Ltd* [1998] Lloyd's Rep IR 151.

Application to subscription and excess policies

5.43 The old law concerning the insured's duty to disclose and not to misrepresent material circumstances developed in respect of relatively simple transactions where a single insured purchased an insurance policy from a single insurer. Except for the insurance of small businesses, in the second half of the twentieth century, commercial insurance usually concerned more complex circumstances involving multiple parties, and the old law had to evolve to meet those new circumstances. Those included multiple parties being insured under the same policy, multiple insurers underwriting the same policy, and multiple insurers underwriting the same risk in different layers. Although the Insurance Act was intended to bring UK insurance law into the twenty-first century, it has addressed only in passing[51] some of the issues that complicate the underwriting of commercial insurance in today's marketplace. The introduction of proportionate remedies for breach of the insured's duty of fair presentation has made the application of the law in practice more, rather than less, complex.

Subscription risks

5.44 The economic and efficient underwriting of commercial insurance business has inevitably meant that some insurers will rely on the skills of others in assessing the risks to be underwritten. The process by which one risk is underwritten by many insurers in a subscription market, particularly the London insurance market, is well known and has been described and analysed in judgments such as those of Kerr LJ in *General Reinsurance Corp. v Fennia Patria*[52] and Hobhouse J in *The 'Zephyr'*.[53] The insured, through the agency of its broker, enters into a contract of insurance with each insurer for that insurer's agreed proportionate share of the risk, to be 'signed down' if necessary so that, if possible, 100 per cent of the risk is underwritten. Each insurer is severally liable for the proportion of the risk that it has underwritten.[54] If there are many insureds, each insured will have a separate insurance contract with each insurer, such that a single policy may embrace a multitude, or 'bundle', of separate contracts.[55]

5.45 To facilitate the insuring of risks in these circumstances, insurers may delegate underwriting authority to a third party (whether an underwriting agent such as a coverholder or managing general agent, or another insurer such as a lineslip[56] or consortium leader), or it may co-insure as a 'follower' where it underwrites a share of a risk on terms which it understands to have been more fully considered and assessed by one or more 'leaders'. A follower may place great trust in the judgement and acumen of the leader, but it is accepted that there is no agency or fiduciary relationship between

51 For instance, the recognition that there may be third-party beneficiaries of a commercial insurance policy: see Insurance Act 2015, s.4(7) and para.3.7 above.

52 [1983] QB 856 (CA), [1983] 3 WLR 318.

53 *General Accident Fire and Life Assurance Corp v Tanter (The Zephyr)* [1984] 1 Lloyd's Rep 58 (CA).

54 See s.8(1) Lloyd's Act 1982: 'An underwriting member shall be a party to a contract of insurance underwritten at Lloyd's only if it is underwritten with several liability, each underwriting member for his own part and not one for another, and if the liability of each underwriting member is accepted solely for his own account.'

55 *Touche Ross v Baker* [1991] 2 Lloyd's Rep 207 (HL).

56 *HIH Casualty & General Insurance Ltd v Chase Manhattan Bank* [2003] UKHL 6, [2001] Lloyd's Rep IR 191, [48]–[49] (Aikens J).

them unless there is an express delegation of authority, such as an authority to agree particular amendments to the terms of cover, in which case the relationship will be confined to the scope of that delegation.[57]

5.46 In these circumstances, the insured's duty of fair presentation is owed to each insurer.[58] Information given to one insurer (for instance, in response to a specific question) will not be deemed to have been given to another insurer underwriting the same risk.[59] In *Aneco Reinsurance Underwriting Limited v Johnson & Higgins*[60] it was held that the fact that there had been a material misrepresentation by the broker to the leader was itself material and should have been disclosed to each of the followers, and that the failure to disclose would have entitled the followers to avoid their contracts of reinsurance. In the absence of fraud on the part of the broker, it is to be doubted that the broker would be taken to know that there had been a misrepresentation which required such disclosure. If the broker was under a duty to disclose the fact of the material misrepresentation to the following market, surely he would have been under the same duty to disclose to the leading underwriter that he had made a misrepresentation to him? Individuals are not usually taken to know of their own negligence. It is even more difficult to see how the following underwriters could rely on a material non-disclosure to the leading underwriter if they themselves were not induced by the non-disclosure. At best, it could be said that there is an implied representation to the following market that there has been a fair presentation to the leading underwriter, but section 3(3)(c) Insurance Act concerns actual, not implied, representations.

5.47 As regards inducement, what one underwriter might have done had particular information been disclosed to him or her may not be the same as that which a different underwriter might have done. The fact that the leader would have imposed an exclusion in the policy had certain circumstances been disclosed by the insured, and the court amends the insurance contract between the leader and the insured to include such an exclusion in accordance with paragraph 4 of Schedule 1 to the Insurance Act, does not mean that the same exclusion will be included in the contracts underwritten by the following market, even though in practice it would have been included had the leader required it at the time of underwriting.

5.48 With the introduction of proportionate remedies in the Insurance Act, it will become even more necessary for each underwriter of a subscription risk where there is an allegation of a qualifying breach of the insured's duty of fair presentation, to give evidence about what they were told on placing and of their reliance on the breach. It will also be necessary for each to say what he or she would have done had the true position been disclosed. If their evidence is that they would have followed the decision

57 See for example *Barlee Marine Corporation v Trevor Rex Mountain (The 'Leegas')* [1987] 1 Lloyd's Rep 471 (Com Ct) and the General Underwriter's Agreement (GUA).

58 Peter MacDonald Eggers, Simon Picken, Patrick Foss, *Good Faith and Insurance Contracts*, 3rd edn (Informa Law, London, 2010), paras 13.33–1345.

59 In the BILA 2002 Report, a BILA Sub-Committee chaired by Adrian Hamilton QC recommended that following co-insurers should be deemed to be induced by misrepresentation or non-disclosure, if all the leading insurers were so induced, para.18.

60 [1998] 1 Lloyd's Rep 565 (Com Ct), [596]–[597] (Cresswell J). Followed in *International Lottery Management Ltd v Dumas & Others* [2002] Lloyd's Rep IR 237, *Brotherton v Aseguradora Colseguros (No 3)* [2003] Lloyd's Rep IR 762 and *International Management Group (UK) Ltd v Simmonds* [2004] Lloyd's Rep IR 247, but cf Longmore J in *Sirius International Insurance Corp v Oriental Assurance Corp* [1999] Lloyd's Rep IR 343 where the following market was not able to rely on a misrepresentation made to the leader.

of the leading underwriter, that may introduce a degree of uniformity, but at the risk of the leader failing to establish a qualifying breach as far as he or she is concerned (because, for example, the leader was put on notice of the need to make further enquiries, and failed to make such enquiries, such that the presentation is deemed to be fair under section 3(4) Insurance Act[61]).

5.49 Co-insurers in a subscription market are concerned that they may follow the terms of an insurance contract that are agreed by a leading underwriter where that underwriter has been misled by a misrepresentation not repeated to the co-insureds. Given the degree of reliance which the co-insurers have on the leading underwriter, the LMA have proposed a standard clause for use in situations of co-insurance whereby the followers are deemed to have relied upon a misrepresentation made to the leader in agreeing to underwrite the risk. LMA Standard Clause 5262 provides as follows:

> **Insurance Act 2015 – Effect of misrepresentations made to any leading insurer – for use in open market subscription placements**
> If, before the conclusion of this insurance contract, the Insured has made any material misrepresentation to any leading insurer underwriting the terms on which this insurance contract is also underwritten, the Insurer shall be deemed to have relied upon such misrepresentation when underwriting this insurance contract, and may therefore have a remedy against the Insured for breach of the duty of fair presentation.[62]

The clause addresses misrepresentation only, rather than non-disclosure, since by its very nature a non-disclosure affects all insurers subscribing to a risk.

Excess insurance

5.50 Excess insurance provides insurance in excess of one or more underlying layers of insurance, including a layer of primary insurance. It is usual for excess insurance to attach and become payable in respect of a loss (or several losses if the excess policy so provides) that exceeds the underlying layer(s) of insurance. It is also common for the terms of the excess insurance to incorporate the terms of the underlying insurance. Often, the excess insurers will be liable to pay only if the underlying insurers have paid their share of the relevant loss or losses in full.

5.51 The introduction of proportionate remedies for breach of the duty of fair presentation may cause complications in the handling of claims under excess insurance. For example:

- If a court or tribunal varies the terms of an underlying policy to include an exclusion clause, is the excess insurance which incorporates the original terms of the underlying policy automatically amended to include the exclusion?
- If the underlying insurer's liability in respect of a loss is reduced in proportion to the additional premium that it would have charged, does the excess insurance drop down to cover the shortfall, or are the excess insurers discharged from liability because the limits of the underlying insurance can never be exhausted by payment by the underlying insurer?

61 See paras 3.33 and 3.34 above.
62 LMA 5262 16 March 2016.

CHAPTER 6

Warranties

9 Warranties and representations

(1) This section applies to representations made by the insured in connection with—
 (a) a proposed non-consumer insurance contract, or
 (b) a proposed variation to a non-consumer insurance contract.

(2) Such a representation is not capable of being converted into a warranty by means of any provision of the non-consumer insurance contract (or of the terms of the variation), or of any other contract (and whether by declaring the representation to form the basis of the contract or otherwise).

10 Breach of warranty

(1) Any rule of law that breach of a warranty (express or implied) in a contract of insurance results in the discharge of the insurer's liability under the contract is abolished.

(2) An insurer has no liability under a contract of insurance in respect of any loss occurring, or attributable to something happening, after a warranty (express or implied) in the contract has been breached but before the breach has been remedied.

(3) But subsection (2) does not apply if—
 (a) because of a change of circumstances, the warranty ceases to be applicable to the circumstances of the contract,
 (b) compliance with the warranty is rendered unlawful by any subsequent law, or
 (c) the insurer waives the breach of warranty.

(4) Subsection (2) does not affect the liability of the insurer in respect of losses occurring, or attributable to something happening—
 (a) before the breach of warranty, or
 (b) if the breach can be remedied, after it has been remedied.

(5) For the purposes of this section, a breach of warranty is to be taken as remedied—
 (a) in a case falling within subsection (6), if the risk to which the warranty relates later becomes essentially the same as that originally contemplated by the parties,
 (b) in any other case, if the insured ceases to be in breach of the warranty.

(6) A case falls within this subsection if—
 (a) the warranty in question requires that by an ascertainable time something is to be done (or not done), or a condition is to be fulfilled, or something is (or is not) to be the case, and
 (b) that requirement is not complied with.

(7) In the Marine Insurance Act 1906—
 (a) in section 33 (nature of warranty), in subsection (3), the second sentence is omitted,
 (b) section 34 (when breach of warranty excused) is omitted.

Background to section 9

6.1 A basis clause typically takes the form of a declaration by the insured that the statements contained in the insurance proposal form the 'basis of the contract'. Such a declaration was formerly held to mean that the insured warranted the truth of the matters stated in the proposal, so that if any of the matters was incorrect, the insured was in breach of warranty and the insurer's liability was permanently discharged. That was the case regardless of whether the inaccurate facts were material to the risk,[1] or whether there was any reference to the basis clause in the policy itself. Under section 9 of the Act, basis clauses will be of no effect in non-consumer contracts,[2] and the parties are not able to contract out of this provision.[3]

6.2 Basis clauses have been in the Law Commissions' crosshairs for some time,[4] having received extensive criticism over the years.[5] The chief complaint was that where they were deployed, any error in the proposal could discharge the insurer's liability with permanent effect, no matter how immaterial the matter was.[6] Basis clauses therefore bypassed the need for an insurer to show that a misrepresentation or non-disclosure was material in order to avoid the policy, since the insurer's liability was in any event discharged even if the inaccuracy was immaterial, as in *Dawsons Limited v Bonnin*.[7] That situation was particularly egregious given the basis clause itself did not need to and did not usually appear in the contract of insurance, leading some to describe them as traps for the unwary.[8] Moreover, there was a concern that buyers of insurance did not understand the effect of signing a declaration that the answers in a proposal formed the basis of the contract.[9] For all of these reasons, there was a broad consensus that basis clauses should be abolished.

Abolition of basis clauses

6.3 Section 9 abolishes basis clauses, and is one of only two provisions in the Act which cannot be excluded by agreement between the parties.[10] Under section 9, any representation made by the insured in connection with a proposed insurance contract (or a variation) cannot be converted into a warranty by means of any term in the

1 *Genesis Housing Association Ltd v Liberty Syndicate Management Ltd* [2013] EWCA Civ 1173, [2013] Bus LR 1399, affirming the decision of Akenhead J at first instance ([2012] EWHC 3105 (TCC), [2012] 2 CLC 837). In that case, the declaration on the proposal form was that the statements therein would form the basis of the contract, which was held to turn the statements into warranties. See also *Condogianis v Guardian Assurance Company* [1921] 2 AC 125, (1921) 7 Lloyd's Rep 155, Lord Shaw of Dunfermline at 129–130.

2 Basis clauses have already been abolished in consumer insurance contracts: Consumer Insurance (Disclosure and Representations) Act 2012, s.6.

3 Consumer Insurance (Disclosure and Representations) Act 2012, s.16(1).

4 Para.7.2 Law Commission's 1980 Report.

5 For example, *Joel v Law Union and Crown Insurance Co* [1908] 2 KB 863, Fletcher-Moulton LJ at 885; *Glicksman v Lancashire and General Assurance Co Ltd* [1927] AC 139, (1926) 26 Lloyd's Rep 69.

6 July 2014 Report, para.13.6 *et seq.*

7 [1922] 2 AC 413, (1922) 12 Lloyd's Rep 237.

8 *Zurich General Accident & Liability Insurance Co v Morrison* [1942] 2 KB 53, (1942) 72 Lloyd's Rep 167, Lord Greene MR at [58].

9 July 2014 Report, para.16.2.

10 Insurance Act 2015, s.16(1). The insurer is also unable to put the insured in a worse position as regards deliberate or reckless breach of the implied term (under s.13A) to pay sums due in respect of an insurance claim within a reasonable time: s.16A(2).

policy or in any other contract. Thus, the classical basis clause in the proposal form will not be able to convert pre-contractual statements into warranties. The effect of section 9 is not limited to representations in a proposal form, but extends to any representation in any document prepared by or on behalf of the insured in connection with the proposal for insurance.[11]

A permissible alternative to the basis clause

6.4 If the proposal form contains a material misrepresentation, that will amount to a breach of the duty of fair presentation for which the insurer may be entitled to the remedies in Schedule 1. However, the insurer may in certain cases wish to have a greater degree of protection in respect of particularly important representations of fact, and may therefore wish to include warranties of specific fact in the policy. The Law Commissions have indicated that section 9 is not intended to and does not prohibit warranties of fact. In many cases, there may be good reasons why an insurer requires the insured to warrant the truth of a particular matter. A typical example is seen in some directors' and officers' liability (D&O) policies, in which the insured warrants that none of the directors or officers has a criminal record. In those circumstances, it is permissible to include in the policy an express term warranting the truth of the matter in question. Such a warranty would probably take the form of a warranty of past or present fact, such as: 'warranted that the insured property is built of brick and slate'.[12] Such terms will be effective provided they are included in the policy itself,[13] and regardless of the fact that the matters warranted are also things which the insured has stated in the proposal form or other disclosed information.[14] On analysis, that appears to be because, when a fact is warranted to be true in the contract which the parties have actually entered into, the representation is no longer one that is made in connection with a 'proposed … insurance contract', but a representation contained in an actual concluded contract. It is also unlikely that an actual warranty of past or present fact is one which has been 'converted into a warranty' in the ordinary meaning of those words, since it is a warranty in its own right. In short, therefore, warranties of past or present fact will not be caught by section 9, and are therefore effective under the Act.

Warranties: the mischief

6.5 An insurance warranty is a term which must be exactly complied with, whether it is material to the risk or not.[15] Before the Act, breach of a warranty caused the automatic[16] and permanent discharge of the insurer's liability under the contract, from the moment of breach.[17] Accordingly, fulfilment of a warranty by the insured

11 July 2014 Report, para.16.10.
12 July 2014 Report, para.16.12.
13 July 2014 Report, para.15.3.
14 July 2014 Report, para.16.11.
15 Marine Insurance Act 1906, s.33(3).
16 In the sense that there was no need for election by the insured.
17 Marine Insurance Act 1906, s.33(3).

was formerly characterised as a condition precedent to the insurer's liability under the policy.[18] It made no difference if the breach of warranty was remedied before any loss occurred,[19] nor did it matter if the breach of warranty was entirely unconnected to the loss which actually occurred. These two aspects of insurance warranties, that is, the inability to remedy their breach and the absence of any requirement that the breach is material to the actual loss, are the chief criticisms of insurance warranties which have attracted the ire of judges, commentators,[20] and the Law Commissions for some time.

6.6 The Law Commissions have cited the old case of *De Hahn v Hartley*[21] as one that exemplifies the problem caused by the irremediable nature of a breach of warranty.[22] That case involved the vessel *Juno*, which was captured off the coast of Africa. In the Law Commissions' view of the case, which appears to be mistaken, the insured warranted that the *Juno* would sail from Liverpool with a crew of at least 50 hands.[23] The vessel in fact sailed from Liverpool with 46 hands, but shortly afterwards picked up six additional men in Anglesey, well before the ship was captured off the coast of Africa. At the moment the ship sailed from Liverpool with fewer than 50 hands the insured was in breach of warranty, and the insurer's liability was permanently discharged. One hundred and twenty years later, the Marine Insurance Act 1906 codified the principle that an insured could not avail itself of the defence that a breach of warranty had been remedied before the loss,[24] and this was one of the Law Commissions' chief criticisms of the law of insurance warranties. They have attempted to remedy the problem in section 10 of the Act.

6.7 The second criticism of the law of insurance warranties was that they permitted insurers to refuse a claim even if the breach of warranty was totally unconnected to the actual loss which occurred. In the hackneyed example, breach of a burglar alarm warranty would discharge the insurer from liability for loss caused by a flood or fire, even though the breach of warranty had nothing to do with the loss.[25] There are a few other striking examples in which a technical breach of warranty discharged the insurer's liability (or could have done so, but for other factors),

18 *Bank of Nova Scotia v Hellenic Mutual War Risk Association (Bermuda) Ltd (The Good Luck)* [1992] 1 AC 233 (HL), Lord Goff at 262[G]–263[B].

19 Marine Insurance Act 1906, s.34(2).

20 For example, Barış Soyer, 'Reforming Insurance Warranties – are we finally moving forward?' in Barış Soyer (ed.), *Reforming Marine & Commercial Insurance Law* (Routledge-Cavendish, 2008), 127; Sir Andrew Longmore, 'Good Faith and Breach of Warranty: Are We Moving Forwards or Backwards?' [2004] LMCLQ 158; Professor Trine-Lise Wilhelmsen, 'Duty of Disclosure, Duty of Good Faith, Alternation of Risk and Warranties: An Analysis of the Replies to the CMI Questionnaire' in CMI Yearbook 2000 (CMI 2000), 392, and Professor Hare, 'The Omnipotent Warranty: England *v* The World' (International Marine Insurance Conference, November 1999).

21 (1786) 1 Term Rep 343, 99 ER 1130.

22 July 2014 Report, para.12.2.

23 In fact, the insured warranted not that the vessel *would* sail with 50 hands, but that the vessel *had* 'sailed from Liverpool with 14 six-pounders, swivels, small arms, and 50 hands or upwards'. There was therefore a breach of warranty of past fact, which might not have been capable of being remedied (a matter discussed below). However, if the warranty had provided as the Law Commissions state, the case would indeed exemplify the problem with not permitting a breach of warranty to be remedied, and would have been decided differently under the Act.

24 Insurance Act 2015, s.10(7)(b), the entirety of s.34 of the Marine Insurance Act 1906 is omitted. All but s.34(2) are replaced in s.10(3) of the Act.

25 July 2014 Report, para.12.4(3).

even though it did not cause or contribute to the actual loss.[26] The mischief is easy to understand but rather more difficult to remedy, as will be seen in the discussion of section 11.[27]

Warranties under the Act

6.8 Section 10 does not change what an insurance warranty is, but what a warranty does if it is breached. An insurance warranty, that is a promissory warranty of the type described in section 33(1) of the 1906 Act,[28] remains a term of the policy which must be exactly complied with, whether it is material to the risk or not.[29] If a term was a warranty under the old law, it will also be a warranty under the Act.[30] That is a question of construction, and the existing authorities on identification of insurance warranties remain good law. In *HIH Casualty and General Insurance Ltd v New Hampshire Insurance Co*,[31] Rix LJ set out three possible tests for whether a term was a warranty: (i) whether it was a term which went to the root of the transaction; (ii) whether it was descriptive of or bore materially on the risk of loss; and (iii) whether damages would be an unsatisfactory or inadequate remedy if the term was breached.[32] This work is restricted to those elements of insurance law which have been altered by the Act, and the reader is referred to detailed commentary on the identification of warranties elsewhere.[33] Section 10 applies to all warranties, including the implied warranties under sections 39 and 41 of the Marine Insurance Act 1906.[34]

6.9 The Insurance Act changes the effect of an insurance warranty from a condition precedent to the insurer's liability to a suspensory condition. Whereas previously, breach of warranty discharged the insurer's liability immediately and permanently,[35] under the Act the insurer's liability is automatically suspended, from the moment of breach. This is achieved through section 10(1), which abolishes any rule of law whereby breach of an express or implied insurance warranty results in automatic

26 *Kler Knitwear v Lombard General Insurance Co Ltd* [2000] Lloyd's Rep IR 47: warranty requiring fire sprinkler system to be inspected 30 days after renewal of the policy, inspected after 60 days and loss caused by storm damage wholly unconnected to the failure to inspect the sprinklers; *Sugar Hut Group Ltd v Great Lakes Reinsurance (UK) plc* [2010] EWHC 2636 (Comm), [2011] Lloyd's Rep IR 198: warranty requiring installation of a burglar alarm which would call a central monitoring station breached because different type of alarm installed, loss caused by fire.

27 Chapter 7.

28 Marine Insurance Act 1906, s.33(1): 'A warranty, in the following sections relating to warranties, means a promissory warranty, that is to say, a warranty by which the assured undertakes that some particular thing shall or shall not be done, or that some condition shall be fulfilled, or whereby he affirms or negatives the existence of a particular state of facts.'

29 Marine Insurance Act 1906, s.33(3).

30 July 2014 Report, paras 15.13–15.14

31 [2001] EWCA Civ 735, [2001] Lloyd's Rep IR 596.

32 [2001] Lloyd's Rep IR 596, Rix LJ at 601.

33 For comprehensive coverage of this topic, see John Birds, Ben Lynch, Simon Milnes, *MacGillivray on Insurance Law*, 13th edn (Sweet & Maxwell, London, 2015) (hereafter *MacGillivray*, 2015), ch.10; Jonathan Gilman and others, *Arnould's Law of Marine Insurance and Average*, 18th edn (Sweet & Maxwell, London, 2013) (hereafter *Arnould*, 18th edn), ch.19; Robert M. Merkin, *Colinvaux's Law of Insurance*, 11th edn (Sweet & Maxwell, London, 2016) (hereafter *Colinvaux*, 2016) B2; Malcolm A. Clarke, *Law of Insurance Contracts*, 4th edn (Lloyd's of London Press, London, 2002), ch.20.

34 Explanatory Notes to the Insurance Act 2015, [91].

35 Subject to waiver and estoppel.

discharge of the insurer's liability.[36] Instead, under section 10(2) an insurer will have no liability under the contract for any loss which occurs, or which is 'attributable to something happening' after the warranty has been breached, but 'before the breach has been remedied'. As before, the insurer may still be liable for losses which occur, or which are 'attributable to something happening' both before the warranty was breached,[37] and after the breach has been remedied (if that is possible).[38] For example, a ship sails into a war zone in breach of warranty, where it damages its propellers. It then sails out of the war zone, remedying the breach of warranty. The insurer is not liable for the damaged propellers, since that loss occurred before the breach of warranty had been remedied.[39] Contrastingly, if the facts of *De Hahn v Hartley*[40] had been as described by the Law Commissions, the case would have been decided differently. When the ship sailed from Liverpool with 46 crew (in breach of a warranty requiring at least 50), the insurer's liability would have been suspended until the collection of additional men at Anglesey, when the insurer's liability would have been restored. In view of this change to the effect of an insurance warranty, Lord Goff's *dicta* in *The Good Luck*, that an insurance warranty is a condition precedent to the insurer's liability, is no longer an accurate statement of the law.[41] Warranties have become suspensive conditions, because their breach will suspend the insurer's liability unless and until the breach is remedied.

The period of suspension of the insurer's liability

6.10 Under section 10(2), the insurer will not be liable for loss occurring or 'attributable to something happening' after a warranty has been breached, but before the breach has been remedied (if it can be remedied). Under section 10(4) the insurer may be liable for loss occurring or 'attributable to something happening' both before a breach of warranty (as under the old law) and after the breach of warranty has been remedied (if it can be). The words 'attributable to' are broader than 'caused or contributed', and will presumably include cases in which there is no strict causal link between the thing that happened and the loss which subsequently occurs. The meaning and effect of these words in sections 10(2) and 10(4) is discussed below.

No liability before the breach is remedied (section 10(2))

6.11 The insurer has no liability for loss occurring or 'attributable to something happening' before a breach of warranty has been remedied. The Law Commissions provide the example of a vessel sailing into a war zone in breach of warranty. Whilst

36 Consequently, s.10(7) of the Act amends s.33(3) of the Marine Insurance Act 1906 by deletion of the second sentence, as follows: 'A warranty, as above defined, is a condition which must be exactly complied with, whether it be material to the risk or not.'

37 Insurance Act 2015, s.10(4)(a).

38 Insurance Act 2015, s.10(4)(b).

39 July 2014 Report, para.17.25 cit. Professor Barış Soyer, 'Reforming Warranties in Business Insurance Contract Law', lecture given to the Association of British Insurers Symposium, London, 25 April 2013.

40 (1786) 1 Term Rep 343, 99 ER 1130.

41 *Bank of Nova Scotia v Hellenic Mutual War Risks Association (Bermuda) (The Good Luck)* [1992] 1 AC 233 (HL), Lord Goff at 262[G]–263[B].

in the war zone, the vessel is torpedoed, following which it sails out of the war zone, and sinks. Assuming the breach of warranty was remedied when the vessel sailed out of the war zone,[42] the insurer will have no liability, because the loss was attributable to something happening (the torpedoing of the vessel) after the warranty was breached, and before the breach was remedied.[43]

6.12 An insured warrants that his collection of fine wine will be stored horizontally in cellar conditions, but the wine is stored vertically in a warm warehouse for three months. During this time, the corks dry out and shrink. The wine is then placed horizontally in a cellar, which the Law Commissions consider to be a remedy of the breach of warranty.[44] Years later, it is discovered that the shrinkage to the corks has caused the wine to become oxidised. The insurer is not liable, because the loss is attributable to the corks shrinking whilst it was in the warehouse, which was 'something happening' before the breach of warranty was remedied. The insurer is therefore not liable under section 10(2).[45]

6.13 A solicitor insured under a professional indemnity policy fails to pay its premium on 1 January, in breach of a premium payment warranty. On 10 January, it gives negligent advice to a client. On 1 February, it pays the premium, thereby remedying its breach of warranty. Later, the client suffers loss as a result of the negligent advice, and brings a negligence claim against the solicitor. The policy will not respond to any legal liability arising from the solicitor's negligence on 10 January, since such loss would be attributable to something happening before the breach of warranty was remedied on 1 February, namely, the giving of negligent advice by the solicitor.[46] In a variation to this example, the insured fails to pay its premium on 1 January, and on 10 January it receives a letter before action from a client threatening a negligence action, which it then notifies to the insurer as a circumstance likely to give rise to a claim. This prompts the insured to pay its premium, which it does on 1 February. The outcome in this example is probably different, because the 'loss' (which in this case is the solicitor's liability to its client) cannot properly be said to be 'attributable to' the receipt of a letter before action, still less to the notification. Although the test of 'attributable to' is wider than one of proximate cause, there must be some form of causal link between the 'something happening' and the loss. The receipt of a letter before action is an incidental precursor to the insured's liability to the client which does no more than to inform the insured that it faces the prospect of liability due to its alleged negligence, and any ensuing loss is not 'attributable to' receipt of such a letter.

6.14 There appear to be limitations to the effect of the words 'attributable to something happening' in section 10(2). For example, a marine policy includes a warranty

42 The breach would in those circumstances be remedied, since the insured had ceased to be in breach of warranty (see Insurance Act 2015, s.10(5)(b)).

43 July 2014 Report, para.17.27.

44 July 2014 Report, para.17.29.

45 Because the loss is 'attributable to something happening … after a warranty … has been breached but before the breach has been remedied' (Insurance Act 2015, s.10(2)).

46 The insured might in those circumstances attempt to rely upon Insurance Act 2015, s.11, in view of the fact that failure to pay premium had nothing at all to do with its giving negligent advice on 10 January (which was ultimately the cause of its legal liability to the client). However, that argument is unlikely to succeed, since a premium payment warranty is not a term designed to reduce the risk of loss, and therefore is not caught by s.11(1).

that a vessel will not sail through a particular strait because of the risk of piracy. The vessel sails safely through the strait and emerges into safe waters, whereupon the breach of warranty is remedied. As a result of having sailed through the strait, the vessel cuts two days off its voyage, causing it to encounter a storm which it would otherwise have missed, and the vessel is damaged in the storm. The Law Commissions consider that the insurer would be liable for the damage in those circumstances, because 'the ship that emerged from the strait represents the same risk as that which entered the strait and which the insurer had agreed to insure. It had not acquired any new characteristics …'.[47] The Law Commissions' conclusion is correct, but their reasoning appears to assume (incorrectly) that this is a time-specific warranty, since the focus is upon whether the risk was restored to that originally contemplated.[48] However, this is a general warranty, and the breach was therefore remedied when the insured sailed out of the strait.[49] The loss was therefore after the breach of warranty had been remedied, and section 10(4)(b) makes clear that the insurer cannot escape liability under section 10(2) for such loss. Could it be said that the loss is attributable to taking a shortcut through the war zone, which was 'something happening' before the breach was remedied? That does not appear to be correct for at least two reasons. First, it amounts to an argument that the 'something happening' could be the breach of warranty itself, but that is inconsistent with the language of section 10(2), which treats the 'something happening' and the breach of warranty as separate incidents. It follows that the 'something happening' must be something other than the breach of warranty itself, such as the torpedoing of the vessel whilst in the war zone, in the example above.[50] Secondly, the loss was attributable to the storm, and that was not 'something happening' before the breach of warranty was remedied.[51] The insurer would therefore be liable.

Liability before the breach of warranty, and after it has been remedied (section 10(4))

6.15 Section 10(4) provides that nothing in section 10(2) shall affect the insurer's liability for loss occurring or attributable to something happening before a warranty is breached, or after the breach has been remedied. For example, an insured vessel hits a submerged buoy shortly before sailing into a strait known for piracy risks, in breach of warranty, where the vessel sinks. The loss is attributable to (indeed, is caused by) the vessel hitting the buoy, which happened before the breach of warranty, meaning the insurer is liable notwithstanding the fact that it is in actual breach of warranty at the time of the loss. This may be regarded as surprising. In a variation of that scenario, the vessel hit the buoy and consequently reduced its speed, because it began slowly to take on water. When it entered the strait, it was therefore more vulnerable to a pirate attack, and was captured by pirates (but did not sink). The loss in those circumstances may be said to be attributable to something happening before the breach of warranty, namely the hitting of a buoy. In those circumstances, it arguably follows

47 July 2014 Report, para.17.36.
48 See para.6.19 below.
49 See paras 6.28–6.30 below.
50 Para.6.11 above.
51 *Arnould*, 18th edn, para.1.3-58.

that the insurer would be liable under section 10(4)(a). However, the loss occurred before the breach of warranty was remedied, meaning the insurer is arguably not liable under section 10(2). It is not clear from the Act which of 10(4)(a) or 10(2) should take precedence in those circumstances, but it would be surprising if the insurer was liable in circumstances where the insured was in actual breach of warranty, and the breach caused the loss. This eventuality does not appear to have been considered by the Law Commissions, and the outcome is uncertain.

6.16 The insurer will be liable for loss occurring or attributable to something happening after a breach of warranty has been remedied.[52] For example, if the insured vessel in the above example sailed out of the prohibited war zone and then hit a buoy and sank, the insurer would be liable because the loss occurred and was attributable to something happening after the breach had been remedied.

The two types of warranty identified in section 10

6.17 When it comes to defining how a breach of warranty may be remedied, the Act distinguishes between two types of warranty. The first is any warranty which requires that, by an ascertainable time, something will or will not be done, or a condition fulfilled, or something will or will not be the case.[53] The Law Commissions have referred to these as 'time-specific warranties',[54] and that phrase is adopted in this work for convenience. The second type of warranty identified in the Act is anything that is not a time-specific warranty, which are referred to herein (and by the Law Commissions) as 'general warranties'.[55] It is likely that the majority of warranties will fall into this category.

6.18 A time-specific warranty is breached if, 'by an ascertainable time', the relevant thing is or is not done, or the relevant state of affairs is or is not existent, as the case may be. The ascertainable time must be in the future.[56] Obvious examples are premium payment warranties, warranties that an inspection or survey will occur, or that specific measures will be put in place by a given time, such as the installation of a burglar alarm by the inception date. The implied warranty of seaworthiness is a time-specific warranty,[57] since it requires the insured vessel to be seaworthy at the commencement of the voyage, and section 10 applies to implied as well as express warranties.[58] The editors of *Arnould* suggest that a warranty prohibiting a vessel from leaving port when a typhoon warning is in force[59] could 'hardly be said to require compliance "by an ascertainable time"', meaning such a clause is a general warranty.[60] That appears to be based upon a presumption that the time must be ascertainable from the terms of the

52 Insurance Act 2015, s.10(4)(b).
53 Insurance Act 2015, s.10(6).
54 July 2014 Report, para.17.40.
55 July 2014 Report, para.17.32.
56 That is indicated in section 10(6)(a) by the repeated use of the future passive voice, viz 'something is *to be done*', 'a condition is *to be fulfilled*', and 'something is (or is not) *to be the case*' (emphases added).
57 Marine Insurance Act 1906, s.39(1).
58 Insurance Act 2015, s.10(1).
59 *Amlin Corporate Member Ltd v Oriental Assurance Corp (The Princess of the Stars)* [2014] EWCA Civ 1135, [2014] 2 Lloyd's Rep 561 in which the warranty provided that 'the carrying vessel shall not sail or put out of Sheltered Port when there is a typhoon or storm warning at that port ...'.
60 *Arnould*, 1st supp. to 18th edn, 1.3-68.

policy.[61] The authors do not share this view: section 10(6)(a) does not provide that the time must be 'ascertainable' from the terms of the policy, and there is nothing in the language of the Act which prevents the time being ascertainable from another source, such as the relevant meteorological authorities who gave the typhoon warning in *The Princess of the Stars.* The relevant term in that case was a warranty that something is not to be done at an ascertainable time, and section 10(6)(a) expressly covers warranties requiring that by (or at[62]) an ascertainable time, 'something is to be done (or not done)'. The typhoon warranty in *The Princess of the Stars* was therefore a time-specific warranty. Under the Act, the insurer's liability would have been suspended when the vessel sailed from port when a typhoon warning was in place.

Remedying breach of a time-sensitive warranty

6.19 If a time-sensitive warranty is breached, it is not possible to remedy the breach in the strict sense of the word, since time cannot be reversed in order to permit compliance with the warranty by the specified deadline. If the insured fails to install a new fire alarm by the appointed day, it does not strictly remedy that breach of warranty if, a month later, it installs the fire alarm. The time for compliance has passed, and it cannot be said that the insured has complied exactly with the warranty, as it was required to do.[63] Section 10(5) therefore provides that breach of a time-sensitive warranty is deemed to have been remedied if 'the risk to which the warranty relates later becomes essentially the same as that originally contemplated by the parties',[64] the meaning of which is discussed below. The Law Commissions have stated that the correct approach to take when considering whether breach of a time-sensitive warranty has been remedied is:

> to look at the purpose for which the warranty was inserted in the contract and ask whether that purpose has been frustrated or whether, due to the actions taken to remedy the breach of warranty, the purpose is still in substance fulfilled and the risk profile is restored to that which the Insurer accepted.[65]

The risk to which the warranty relates

6.20 In order to ascertain whether breach of a time-specific warranty has been remedied, one must ascertain the 'risk' to which the warranty relates. In many cases, this will be straightforward, since many promissory warranties clearly relate to a specific risk or risks insured under the policy. A warranty requiring a fire alarm to be installed by a given date relates to the risk of loss caused by fire, for example. The warranty in *The Princess of the Stars*, discussed above, related to the risk that the vessel would be lost or damaged in a typhoon.[66] In many cases, the risk to which the warranty relates

---

61 *Arnould*, 1st supp., to 18th edn (see fn.60 above), 1.3-65.

62 A warranty which is to be complied with 'by' an ascertainable time is not the same as one to be complied with 'at' an ascertainable time, but the courts are likely in practice to interpret s.10(5)(a) in a broad way: see *Arnould*, 18th edn, 1.3-65.

63 Marine Insurance Act 1906, s.33(3).

64 Insurance Act 2015, s.10(5)(a).

65 July 2014 Report, para.17.48.

66 *Amlin Corporate Member Ltd v Oriental Assurance Corp (The Princess of the Stars)* [2014] EWCA Civ 1135, [2014] 2 Lloyd's Rep 561.

will be obvious. However, section 10(5)(a) appears to proceed on the basis that all time-sensitive warranties relate to a risk, and this may cause difficulties if the warranty in question does not relate to a risk at all. A common example is the premium payment warranty, under which the insured warrants that it will pay premium by a specified time. This is not a warranty that relates to a particular risk, such as that of fire or loss of a vessel. Rather, it is a warranty which goes to the mechanics of the bargain between the parties, namely the deadline for payment of the premium. Assuming that breach of a premium payment warranty can be remedied (and there is no reason it should not be possible, subject to any contrary term in the policy), it should be remedied when the premium is paid, albeit late. However, that conclusion is not easily squared with section 10(5)(a), which provides that a time-specific warranty is remedied if the risk to which the warranty relates becomes essentially the same as originally contemplated.

6.21 Suppose a shipowner does not pay its premium until he hears a hurricane warning which threatens his vessel, causing the insured to pay the premium before the hurricane strikes. Shortly afterwards, the vessel is lost in the hurricane. It is not immediately clear whether, and if so how, section 10(5)(a) will prevent the insured from seemingly playing the system in this way. As identified, a premium payment warranty does not relate to a 'risk', so one cannot readily conclude whether the 'risk to which the warranty relates' has become 'essentially the same as that originally contemplated by the parties'. A potential solution in those circumstances is that the relevant 'risk' should be the risk(s) insured under the policy in question, which in that example would include perils of the sea. If that is right, the risk at the time when the premium is paid has not become essentially the same as that originally contemplated by the parties, who presumably did not envisage, when the contract was entered into, that there would be an approaching hurricane which threatened the vessel. The insured should not, therefore, be taken to have remedied its breach of warranty by paying the premium shortly before the hurricane struck. This outcome requires a somewhat strained reading of the words 'the risk to which the warranty relates' in section 10(5)(a), but it is not inconsistent with those words, or with the purpose behind section 10.

Risk becomes essentially the same as originally contemplated

6.22 As discussed above, breach of a time-specific warranty cannot be remedied in the strict sense, since the time for compliance has passed. For this reason, the Act deems that breach of a time-specific warranty has been remedied if the risk later becomes 'essentially' the same as originally contemplated. The words 'originally contemplated' mean the risk as contemplated by the parties at the time when the policy containing the warranty was entered into or, if the warranty was inserted by a variation, at the time it was agreed.[67] It is submitted that if the risk to which the warranty relates has been increased by any material degree, then, notwithstanding any attempt to remedy the breach of warranty, the insured will remain in breach and the insurer's

67 This is implicit in Law Com No 353 (July 2014 Report), para.17.44, which explains that in order to remedy breach of a time-specific warranty, the risk must be 'restored to the state in which the insurer accepted it', which means the time when the contract or variation was concluded.

liability will remain suspended unless and until the risk becomes essentially the same as originally contemplated. That is consistent with the fact that warranties are terms of the contract which must be exactly complied with.[68]

6.23 Certain breaches of warranty are incapable of being remedied, and this is expressly acknowledged in section 10(4) of the Act,[69] and by the Law Commissions.[70] It will be impossible to remedy breach of a time-sensitive warranty if the risk cannot be made essentially the same as originally contemplated by the parties, such as where the breach of warranty has permanently and irreversibly increased the risk of loss. If, following a breach of warranty, the risk later becomes better than that originally contemplated by the parties, such as where the insured exceeds what it was required to do under a warranty, the breach of warranty should be taken as remedied. That is consistent with the purpose of section 11, which is to prevent an insured from being deprived of cover for a technical breach of warranty which has been remedied. If the insured has exceeded what it was required to do under the warranty, thereby improving the risk, there is no good reason why it should not be taken to have remedied its breach of warranty.

Examples involving time-specific warranties

6.24 An insured warrants that by 1 January it will install a fire detection system which dials through directly to the local fire station when a fire is detected. The risk to which this warranty relates is the risk of fire; the purpose of the warranty is to enable fire to be detected and extinguished. The insured does not install the system on 1 January, but does so on 20 January. At that later time, the risk to which the warranty relates has become essentially the same as originally contemplated, because the new system has been installed, and the risk of loss by fire has (presumably) diminished.

6.25 An insured warrants that it will install five-lever mortise locks on all doors to its premises by 1 January, but fails to do so. On 1 February, it installs three-lever mortise locks on the doors. The breach of warranty has not been remedied, because a three-lever mortise lock does not afford the same protection as the five-lever lock required under the warranty, meaning the risk has not become essentially the same.[71] It is also relevant that a warranty is a term which must be exactly complied with,[72] and installation of a three-lever lock is not exact compliance.

6.26 In a liability policy, the insured warrants that it will notify any circumstances likely to give rise to a claim within 10 days of gaining knowledge.[73] One of the purposes of such a warranty may be to allow the insurer to intervene in any proceedings against the insured, thereby reducing the risk that the insured will suffer loss in the

---

68 Marine Insurance Act 1906, s.33(3).

69 Insurance Act 2015, s.10(4)(b): '*if the breach can be remedied*, after it has been remedied.'

70 July 2014 Report, para.17.49.

71 That question could turn upon factual and expert evidence.

72 Marine Insurance Act 1906, s.33(3).

73 It is acknowledged that a notification warranty would be very rare, and such a term is more likely to be drafted as a condition precedent to the insurer's liability. Such terms are discussed below at paras 6.36–6.40.

form of legal liability to a third party.[74] The risk to which the warranty relates is therefore the risk that the insured will be found liable. If the insured fails to notify the insurer for 30 days, the breach of warranty will be taken to be remedied unless the failure to notify has permanently increased the risk of loss. For example, if during the intervening period default judgment was entered against the insured, the breach of warranty might not be remedied, because the purpose behind the warranty has been frustrated.[75] However, if the risk of liability has not increased in the intervening period, the breach of warranty will be remedied as soon as the notification is given, because the risk has been restored to that which the insurer accepted.

6.27 In a cyber policy, the insured company warrants that it will delete the profiles all non-employees by 1 January. In breach of warranty, the insured fails to delete the profile of a temporary intern, who steals confidential material about the company's top clients. On 1 March, the company deleted the intern's profile. Later, the intern sells the confidential material to a newspaper, causing the company to suffer loss. The warranty relates to (amongst others) the risk that non-employees will access confidential material stored on the IT system. Although the company deleted the intern's profile on 1 March, the risk did not and could not become essentially the same as originally contemplated, because the intern had taken the confidential material for good. The breach of warranty was therefore incapable of being remedied.

Remedying breach of a general warranty

6.28 Breach of a general warranty will be remedied if the insured ceases to be in breach of the warranty.[76] In most cases, this will be a relatively straightforward matter. For example, if the insured breaches a warranty prohibiting the vessel from sailing in specified waters, the breach will be remedied at the moment the vessel leaves the forbidden area, because the insured has ceased to be in breach of warranty.[77] Like time-specific warranties, certain breaches of general warranties cannot be remedied. For example, breach of a warranty of confidentiality cannot be remedied if the insured compromises confidentiality, since this is akin to a continuing breach of warranty in that, once confidentiality has been lost, its loss is continuous and cannot be undone.[78] If it is impossible to remedy a breach of warranty, the insurer's liability will remain permanently suspended, but the insured will still have to meet its other obligations under the contract, including any duty to pay premium.

6.29 Particular difficulties may arise where the insured slips in and out of breach over a sustained period of time. In *Murray v Scottish Automobile and General Insurance*

74 Under a liability policy, loss usually occurs when the insured's liability is established by judgment, award or settlement: see *Post Office v Norwich Union Fire Insurance Society Ltd* [1967] 2 QB 363, [1967] 1 Lloyd's Rep 216; *Bradley v Eagle Star Insurance Co Ltd* [1989] AC 957, 1 Lloyd's Rep 465.

75 July 2014 Report, para.17.48, which indicates that the correct approach when considering whether breach of a time-specific warranty has been remedied is to look at the purpose for which the warranty was inserted in the contract and ask whether that purpose has been frustrated or whether, due to the actions taken to remedy the breach of warranty, the purpose is still in substance fulfilled and the risk profile is restored to that which the insurer accepted.

76 Insurance Act 2015, s.10(5)(b).

77 July 2014 Report, para.17.33.

78 July 2014 Report, para.17.49.

Co,[79] a motor policy contained a condition that the insurance applied 'only to a Car for private personal use', and another that excluded liability for loss when the car was 'being used in connexion with any trade or business or otherwise than for the private personal purposes of the assured'.[80] Had they been warranties, these would have been general warranties, since they did not require something to be done (or not done) by an ascertainable time, but instead related to the entire period covered by the policy.[81] The car was habitually used in a private hiring business conducted by the owner, and was only rarely put to personal use. After returning from a hire one night, the insured put the car in a garage, and shortly afterwards it was destroyed in a fire. A majority of the Inner House of the Court of Session held that, at the time of the fire, the car was being used in connection with or for purposes ancillary to its use for trade or business, meaning the insurer was not liable.[82] It appears that the majority thereby treated the breach as a continuing one which had not been remedied by the time of the loss. However, Lord Blackburn (dissenting) was unable to characterise the breach as continuing since, at the time the car was in the garage, it was not being used for any commercial hiring purpose, meaning there should have been cover.[83]

6.30 The Law Commissions have said that section 10 is not intended to protect those who 'play the system' as the insured did in *Murray.* They have stated that under section 10, the breach should not be remedied unless and until the car's 'use for commercial purposes was stopped entirely, or at least reduced to a level where personal use dominated'.[84] Whilst this outcome may be desirable, it does not appear to be reflected by section 10(5)(b), which provides that breach of a general warranty is remedied if the insured ceases to be in breach of warranty. If the Law Commissions are correct that the breach would be remedied when personal use became dominant, ascertaining the precise time when the insured ceased to be in breach of warranty would be fraught with uncertainty. The suggestion that the breach of warranty could be remedied by reducing use of the car to a level where personal use dominated is also difficult to reconcile with the fact that a warranty is a term of the policy which must be exactly complied with, in view of which any commercial use of the car ought to be impermissible. In the authors' view, the breach of warranty in *Murray* was indeed a continuing one which had not been remedied at the time of the loss, since the car was used habitually for a commercial purpose. In order to overcome this, the insured would need to prove that it had ceased using the car for commercial purposes, failing which it would be in continuing breach of warranty. If the insured habitually breached a warranty, it would face a relatively high burden to prove that at the time of loss it had ceased to be in breach. For example, if the insured in *Murray* could prove that

79 *Murray v Scottish Automobile & General Insurance Co Ltd* 1929 SC 48 (IH), 1929 SLT 114.

80 Neither term was a warranty, but the reasoning is nonetheless relevant for the reasons explained below.

81 That may be contrasted with, for example, a warranty requiring a night watchman to be posted after sunset, which might be said to be a time-specific warranty. However, the better view appears to be that warranties requiring continuing compliance over specific periods of time should be treated as general warranties, not least because it is doubtful whether such warranties require compliance by an 'ascertainable' time.

82 *Murray v Scottish Automobile & General Insurance Co Ltd* 1929 SC 48 (IH), 1929 SLT 114, Lord Clyde, at 52, (at the time of the loss, the car was being used 'in connexion with the hiring business'); Lord Sands, at 54, (at the time of the loss, the car was being put to a use which was 'ancillary' to the hiring business). Lord Morrison, at 54, agreed with the majority.

83 Ibid., Lord Blackburn, at 54.

84 July 2014 Report, para.17.39.

it had acquired a separate car which it used for commercial hiring, that might indicate that it had stopped using the insured car for anything other than personal use. Such issues are of course highly fact-sensitive.

6.31 Unlike time-specific warranties, there is no requirement that the risk to which a general warranty relates must become essentially the same as originally contemplated by the parties in order for the breach to be remedied. It is possible, therefore, that something may take place whilst the insured is in breach of warranty which increases the risk of loss or causes loss to occur, notwithstanding which the breach of warranty may be remedied for the purposes of the Act. However, in those circumstances the insurer may be able to rely upon section 10(2), under which it has no liability for loss attributable to something happening before the breach of warranty has been remedied.[85]

Warranties of past and present facts

6.32 It is likely that breach of a warranty of past or present fact cannot be remedied, at least in the majority of cases. If, for example, an insured warrants (incorrectly) that he has never had a criminal conviction, the breach of warranty cannot be remedied, since the insured cannot go back in time and remove the criminal conviction. Similarly, in *Yorkshire Insurance Co v Campbell* the insured warranted (incorrectly) that a horse was of a particular pedigree.[86] That breach of warranty of past and present fact could not be remedied,[87] since the insured could not go back in time and alter the breeding of the horse. It has been suggested that all warranties of past or present fact are incapable of being remedied if they are breached. [88] That appears to be correct in many (and perhaps all) cases because, if a matter of fact is warranted to be true when it is not, it is not easy to see how the insured could ever cease to be in breach of warranty under section 10(5)(a). However, this point is uncertain, and there may be cases in which breach of a warranty of past or present fact could be remedied. The contrary view is based in part upon the *dicta* of Lord Goff in *The Good Luck,* to the effect that where a warranty of past or present fact is breached the risk does not attach in the first place, because a warranty is a condition precedent to the insurer's liability.[89] However, the reasoning of Lord Goff in that case was based upon section 33(3) of the Marine Insurance Act, which previously provided that a warranty was a condition which must be exactly complied with, failing which 'the insurer is discharged from liability as from the date of the breach of warranty'. Having quoted section 33 of the 1906 Act, Lord Goff said:

> So it is laid down in section 33(3) that, subject to any express provision in the policy, the insurer is discharged from liability as from the date of the breach of warranty. Those words

85 See paras 6.11–6.14 above.

86 *Yorkshire Insurance Co Ltd v Campbell* [1917] AC 218.

87 The warranty may be regarded as one of both past and present fact, since it was a promise that the horse had been born of a particular sire and dam, but also that it was at the present time a horse of a particular pedigree.

88 *Arnould*, 18th edn, para.1.3-51; Law Com No 353, para.17.50.

89 Para.17.50, July 2014 Report and *Arnould*, 18th edn, para.1.3-49, citing *The Good Luck* [1992] 1 AC 233, Lord Goff at 262[G]–263[B]

> are clear. They show that discharge of the insurer from liability is automatic and is not dependent upon any decision by the insurer to treat the contract or the insurance as at an end … Section 33(3) of the Act reflects what has been described, in successive editions of *Chalmers, The Marine Insurance Act 1906*, as the inveterate practice in marine insurance of using the term 'warranty' as signifying a condition precedent …
>
> Once this is appreciated, it becomes readily understandable that, if a promissory warranty is not complied with, the insurer is discharged from liability as from the date of the breach of warranty, for the simple reason that fulfilment of the warranty is a condition precedent to the liability of the insurer … and it follows that the immediate effect of a breach of a promissory warranty is to discharge the insurer from liability as from the date of the breach.[90]

6.33 As explained above, the critical words in section 33(3) upon which Lord Goff's analysis rests have been deleted by section 10(7) Insurance Act,[91] and warranties have now been recast as suspensory conditions.[92] The *dicta* of Lord Goff in *The Good Luck* are no longer good law, therefore.

6.34 Under section 10, if a fact was incorrect when the warranty was given but later became substantially correct, it is possible that the breach of warranty has been remedied. For example, in *De Hahn v Hartley*, the insured warranted that the vessel had sailed from Liverpool with a crew of 50 hands or more, which was a warranty of past fact.[93] It was untrue, since the vessel had only 46 crew, until it picked up more men at Anglesey shortly after leaving Liverpool. That is a general warranty, since it is not a warranty that something will be done in the future.[94] In view of the Law Commissions' analysis of that case, albeit premised on an apparent mistake, it is plainly their intention that the picking up of further men at Anglesey ought to mean that the insured remedied its breach of warranty. It ought to make no difference that this was a warranty of past fact rather than future conduct. Whilst this may be difficult to reconcile with section 10(5)(a), it must be recalled that section 10 operates on the basis that breach of a general warranty is deemed to have been remedied,[95] so it should not necessarily matter that the fact was untrue when the warranty was given. Taking a purposive approach to section 10, it is not clear why the insured should lose its cover merely because the warranty was phrased as one of past fact rather than future conduct, particularly given (as the Law Commissions have inadvertently demonstrated) the difference between the two types of warranty may be very subtle.[96] It would be potentially problematic if section 10 could be circumvented by drafting a warranty as one of past fact ('the burglar alarm was working on the inception date') rather that one of future conduct ('the burglar alarm will be working on the inception date'). There is therefore a possibility that breach of a warranty of past or present fact may be capable of being remedied.

---

90 *The Good Luck* [1992] 1 AC 233, Lord Goff at 262[G]–263[B].

91 Insurance Act, s.10(7) amends Marine Insurance Act 1906, s.33(3) by deletion of the second sentence, as follows: 'A warranty, as above defined, is a condition which must be exactly complied with, whether it be material to the risk or not.'

92 Para.6.9 above.

93 See para.6.6 above.

94 See para.6.17 above.

95 Insurance Act 2015, s.10(5)(b): '… a breach of warranty *is to be taken as remedied* … if the insured ceases to be in breach of warranty.'

96 See para.6.6 above; the Law Commissions appear to have misread the warranty in *De Hahn* as being one of future conduct rather than past fact.

6.35 Certain warranties of present fact may be construed as promissory warranties of future conduct, and such warranties should be capable of being remedied if they are breached. This is a question of construction in every case. For example, in *Agapitos v Agnew (No 2)*, the insured warranted that its vessel had certain approvals certified by the London Salvage Association and, whilst this was true at the time the contract was entered into, the approval certificate later expired and was not renewed. Moore-Bick J held that this was a breach of a continuing warranty.[97] Under the Act, if the insured had later renewed the certificate, this would have remedied the breach of warranty. Similarly, in *Hales v Reliance Fire Assurance*, the insured was asked in the proposal for insurance on a general shop: 'Are any inflammable oils or goods used or kept on the premises?', and answered (only) 'lighter fuel'. This was a warranty by reason of a basis clause in the proposal form. A fire subsequently occurred whilst the insured was keeping fireworks on the premises, which he customarily did in the weeks leading up to 5 November. McNair J held that the answer was a continuing warranty which had been breached.[98] Under the Act, if the insured had ceased to store fireworks in the shop by the time of the fire, the breach of warranty would have been remedied.

Conditions precedent to liability

6.36 There appears to be some confusion over whether a condition precedent to liability will be treated as an insurance warranty, and therefore subject to section 10 Insurance Act. That confusion may stem from Lord Goff's observation in *The Good Luck* that an insurance warranty is a condition precedent to the insurer's liability under the policy.[99] However, Lord Goff was saying that a warranty was (under the old law) a condition precedent to any liability which post-dates a breach of warranty, and not that any term which refers to itself as a 'condition precedent to liability' is therefore an insurance warranty. Conditions precedent to liability in insurance contracts generally address either the insured risk, such as a condition precedent that the insured will make reasonable endeavours to maintain his taxi in a roadworthy condition,[100] or the mechanics of the policy, such as a condition precedent that notice of loss be given or premium paid within a specified time. In certain cases, there will be a term providing that compliance with every condition in the policy is a condition precedent to the insurer's liability.[101] The meaning and effect of any condition precedent is a matter of construction in every case, and there is no universal rule about the effect of breaching a condition precedent to liability.[102] Generally speaking, however, these terms are not warranties, and breach of them will not discharge the insurer's liability under the

97 *Agapitos v Agnew (No 2) (The Aegeon)* [2002] EWHC 1558 (Comm), [2003] Lloyd's Rep IR 54.

98 *Hales v Reliance Fire & Accident Insurance Corporation Ltd* [1960] 2 Lloyd's Rep 391.

99 Although, as has been explained, this proposition appears no longer to be good law in view of Insurance Act 2015, s.10(7)(a).

100 *Conn v Westminster Motor Insurance Association* [1966] 1 Lloyd's Rep 407.

101 For examples, see *Farrell v Federated Employers' Insurance Co* [1970] 1 WLR 498 at 500; *Cox v Orion Insurance Co* [1982] RTR 1.

102 A condition precedent to liability is contrasted with a condition precedent to the contract, breach of which means the contract never comes into effect at all, and breach of a condition precedent to inception of the risk, breach of which will mean that the contract is in effect, but the insurer never comes on risk.

policy in respect of all future claims,[103] as a breach of warranty would have done under the old law. If a condition precedent to liability is breached, the insured will generally be prevented from recovering (only) the particular loss in respect of which there has been a breach of the term,[104] regardless of whether it was remedied before or causally connected with the loss.[105] The insured will nonetheless be free to pursue a separate claim, provided it has complied with the condition precedent in respect of that loss.

6.37 For example, a policy provides that it is a 'condition precedent to the insurer's liability that the insured shall give written notice of loss within 10 days'. The insured, who owns a computer shop, fails to notify the insurer that a laptop was stolen from the shop until 60 days after the theft. *Prima facie*, there will be no cover for the stolen laptop, since the insured has breached a condition precedent to liability. Subsequently, thieves steal many items from the shop, and the insured gives written notice of the loss to the insurer the next day. Notwithstanding the previous breach of condition precedent, the insured will recover for the subsequent loss, since there was no breach of the condition precedent in the context of that loss. The condition precedent prevents the insured from recovering any loss in respect of which there has been a failure to notify, but breach does not discharge (or suspend) the insurer's liability for all future losses. That is because the condition precedent to liability is not (without more) a warranty, albeit the two types of term share certain similarities.

6.38 Similarly, in *Welch v Royal Exchange Assurance*,[106] a fire insurance policy contained a condition that on making a claim, the insured should 'give to the [insurer] all such proofs and information with respect to the claim as may reasonably be required' and that 'no claim under this policy shall be payable unless the terms of this condition shall have been complied with'. The insured made a claim following a fire, and the insurer asked for information which the insured refused to provide until he was cross-examined at trial. The primary issue in the case was whether this late provision of the information remedied the breach of condition precedent (which it did not). However, MacKinnon LJ said that breach of the condition precedent only prevented the insured from recovering for loss caused by that specific fire, and not if there were later fires in respect of which the insured did not breach the condition precedent.[107]

6.39 What if the condition precedent to liability is framed more broadly, such as 'it is a condition precedent to any liability to make any payment under this policy that the insured shall give notice of any loss to the insurer within 10 days of loss'? If loss occurred and the insured failed to give notice within 10 days, does it follow that the insurer's liability is discharged for all future losses, even if the insured gave timely notice of such losses? If interpreted literally, non-fulfilment of such a term suggests that the insurer is altogether discharged from liability under the policy, and not merely in respect of the particular claim.[108] However, before the Act it was seen as unlikely that a court would read a condition precedent to liability as discharging the insurer from

103 *Colinvaux*, 2016, B-0089.

104 Ibid., B-0082.

105 *Conn v Westminster Motor Insurance Association* [1966] 1 Lloyd's Rep 407 at 414; *Provincial Insurance Co v Morgan* [1933] AC 240.

106 [1939] 1 KB 294.

107 Ibid., MacKinnon LJ at 312.

108 *MacGillivray*, 2015, para.10-011.

all future liability, absent very clear words,[109] and the courts strained against such an interpretation in a number of cases.[110] The courts are likely to adopt the same approach under the Act. Otherwise, the condition precedent to liability would be accorded the same draconian effect as a warranty under the old law, even though it is not a warranty, and therefore not capable of being remedied under section 10. Moreover, the insured could not rely upon section 11 Insurance Act (at least in this example), since the term is not one which, if complied with, would tend to reduce the risk of loss (see Chapter 7).

6.40 It follows that where a warranty has been recast as a condition precedent to liability, perhaps in an attempt to retain the old effect of a warranty without the need formally to contract out of section 10, the term will not be treated as an insurance warranty unless it is clear from the words of the term that the parties intended it to have that effect.

Excuses for breach of warranty

6.41 The circumstances in which a breach of warranty will be excused remain unaltered in all but one respect,[111] although they are now contained in section 10(3) of the Insurance Act rather than in section 34 of the Marine Insurance Act 1906, which has been repealed. A breach of warranty will be excused where a change in circumstances causes the warranty to cease to be applicable to the circumstances of the contract;[112] where a change of the law renders compliance with the warranty unlawful;[113] and where the insurer waives the breach of warranty.[114] The cases and legal principles governing each of these excuses will remain good law, and are not altered by the Insurance Act. In addition, the Insurance Act effectively introduces a new excuse for a breach of warranty; namely, where the breach has been remedied before the loss occurs.

109 Ibid., para,10-094, fn.320.

110 *Welch v Royal Exchange Assurance* [1939] 1 KB 294; *Kazakstan Wool Processors v Nederlandsche Credietverzekering Maatschappij* [2000] Lloyd's Rep IR 371.

111 The exception is s.34(2) of the 1906 Act, which previously provided that when a warranty is breached, the insured cannot avail itself of the defence that the breach was remedied before the loss.

112 Formerly s.34(1) of the Marine Insurance Act 1906; now s.10(3)(a) of the Act.

113 Formerly s.34(1) of the Marine Insurance Act 1906; now s.10(3)(b) of the Act.

114 Formerly s.34(3) of the Marine Insurance Act 1906; now s.10(3)(c) of the Act.

CHAPTER 7

Terms not relevant to the actual loss

11 Terms not relevant to the actual loss

(1) This section applies to a term (express or implied) of a contract of insurance, other than a term defining the risk as a whole, if compliance with it would tend to reduce the risk of one or more of the following—

(a) loss of a particular kind,

(b) loss at a particular location,

(c) loss at a particular time.

(2) If a loss occurs, and the term has not been complied with, the insurer may not rely on the non-compliance to exclude, limit or discharge its liability under the contract for the loss if the insured satisfies subsection (3).

(3) The insured satisfies this subsection if it shows that the non-compliance with the term could not have increased the risk of the loss which actually occurred in the circumstances in which it occurred.

(4) This section may apply in addition to section 10.

Section 11: the mischief

7.1 Section 11 is intended to prevent an insurer from disputing a claim for any non-compliance with a term which is unconnected to the actual loss.[1] Under the old law, if the insured breached a warranty, the insurer's liability was automatically discharged from the moment of breach, regardless of whether the breach caused, contributed to or was in any way connected to the actual loss.[2] An insurer's liability could therefore be discharged for breach of a burglar alarm warranty where the actual loss was caused by a storm[3] or a fire,[4] or for breach of a warranty requiring the deployment of a nightwatchman where the loss occurred during the day.[5] In

1 The word 'unconnected' is used herein as shorthand for the test set out in s.11(3). The Act uses the words 'not relevant' in the heading of s.11.

2 Marine Insurance Act 1906, s.33(3). See Chapter 6 above.

3 *Kler Knitwear v Lombard General Insurance Co Ltd* [2000] Lloyd's Rep IR 47.

4 *Printpak v AGF Insurance Ltd* [1999] 1 All ER (Comm) 466 (CA), [1999] Lloyd's Rep IR 542. The Court of Appeal averted a seemingly harsh result in that case by construing the warranty as applying only to the section of the policy which covered theft risk, and not the section covering fire risk. See also *Sugar Hut Group Ltd v Great Lakes Reinsurance (UK) plc* [2010] EWHC 2636 (Comm), [2011] Lloyd's Rep IR 198.

5 *Century Insurance Company of Canada v Case Existological Laboratories Ltd (The Bamcell II)* [1984] 1 WWR 97 (SCC), in which the owners of a vessel warranted that a watchman would be stationed on board at night. The warranty was breached, and the barge suffered fire damage during the day. Seemingly in attempt to mitigate the harshness of the law of insurance warranties, the Supreme Court of Canada decided that the term was not a warranty, in spite of its clear wording to the contrary. 1 WWR 97 (SC) 104 (Richie J). See also Barış Soyer, *Warranties in Marine Insurance*, 2nd edn (Routledge-Cavendish, 2006), 45.

Forsikringsaktieselskapet Vesta v Butcher,[6] a Norwegian insurer insured a salmon farm, and the insured warranted that it would keep a 24-hour watch at the farm. The warranty was breached, and many fish were lost in a severe storm. Under Norwegian law, the insurer was liable to pay the claim on the primary insurance. However, the reinsurance was governed by English law, and the reinsurer argued that it was not liable in view of the breach of warranty. The Court of Appeal rejected the reinsurer's case, but only after finding that the reinsurance was governed by Norwegian law on this particular issue. It therefore appears that the courts have occasionally been willing to adopt a creative approach to contractual construction or applicable law in order to mitigate the harshness of insurance warranties, in particular the absence of any need for a nexus between the breach of warranty and the actual loss. However, the Law Commissions considered that a more permanent and comprehensive solution was required, which is now seen in section 11 of the Act. Although borne of the Law Commissions' dissatisfaction with warranties, section 11 applies to a substantially wider range of risk mitigation terms.

Historical background to section 11

7.2 Although relatively short, section 11 is of considerable uncertainty, particularly as regards the terms to which it applies, and the effect where it does apply. Since at least 1980, the Law Commission(s) have been considering the introduction of a requirement for some kind of nexus between breach of a policy term[7] and the actual loss which has occurred, if the insurer wishes to rely upon the breach to extinguish or reduce its liability. The evolution of this concept might well be instructive as to the meaning and effect of section 11, and it is therefore considered in some detail below.

Law Commission proposals of 1980

7.3 In its Report of 1980, the Law Commission criticised as unjust the fact that an insurer could reject a claim for breach of warranty no matter how irrelevant the breach may have been to the loss.[8] Of its various criticisms of insurance warranties, this was seen as the most important defect,[9] because it was unacceptable that an insurer was able to reject a claim for a breach which was 'totally unconnected' with the loss.[10] The Law Commission therefore proposed (amongst other measures) that an insurer should not be entitled to reject a claim if the insured proved that its breach of warranty could not have increased the risk that the loss would occur in the way it did in fact occur,[11] which was referred to as the 'nexus test'. It was set out in section 10(5)(b) of a Draft Insurance Law Reform Bill, which provided that the insurer would be liable to meet a claim notwithstanding a breach of warranty, if the insured could prove that 'the

6 [1988] 3 WLR 565, [1988] 1 Lloyd's Rep 19, affd [1989] AC 852, [1989] 1 Lloyd's Rep 331.

7 Albeit that the Law Commission's initial consideration of the law in this area, in 1980, focused exclusively on warranties.

8 Law Commission's 1980 Report, para.6.9(b).

9 Ibid., para.6.11.

10 Ibid., para.6.15.

11 Ibid., paras 6.21 and 6.22(b).

breach of warranty could not have increased the risk that the event which gave rise to the claim would occur in the way in which it did in fact occur'.[12] This is strikingly similar to the language of section 11(3), which provides that the insurer may not rely upon non-compliance with a term if it 'could not have increased the risk of the loss which actually occurred in the circumstances in which it occurred'. There is, however, a potentially significant difference between the two clauses; whereas the 1980 version speaks of 'the *way* in which it did in fact occur', section 11 speaks of '*the circumstances* in which it occurred'. The relevance of this distinction is discussed below, since it appears to have been in the minds of the Law Commissions when drafting section 11(3).

7.4 The 1980 nexus test was intended to prevent an insurer from relying upon a breach of warranty in circumstances where the breach could have no connection with the actual loss. For example, a warranty in a factory's fire insurance policy requires an efficient sprinkler system to be maintained throughout the premises. A fire occurs in a workshop at one end of the factory where the sprinkler system is working, but there is no working sprinkler in a workshop at the other end of the factory, to which the fire does not spread. The Law Commission considered that the insured should recover in those circumstances, because 'the breach could have had no possible connection with the way in which the actual loss occurred'.[13] Presumably, that is because the absence of a working sprinkler in a separate part of the factory could not have increased the risk of the actual loss, which occurred in a different part of the factory where there was a working sprinkler. This example suggests that the nexus test proposed by the Law Commission in 1980 resembled a causation test, or at least did not prevent causation-type arguments. However, it was not the same as a causation test, since the insured had to prove that the breach *could* not have increased the risk of loss, rather than proving that it *did* not increase the risk of loss.

7.5 In a further example, an insured under a fidelity policy warranted that it would not employ anybody without first obtaining satisfactory references. In breach of warranty, the insured employs A, who has no references. Following this, a different employee, B, steals money from the company. B had supplied satisfactory references. On these facts, the insurer should be liable, because even though the general likelihood of loss by theft is reduced if the insured had complied with the warranty in respect of A, the breach could have had no possible connection with the way in which the actual loss occurred, because the failure to obtain a reference related to a different employee.[14] Taking the same warranty and breach, the outcome would be different if A stole the money. In those circumstances, the insurer should not be liable, since failing to obtain the reference could have increased the risk of loss through theft (in general), and the way in which the actual loss occurred was through theft committed by A.[15] The insured may contend that if A had been asked for references, he would have provided satisfactory (or forged) references. The Law Commission considered that the insurer would nonetheless not be liable, because the breach of warranty could have increased the risk of the loss which actually occurred, even if it was not causative of

12 Ibid., p.142.
13 Ibid., para.6.21(j).
14 Ibid., para.6.9(h).
15 Ibid., para.6.9(e).

the actual loss in that case.[16] The risk of loss was increased because failing to obtain references for A increased the risk that the company was employing a dishonest person who would steal from it.[17] This indicates that, under the 1980 nexus test, it was sufficient if the breach of warranty could realistically have increased the risk of the actual loss, even if it did not cause the loss in question. It was therefore distinct from a causation test, under which a realistic possibility that the breach could have increased the risk of the actual loss would be insufficient. Given the similarities in formulation and rationale behind the 1980 proposals and section 11 of the Act (amongst other things), the same outcome should result under section 11.

Law Commissions' proposals of 2006/2007

7.6 In 2006, the Law Commissions considered the unrealised proposals of 1980 to fall short in a number of respects. Firstly, the 1980 proposal would have applied only to warranties, meaning it may have been evaded by recasting warranties as exclusions, conditions precedent or other terms.[18] The Law Commissions saw no reason why the nexus test should apply only to warranties.[19] It was therefore considered necessary for the proposal to extend to a wider range of terms, including those which were 'descriptive of the risk',[20] such as a term in a motor policy that a car is for personal use only, rather than commercial use.[21] It was also proposed that the test should apply to warranties of specific fact and of future conduct, and terms which 'limit the risk', such as exclusion clauses.[22] In other words, the Law Commissions proposed that the nexus test should apply to a wider range of terms, not only warranties. Secondly, the 2006 report rejected the nexus test set out in the 1980 report and draft Bill, and instead adopted a causation test which required that 'the claim must be causally connected to the breach'.[23] Before doing so, the Law Commissions considered the form of this test in detail, noting the distinctions between the 1980 proposal and the equivalent provisions under New Zealand and Australian Law. In summary, the equivalent New Zealand statute provides that the insured must prove that the breach did not 'cause or contribute to' the loss,[24] whilst the Australian test was that the insured must prove that the breach did not 'cause' the loss.[25]

7.7 In analysing the difference between these tests, the Law Commissions considered the Australian Law Reform Commission's (ALRC's) 1982 analysis of the 1980 nexus test. The ALRC considered that test to be deficient because it risked doing injustice to

16 Ibid., para.6.9(i).
17 Ibid., para.6.9(i).
18 Insurance Contract Law Issues Paper 2, Warranties (November 2006), para.3.16.
19 Ibid., para.3.24.
20 Ibid., para.3.20.
21 Ibid., paras 3.17–3.20.
22 Ibid., para.7.8.
23 Ibid., para.7.6.
24 Under the New Zealand Insurance Law Reform Act 1977, s.11, the insured has a right to be indemnified if it can prove on the balance of probabilities that the loss was not 'caused or contributed to by the happening of such events or the existence of such circumstances'.
25 Under the Australian Insurance Contracts Act 1984, s.54(3), where the insured proves that 'no part of the loss that gave rise to the claim was caused by the act, the insurer may not refuse to pay the claim by reason only of the act'.

some insureds by permitting an insurer to rely upon a breach of warranty where the breach did not cause or contribute to the loss.[26] It gave the example of a motor policy containing a warranty that the insured will not modify the car, which the insured breaches by making modifications which increase the risk that the brakes will fail. The insured fails to keep a proper lookout, applies the brakes too late, and crashes the car. The crash is caused entirely by the driver's carelessness, and the brakes worked flawlessly.[27] The ALRC considered that under a causation test the insured would recover, but under the 1980 nexus test it would not,[28] because the insured would be 'unable to prove that his breach could not have increased the risk that the loss would occur in the way in which it did in fact occur'.[29] Presumably, that was because the ALRC considered that the breach could have increased the risk of a crash, and the 'way in which' the loss did in fact occur was through a crash.[30] It does not matter if the crash was not in fact caused by a failure of the brakes, since under the 1980 nexus test the fact that the modifications 'could' in theory have increased the risk of a crash is sufficient. If that is a correct application of the 1980 test, which the Law Commissions acknowledged it might not be,[31] the ALRC's criticism of that test is readily understandable.

7.8 The Law Commissions therefore concluded that the 1980 nexus test should be replaced by a causation test, under which the insured would be entitled to recover 'if it can prove on the balance of probability that the event or circumstances constituting the breach of warranty did not contribute to the loss'.[32] That drew on the Australian approach,[33] under which the insured may recover if it proves that no part of the loss was caused by the breach of warranty. The proposal was repeated by the Law Commissions in 2007, when it was proposed that the insured should be entitled to cover if it could prove on the balance of probabilities that the event or circumstances constituting the breach of warranty did not contribute to the loss.[34]

7.9 The operation of the 'did not contribute' test was illustrated by reference to some of the scenarios previously cited by the Law Commission in 1980. In the motor insurance example involving a breach of warranty through modification of the car,[35] the insured would recover under the causation test, since it would be able to show that the modifications did not in fact contribute to the accident, because the brakes worked properly and the accident was a result of negligence alone. Unlike the nexus test, there was no scope under the causation test for consideration of whether the breach of warranty could have increased the risk of the loss which actually occurred. Similarly, in the fidelity insurance example in which the insured failed to obtain references for employee A, who then stole from the company, the Law Commissions suggested that the insured would recover if it could prove that the employee would have provided

---

26 Australian Law Reform Commission No 20 (1982), para.228.
27 Ibid.
28 Ibid.
29 Ibid.
30 Ibid., cit. Insurance Contract Law Issues Paper 2, Warranties (November 2006), para.7.72.
31 Insurance Contract Law Issues Paper 2, Warranties (November 2006), para.7.73.
32 Ibid., para.7.76.
33 Ibid., para.7.73.
34 Law Commissions' 2007 Joint Consultation Paper, para.12.55.
35 See para.7.7 above.

satisfactory or forged references when asked for them.[36] That avenue was not open to the insured under the 1980 nexus test.

2012 and 2014 proposals

7.10 In 2012, the 'did not contribute' test proposed in 2007 was rejected, because a causation test was thought to introduce unnecessary complexity into the law, and threatened to increase litigation.[37] The Law Commissions also considered that it was inappropriate to apply a causation test to all contractual terms, but that it 'would generate too much uncertainty to attempt to apply such a test to some terms and not others'.[38] The 'did not contribute' test was therefore rejected in the Law Commissions' proposals of June 2012.[39] Instead, it was proposed that breach of a term which concerns a particular type of loss, or loss at a particular time or place, should give the insurer a remedy only in respect of that type of loss or loss at that time or place. This proposal would apply to any term designed to reduce the risk of loss of a particular type or at a particular location or time, and not only to warranties.[40] The test was set out in the first published version of the Insurance Bill in the following terms:[41]

> **11 Terms relevant to particular descriptions of loss**
> (1) This section applies to any term (express or implied) of a contract of insurance compliance with which would tend to reduce the risk of one or more of the following –
> (a) loss of a particular kind,
> (b) loss at a particular location,
> (c) loss at a particular time.
> (2) Breach of such a term may not be relied upon by the insurer to exclude, limit or discharge its liability for, respectively –
> (a) loss of a different kind,
> (b) loss at a different location,
> (c) loss at a different time.
> (3) This section may apply in addition to section 10.

7.11 The new proposal would have applied to any term which fitted the description in subsection (1), and not only warranties. The Law Commissions explained that it was not intended to apply to terms which 'defined the whole contract', such as terms restricting the use of a vehicle or property to private rather than commercial use.[42] This was not explicit in the draft Bill, and the Law Commissions have attempted to address this matter in section 11(1) by reference to terms defining the risk as a whole.

7.12 In view of the concerns over causation, the Law Commissions insisted that section 11 of the draft Insurance Bill did not introduce a causation test;[43] indeed, it was adopted as an alternative to such a test. The new test was said to be whether the term in question was relevant to a particular kind of loss, or loss at a particular time

36 Insurance Contract Law Issues Paper 2, Warranties (November 2006), para.7.75.
37 Law Commission Consultation Paper 204 (Summary) June 2012, paras S.100–S.101.
38 Law Commissions' 2012 Joint Consultation Paper, para.14.57.
39 Law Com No 204, para.17.60.
40 Law Commissions' 2012 Joint Consultation Paper, para.15.1(3).
41 July 2014 Report, p.356.
42 Law Commissions' 2012 Joint Consultation Paper, para.18.6.
43 Law Commissions' 2012 Joint Consultation Paper, para 18.5; July 2014 Report, para.14.27.

or place, in which case the insurer could not rely upon breach of the term for loss of a different kind, or at a different time or place.[44] The Law Commissions said that the term in question:

> should not be considered in light of what has actually happened. That is, when assessing the result that compliance would tend to have, whether or not breach of the term actually contributed to the loss which has occurred is not relevant. It is sufficient that the term is relevant to the particular kind, time or place of loss. If that is the case, the insurer is not liable for the actual loss. The insurer therefore retains a broader remedy than it would have under a causation test.[45]

For example, compliance with a term requiring the insured to fit a particular type of lock on the door of its premises would tend to reduce the risk of theft. If the relevant door lock was not fitted and there was a break in through a window, the Law Commissions considered that the insurer could nonetheless rely upon breach of the term.[46] That is because compliance with the term would tend to reduce the risk of theft (i.e. 'loss of a particular kind'), meaning the insurer would not be prohibited under subsection 11(2) from relying on the breach, since the actual loss was of the same kind. The fact that loss was caused by thieves gaining access through a window, not the door, was not relevant to the analysis, since this was not a causation test.

7.13 Notwithstanding the Law Commissions' indication that the term should not be considered in the light of what has actually happened, it was not clear what would prevent the insured from saying that compliance with the term in the Law Commissions' example would tend to reduce the risk of (specifically) theft caused by thieves gaining access through the door, rather than theft in general. In that case, loss caused by thieves breaking in through the window would be 'loss of a different kind', and the insurer would be prohibited from relying on the breach. This would effectively introduce a causation test by the back door, which was contrary to the Law Commissions' stated intention.

The Law Commissions' proposal of 7 November 2014

7.14 There was significant opposition to clause 11 on the basis that it was uncertain[47] and too broad in scope.[48] The Treasury therefore asked the Law Commissions to redraft the provision, and a new draft of clause 11 was produced on 7 November 2014,[49] along with a short explanatory note, which was presented as written evidence to the Special Public Bill Committee of the House of Lords.[50] As explained in more detail in Chapter 1,[51] even the revised version of clause 11 was initially considered too controversial, and it was not included in the Bill published by the Special Public Bill Committee on 18 December 2014.[52] However, there was an apparent change of heart over Christmas, and the version of the Bill published on 9 January 2015 included the

44 Law Commissions' 2012 Joint Consultation Paper, para 15.1(3); July 2014 Report, para.18.39.
45 July 2014 Report, para.18.39.
46 July 2014 Report, para.18.40.
47 HL Paper 81, p.78 (Memorandum submitted by the Law Commissions, David Hertzell, para.17).
48 HL Paper 81, p.78 (Memorandum Submitted by BILA, para.39).
49 HL Paper 81, p.46.
50 HL Paper 81, p.46 *et seq.*
51 Para.1.21 *et seq.*
52 HL Bill 72 2014–2015.

Table 7.1 Comparison between tests in 1980 Bill and the Act

1980 Draft Insurance Bill	*Insurance Act 2015*
'… the breach of warranty could not have increased the risk that the event which gave rise to the claim would occur *in the way* in which it did in fact occur.'	'the non-compliance with the term could not have increased the risk of the loss which actually occurred *in the circumstances* in which it occurred.'

revised version of clause 11,[53] which survived up to and including Royal Assent. The 'new' version of section 11 therefore appears in the Insurance Act.

7.15 The test in section 11(3) is very similar to the test originally proposed in the Insurance Law Reform Bill of 1980,[54] as illustrated in Table 7.1 above.

7.16 Unlike the draft Bill of 1980, section 11 of the Act applies not only to warranties, but to a broader range of terms. That reflects the Law Commissions' earlier conclusion that to apply a nexus requirement to some terms but not others would cause confusion.[55] Section 11(3) also replaced the words 'in the way' (1980) with 'in the circumstances' (2015). The Law Commissions considered this to be a material difference which was intended to underline the fact that this was not a causation test:

> The reference to 'the circumstances' in which the loss occurred is intended to look at the issue in a broad way. There is less suggestion of causation in these words, as there would be if the court was required to consider 'the way' in which the loss occurred.[56]

Not applicable to terms defining the risk as a whole (section 11(1))

7.17 Section 11 applies to any term which, if complied with, would tend to reduce the risk of loss of a particular kind, or loss at a particular place or time. For convenience, these will be referred to as 'risk mitigation terms'. However, before considering the risk mitigation terms which are subject to section 11, it is convenient to identify those terms to which it will not apply, namely any 'term defining the risk as a whole'.[57] The logical starting point in any enquiry over section 11 is to determine whether the term defines the risk as a whole, in which case section 11 does not apply even if it is also a risk mitigation term. A term may be both a term 'defining the risk as a whole' and a risk mitigation term, in which case section 11 will not apply. For example, a term that a vessel is prohibited from sailing in the Gulf of Aden is one which, if complied with, would tend to reduce the risk of loss at a particular location, and also (perhaps) loss of a particular kind, i.e. loss caused by piracy. However, the term also defines the geographical scope of cover, and is therefore said by the Law Commissions to be a 'term defining the risk as a whole', which is therefore not subject to section 11.[58] It does not matter that the term is also a risk mitigation term which would otherwise be subject to section 11.

53 HL Bill 76 2014–2015.
54 Para.7.3 above.
55 Law Commissions' 2012 Joint Consultation Paper, para.14.57.
56 HL Paper 81, p.47, para.1.17.
57 Insurance Act 2015, s.11(1).
58 HL Paper 81, p.47, para.1.8(2).

7.18 The meaning of 'term defining the risk as a whole' is unclear, and in view of its late introduction has been subject to less commentary from the Law Commissions than other parts of the Act. Its boundaries are likely to be tested in litigation; indeed, that appears to be the intention of the Law Commissions.[59] A term is likely to define the risk as a whole if it delineates the overall scope of cover which the insurer agrees to provide under the policy, rather than targeting a narrow or specific risk.[60] It has been suggested that a term defines the risk as a whole if it goes to the heart of the risk profile which the insurer is willing to accept.[61] The Law Commissions have drawn upon a report by the New Zealand Law Commission in providing examples of terms which might be said to define the risk as a whole, according to which such terms include the following categories:[62]

(i) **A term which defines the geographical limits of the policy**. Such a term may achieve this by stating the geographical area in which the insured person or chattel may or may not enter, or in which the insured activity may or may not occur, if the insurer is to be liable.[63] For example, marine insurance policies usually contain territorial limits, and if the insured vessel sails outside those limits there is no cover under the policy. Such terms have been said by the Law Commissions to define the risk as a whole.[64] The territory in which the insurer agrees to cover loss does appear to go to the overall scope of cover rather than a narrow or specific risk.[65] In addition, certain terms defining the geographical limits of the policy are not terms with which the insured is required to comply, and that is a touchstone of the applicability of section 11(1).[66] For example, a travel insurance policy contains an exclusion on all losses in any country subject to a Foreign and Commonwealth Office travel warning. If the insured enters such a country, it does not follow as a matter of ordinary language that the term has not been complied with, since the term did not call for the insured to do or refrain from doing anything in the first place. This is a matter of construction in every case.

(ii) **A term which defines the use to which insured property may be put**. The Law Commissions' example is a term which forbids the insured from using an insured chattel, such as a car, yacht or aircraft, from being used for commercial as opposed to personal purposes.[67] Similarly, a term restricting cover to a farming business, not tourism, has been said to define the risk as a whole.[68] The Law Commissions have suggested that such terms define the risk as a whole because they go 'more generally to the risk the insurer was prepared to take, rather than targeting particular types of loss which might occur'.[69] As with terms defining

59 July 2014 Report, para.18.35.
60 Ibid., para.18.23.
61 Ibid., para.18.34.
62 July 2014 Report, para.18.33, cit. *Some Insurance Law Problems* (1998) NZLC R46, pp.28–29.
63 HL Paper 81, p.47, para.1.8(2).
64 July 2014 Report, para.18.33; Explanatory Notes Insurance Act 2015, para.94.
65 July 2014 Report, para.18.23.
66 Because Insurance Act 2015, s.11(1) is expressed to apply to a term 'if *compliance* with it would tend to reduce the risk of …' loss of a particular kind, or at a particular time or place.
67 July 2014 Report, para.18.33; Explanatory Notes Insurance Act 2015, para.94.
68 Law Commissions' 2012 Joint Consultation Paper, para.15.38.
69 July 2014 Report, para.18.23

the geographical scope of cover, such terms might not be ones which call for compliance. For example, if there is an exclusion of liability where a yacht is used for a commercial voyage, it does not necessarily follow that the insured fails to comply with the exclusion if he charters the yacht for reward, since the clause did not as a matter of construction call for 'compliance' by the insured.

A further example may be seen from *Murray v Scottish Automobile and General Insurance Co.*, in which a motor policy contained a term that the insurance applied 'only to a Car for private personal use', and another that excluded liability for loss when the car was 'being used in connexion with any trade or business or otherwise than for the private personal purposes of the assured'.[70] In the context of a motor insurance policy, it is readily understandable why such terms might be said to define the risk as a whole, since they go to the overall risk profile which the insurer agreed to accept. Generally speaking, commercial motor insurance will be more expensive than the equivalent personal insurance, and terms such as those in *Murray* reflect the fact that in the latter category, the risk insured does not include commercial use of the vehicle.

(iii) **A term which defines the age, identity, qualification or experience of the operator of a vehicle, aircraft, vessel or chattel.**[71] For example, a term in an agricultural machinery insurance policy provides that none of the machinery may be operated by a minor. That is a term which might be said to go to the relatively narrow and specific risk that a piece of machinery will be damaged whilst being operated by a minor, and therefore not one that defines the risk as a whole. However, it is also a term relating to the age and possibly the experience of a person operating an insured vehicle, and on this basis the Law Commissions consider it to be a term defining the risk as a whole.

(iv) **A term requiring a vessel to maintain class**. The Law Commissions have said that such a term has an impact on the insurer's overall assessment of the risk, and that it is therefore a term defining the risk as a whole.[72] It ought to follow that a term requiring any insured chattel to be kept in a particular condition, such as a term requiring the insured to maintain his car in a roadworthy condition, is a term defining the risk as a whole, since it affects the insurer's overall assessment of the risk. Similarly, the implied warranties of seaworthiness and fitness to carry cargo under sections 39 and 40 of the Marine Insurance Act 1906 should be regarded as terms defining the risk as a whole.

7.19 This list of terms which define the risk as a whole is non-exhaustive, and it is the Law Commissions' express intention that the list will continue to be developed by the courts.[73] Further examples of terms which appear likely to define the risk as a whole or to fall outside the ambit of section 11 for other reasons include the following:

(i) **Premium payment warranties or similar terms**. A term under which the insured warrants or otherwise promises to pay the premium by a defined time has no

70 1929 SC 48 (IH), 1929 SLT 114.
71 July 2014 Report, para.18.33(3).
72 July 2014 Report, para.18.24.
73 July 2014 Report, para.18.34.

bearing on the risk of loss, and does not fall under section 11.[74] If the insured has failed to pay its premium and suffers loss, the insurer may be entitled (subject to the terms of the policy) to rely upon a premium payment warranty to discharge its liability for the loss.

(ii) **A term which goes to the mechanics of the insurance, and has no bearing on the risk**. A premium payment warranty (or equivalent) is one such example, since it goes to the mechanics of the insurance, not the risk. Another example, depending upon the circumstances, could be a term requiring the retention of written records by the insured, which is unlikely to be subject to section 11, unless it has some bearing on the risk of loss.[75] In most cases, a notification clause is also unlikely to be subject to section 11. However, in the context of liability insurance, it is possible that a notification clause (or similar) might be subject to section 11. For example, some liability policies contain a condition precedent requiring the insured to notify the insurer of circumstances likely to give rise to a claim. Such a term is intended to enable the insurer to intervene in the insured's defence, thereby potentially reducing the risk of loss in the form of legal liability to a third party.[76] Compliance with a notification condition precedent or similar term in a liability policy is therefore likely to be subject to section 11, though this will be a matter of construction in every case.

(iii) **A term addressing moral hazard**. For example, in a directors' and officers' liability (D&O) policy, it is common for the insured to warrant that none of the directors or officers has a criminal record. If such a term is one with which the insured can properly be said to comply, it has been suggested that it nonetheless defines the risk as a whole,[77] and therefore falls outside section 11.

Exclusion clauses

7.20 There is uncertainty over the application of section 11 to most exclusion clauses.[78] The Law Commissions have stated that section 11 could apply to exclusion clauses,[79] and subsection 11(2) appears to recognise this possibility, since it provides that 'the insurer may not rely on the non-compliance *to exclude* ... its liability'. If section 11 is not applicable to exclusion clauses, it would enable warranties and other terms to be rephrased as exclusion clauses in order to circumvent the effects of section 11. For example, a warranty that the insured will install a burglar alarm could be redrafted as an exclusion on all losses which occur before the burglar alarm is installed. If that is enough to take the term outside the ambit of section 11 without the need to contract out, the potency of the Law Commissions' reforms could be reduced

74 Law Commissions' 2012 Joint Consultation Paper, para.15.38.

75 Ibid., para.18.6.

76 Under a liability policy, loss occurs when the insured's liability is ascertained through a judgment, award or settlement: *Post Office v Norwich Union Fire Assurance Society Limited* [1967] 2 QB 363 (CA), [1967] 1 Lloyd's Rep 216, [219] (Lord Denning MR); *Bradley v Eagle Star Insurance Co Ltd* [1989] 1 Lloyd's Rep 465, [468] (Lord Brandon).

77 Law Commissions' 2012 Joint Consultation Paper, para.15.38.

78 See paras 7.18(i) and 7.18(ii) above.

79 Explanatory Notes to the Insurance Act 2015, para.94.

substantially. However, the authors consider that most, if not all, exclusion clauses are unlikely to be subject to section 11. Many exclusion clauses define the risk as a whole, since they delimit the scope of cover provided under an insurance contract. Obvious examples have already been identified, such as exclusions for loss in certain geographical areas, or where a chattel is used for commercial rather than private purposes.

7.21 If a given exclusion clause does not define the risk as a whole, it is nonetheless unlikely to be subject to section 11. Subsection 11(1) is concerned with a term only 'if *compliance* with it' would tend to reduce the risk of loss, and sub-section 11(2) is triggered only if a loss occurs and the relevant term has 'not been *complied* with'. To engage section 11, one must therefore have a term which calls for compliance, and a failure to comply with that term. It ought to follow that if, on a true construction, the term is not one with which the insured (or anybody else) may or may not comply, it does not qualify as a risk mitigation term under subsection 11(1) of the Act, and cannot engage the protection afforded by subsection 11(2). For example, many marine policies exclude loss 'arising out of strikers, locked-out workmen, or persons taking part in labour disturbance, riots or civil commotions'. If a riot occurs and the insured suffers loss, it is artificial to say that there has been non-compliance with the term, since the term did not call for compliance in the first place, and the insured has not failed to comply with it. Section 11 should not apply to this exclusion, therefore. Similarly, many liability policies contain an exclusion clause along the following lines:

> The insurer will have no liability to indemnify the insured in relation to any civil liability or related defence costs arising from any dishonest act or omission committed by the insured.

7.22 That is not, on a true construction, a term which calls for compliance by the insured: it does not (for example) say that the insured is prohibited from acting dishonestly (although it may well have that effect in practice). If the insured commits an act of dishonesty, it does not follow as a matter of ordinary language that there has been any failure to comply with the exclusion clause. Rather, as a result of the exclusion clause, there will be no cover for liability arising from the dishonesty, because the term limits the scope of cover to that extent. Whilst it will be a question of construction in every case, a similar analysis would appear to apply to many other exclusion clauses, such as those which exclude liability for fines and penalties (another common clause in a liability policy). There is a further reason why it might be thought undesirable for section 11 to apply to an exclusion clause, since if it does apply it would have the surprising effect of reversing the burden of proof applicable to exclusion clauses. If it is to rely on an exclusion clause, the insurer must demonstrate that the loss falls within the ambit of the exclusion. For example, it must show (in the above example) that the loss arose from a riot or civil commotion. If an exclusion clause is subject to section 11, the insured would have the burden of proving that non-compliance with the term could not have increased the risk of the loss that actually occurred, in the circumstances in which it occurred.[80] That would be a surprising and, in the authors' view, an undesirable result.

80 See Insurance Act 2015, ss.11(2) and 11(3), under which the burden is on the insured to show that non-compliance with the term could not have increased the risk of the loss which actually occurred in the circumstances in which it occurred.

Risk mitigation terms which are subject to section 11

7.23 Although the genesis of section 11 lies in the mischief of the law of warranties, discussed above, it potentially applies to a much wider range of terms. That includes warranties, though it could also apply to conditions, conditions precedent, and (subject to the discussion above) exclusion clauses. The Law Commissions have indicated that section 11 'only applies to terms which could affect the risk of a specific type of loss taking place at all, or the risk that a particular type of loss would be more extensive'.[81] It bears repeating that a term may be both a risk mitigation clause and a term defining the risk as a whole, in which case section 11 will not apply.[82] For example, terms in a marine insurance policy relating to the vessel's class, the qualifications of the captain and the use to which the ship may be put (such as commercial or private) have been said to affect either the whole risk or a significant part of the risk, meaning they are terms defining the risk as a whole, and therefore outside the ambit of section 11. However, a term relating to the type of locks installed on the vessel would only affect the risk of intruders in the locked part of the ship, and is therefore likely to fall within section 11, since compliance would tend to reduce the risk of loss of a certain type. Similarly, a term requiring that a working fire sprinkler system be installed has been said to relate only to the risk or extent of fire damage, and is therefore likely to be subject to section 11.[83]

7.24 In assessing whether a term is a risk mitigation term, or something which defines the risk as a whole, the overall nature of the cover provided under the policy in question appears to be relevant. For example, in view of the heightened risk of fire at an oil refinery, an insured buys a bespoke fire insurance policy which covers (only) the risk of loss caused by fire. The insured warrants that there will be a qualified fire officer on watch at all times when the refinery is operational. Would section 11 apply to such a term? Because the specific (indeed, the only) risk being insured against is fire, one might say that the term 'defines the risk as a whole', because it would 'tend to affect either the whole risk, or a significant part of the risk'.[84] However, the term is also a risk mitigation clause since, if complied with, it would tend to reduce the risk of loss of a particular type (loss caused by fire), or at a particular time (loss during the refinery's hours of operation). Whether section 11 applies appears to turn in part on the overall scope of cover provided by the policy: if it is narrow (i.e. only fire risks) then section 11 may not apply, because the term may be said to define the risk as a whole. If, however, the cover were to be broader, an equivalent term might be subject to section 11, because in that context it would only affect the particular risk of a specific type of loss. The application of section 11 may therefore turn in part upon a consideration of the relevant term in the context of the risks insured under the policy as a whole.

The effect of section 11 on terms which are irrelevant to the loss

7.25 Section 11(2) provides the insured with the prospect of protection if there has been non-compliance with a term subject to section 11. If the insured satisfies

81 HL Paper 81, p.47, para.1.7.
82 See para.7.17 above.
83 HL Paper 81, p.47, para.1.9.
84 Ibid.

section 11(3), the insurer will be prohibited from relying on non-compliance with the term in order to reduce or extinguish its liability under the policy. There is a good deal of uncertainty about the meaning and effect of section 11(3). Broadly speaking, the insured will satisfy the test if it shows that non-compliance with the term was 'totally irrelevant' to the loss.[85] That means the non-compliance could not have increased the risk of the actual loss occurring in the circumstances in which it occurred. A straightforward example is where an insured warrants that a specific type of window lock must be fitted. The insured fails to install such locks, and the property is damaged by flooding. The insured would in all likelihood be able to show that its failure to use the required window locks could not have increased the risk of flooding, meaning the breach of warranty was irrelevant to the actual loss, and the insured would recover.[86]

7.26 As with its predecessor in 1980,[87] section 11(3) does not call for the insured to prove that non-compliance with the relevant term did not cause or contribute to the actual loss. The Explanatory Notes to the Insurance Act state emphatically that 'a direct causal link between the breach and the ultimate loss is not required. That is, the relevant test is not whether the non-compliance actually caused or contributed to the loss which has been suffered'.[88] The Law Commissions previously considered but ultimately rejected a causation test. Indeed, section 11(3) was intended to clarify that there was no causation requirement, which is reflected by use of 'the circumstances' instead of 'the way' in which the actual loss occurred.[89] Rather than a causation test, the insured will satisfy section 11(3) if it is able to show that non-compliance with the term could not have increased the risk of the actual loss. The Law Commissions explained the meaning and effect of section 11(3) in the following way:

> Neither the insured nor the insurer would have to prove what actually caused the loss, or what would have happened if the term had been complied with, so evidential matters are far less important than they would be under a causal test. Even if an insured can show that compliance with the warranty would not have actually made a difference to the loss (thus satisfying a causation test), the fact that it could have made a difference means that an insurer does not have to pay. Instead, there would be a more objective assessment of whether it is obvious that the breach could not have made any difference – and the onus is explicitly on the insured to show this. This keeps the focus looking forward from when the risk was underwritten (the breach could not have increased the risk of the loss) – as opposed to looking backwards from the actual circumstances of the claim (whether it contributed to the loss which occurred – a causation test).'[90]

7.27 If there is a possibility that non-compliance with the term could have increased the risk of loss, the insured will not satisfy the test in section 11(3). That question falls to be considered in the context of the facts of the actual loss, meaning that a purely theoretical chance that the non-compliance will increase the risk is unlikely to qualify. For example, in the scenario involving the insured factory owner who fails to install a

85 HL Paper 81, p.47, para.1.11.
86 Explanatory Notes to the Insurance Act 2015, para.95.
87 Paras 7.3–7.5 above.
88 Explanatory Notes to the Insurance Act 2015, para.96.
89 See paras 7.14 and 7.15 above.
90 HL Paper 81, p.47, para.1.16.

working sprinkler in a room at one end of the factory (in breach of warranty), where a fire breaks out in another part of the factory and does not spread to the room where there is no sprinkler, the insured ought to satisfy section 11(3). Whilst not having a sprinkler in one part of the factory could in theory increase the risk of loss by fire, the circumstances of the loss were that the fire was in a separate part of the factory, where the sprinkler system had been installed.

Examples of the operation of section 11(3)

7.28 The Law Commissions have attempted to explain the meaning and effect of section 11(3) in a series of examples,[91] some of which are problematic. In the first, there is a warranty requiring the insured to install five-lever mortise locks on all the doors. This is breached because the lock on one door (door A) has only three levers. Thieves break in through door A. According to the Law Commissions, the insurer is entitled to rely upon the breach of warranty, because 'the lock might have made a difference given the circumstances of the loss (which are that the door did not have the requisite lock, and the thieves broke in through it)'.[92] It is (apparently) not open to the insured to argue that the thieves would have found another way into the premises even if the correct lock had been fitted, or that they would in any event have been able to batter down the door, because that is a causation argument which is not permitted.[93] In the second scenario involving the same warranty and breach, the thieves break in through a window, or a different door which was fitted with the correct five-lever lock. The Law Commissions say that 'in these circumstances, it would not have made any difference if door A had had a different lock', meaning the insurer should be liable.[94] Presumably, that is because 'the circumstances' of the actual loss were that the thieves were able to enter through a window, or a different door. That sounds very like a causation argument, because it distinguishes between the two scenarios based on the way in which the loss occurred (even if one refers to this as 'the circumstances'). It is also (surprisingly) at odds with the outcome under the earlier test proposed in the initial draft Insurance Bill, under which the Law Commissions said that the insured would not be entitled to recover in those circumstances.[95] That is in spite of the fact that the final formulation of section 11(3) was supposed to take the Act further away from causation, not closer to it.

7.29 In another example, the insured warrants that the insured vehicle will be roadworthy. The warranty is breached because one of the headlights is defective. In the first scenario, the vehicle collides with a truck in broad daylight. The Law Commissions say that 'there is no possibility that the defective headlight contributed to the accident given the circumstances in which it happened (it was daylight and the headlights would not have needed to be on even if they were working properly)'. As a result, the insurer

91 HL Paper 81, pp.47–48, para.1.18(1) *et seq.*

92 Ibid., fn.61. In this example, it is not easy to discern the difference between the 'circumstances' of the loss and the 'way' it occurred.

93 Ibid.

94 Ibid.

95 Law Com No 353 (July 2014), para.18.40.

should not be able to rely upon the breach of warranty.[96] This appears to be the right conclusion, but the reasoning is unhappily expressed. Under section 11(3), the insured is not required to show whether the breach of warranty 'contributed' to the loss, but must prove that the breach could not have increased the risk of loss in the circumstances in which it occurred. The circumstances were that the collision took place in broad daylight, and the risk of this could not have been increased by the fact that one of the headlights was not working.

7.30 In a variation of that scenario, the warranty and breach are the same, but the car skids on black ice in the dark, and crashes. The Law Commissions' analysis is that although the faulty headlight did not cause the accident, 'it is possible that it could have contributed, given the circumstances of the loss (that is, that it was dark, and a headlight was defective)'.[97] On that basis, the insurer may rely upon the insured's non-compliance, and is not liable. This analysis is questionable, however. Under section 11(3), the insured is not required to show whether the breach of warranty 'could have contributed' to the loss, but that it could not have increased the risk of loss in the circumstances in which it occurred. The circumstances of the loss were that the car skidded on black ice, which is invisible. It should follow that a defective headlight could not have increased the risk of loss in the circumstances in which it occurred, because the ice would have been invisible in any event. The faulty headlight made no difference at all. The Law Commissions have suggested that 'this would be a causation type debate, which we do not want'.[98] If that is right, the line of argument above may not be open to the insured, in which case the insurer may rely upon the breach of warranty, even though it appears to have been irrelevant to the actual loss.

7.31 Finally, it is worth revisiting the example raised by the Australian Law Reform Commission in 1982. A motor insurance policy contains a term that the insured will not modify his car, which he breaches by making modifications. This increases the risk that the brakes will malfunction. The driver fails to keep a proper look-out, applies the brakes too late, and an accident occurs, even though the brakes work perfectly.[99] The insured's failure to comply with the term did not cause or contribute to the loss, which was a result of the insured's negligence. The insured could therefore satisfy a causation test of the type previously proposed by the Law Commissions. However, applying the test under section 11 might lead to a different result, and the ALRC thought that it would, albeit under the slightly different wording of the 1980 test.[100] The circumstances of the actual loss were that the car collided with another vehicle, and the risk of that type of loss could have been increased by the modifications which had been made, even though the modifications did not in fact cause or contribute to the crash.[101] The outcome under section 11(3) is therefore different and less favourable to the insured than under a causation test. If the ALRC's assessment

---

96 HL Paper 81, p.48, para.1.18(2).

97 Ibid.

98 HL Paper 81, p.48, fn.62.

99 Australian Law Reform Commission No 20 (1982), para.228, cit. Insurance Contract Law Issues Paper 2, Warranties (November 2006), para.23.

100 Para.7.7 above.

101 Insurance Contract Law Issues Paper 2, Warranties (November 2006), para.6.24.

is correct, the mischief which the Law Commissions intended to eliminate might survive in certain cases, namely those where the non-compliance could have increased the risk of loss, even if it did not in fact cause or contribute to it. In view of this, and given the ambiguity of section 11(3), there is at least a prospect that a court would take an alternative view of its effect, so as to treat it as (in effect) a causation test. Regrettably, therefore, it is impossible to form more certain conclusions on the effect of section 11(3).

7.32 In any event, the protection afforded to the insured by section 11 is far from toothless. Taking the same warranty and breach, assume the loss is caused by a tree falling on the car whilst it is parked. In those circumstances, the insured should be able to satisfy section 11(3). The risk of a tree falling on the car could not have been increased by the modifications, and the insured would therefore be afforded the protection in section 11(2). One would expect a similar result if the car were stolen, or set alight by arsonists, because it is unlikely in either case that the modifications could have increased the risk of either eventuality.

Interaction between sections 10 and 11

7.33 A warranty falling under the ambit of section 11 will also be subject to section 10.[102] If the insured breaches such a warranty, but the breach is remedied before the loss, the insurer will be liable regardless of whether the insured is able to satisfy section 11(3), because the insured had ceased to be in breach of warranty at the time of the loss. If, however, the insured has failed to remedy its breach of warranty before the loss, it will nonetheless be entitled to recover if it shows that the breach could not have increased the risk of loss which actually occurred, in the circumstances in which it occurred. The potential interaction between sections 10 and 11 may be seen through the old case of *Hibbert v Pigou*,[103] in which the insured warranted that the ship *Arundel* would depart from Jamaica with a convoy. Such warranties were traditionally included in marine policies because they reduced the risk of the vessel being captured or attacked. The *Arundel* arrived late at Jamaica, and therefore missed the departure of the convoy, later sailing with only one other ship. A few days later, the *Arundel* caught up with and joined the convoy off the coast of Cuba, but was later separated from the convoy in a storm, and was subsequently taken.[104] Sailing from Jamaica without the convoy was a breach of warranty which immediately discharged the insurer's liability.[105] Were that case to be decided under the Act, it is likely that the breach of warranty would be taken as remedied when the *Arundel* joined the convoy off the coast of Cuba.[106] However, if that was not the case, the insured

102 Insurance Act 2015, s.11(4).

103 (1783) 3 Doug KB 224, 99 ER 624.

104 It is not clear from the report by whom or how the *Arundel* was taken.

105 (1783) 3 Doug KB 224, 99 ER 624, 626 (Lord Mansfield) and 627 (Buller J).

106 The warranty would probably be treated as a time-specific warranty, meaning it was remedied when the risk to which it related became essentially the same as originally contemplated, which would have been at the moment when the *Arundel* actually joined the convoy off the coast of Cuba. The fact that the vessel was subsequently separated from the convoy in a storm does not alter this, since by then the breach of warranty had been remedied, and the separation in a storm is not a fresh breach of warranty.

would nonetheless have a potential line of argument under section 11.The risk of the *Arundel*'s being taken could have been increased by the breach of warranty, since sailing outside a convoy increased this risk. However, given the circumstances of the loss, the insured would be likely to succeed under section 11(3), since by the time of the loss the *Arundel* had in fact re-joined the convoy, but had later become separated from it in a storm. Therefore, the departure from Jamaica without the convoy could not have increased the risk of loss in the circumstances in which it occurred.

CHAPTER 8

Contracting out of the Act

15 Contracting out: consumer insurance contracts

(1) A term of a consumer insurance contract, or of any other contract, which would put the consumer in a worse position as respects any of the matters provided for in Part 3 or 4 of this Act than the consumer would be in by virtue of the provisions of those Parts (so far as relating to consumer insurance contracts) is to that extent of no effect.

(2) In subsection (1) references to a contract include a variation.

(3) This section does not apply in relation to a contract for the settlement of a claim arising under a consumer insurance contract.

16 Contracting out: non-consumer insurance contracts

(1) A term of a non-consumer insurance contract, or of any other contract, which would put the insured in a worse position as respects representations to which section 9 applies than the insured would be in by virtue of that section is to that extent of no effect.

(2) A term of a non-consumer insurance contract, or of any other contract, which would put the insured in a worse position as respects any of the other matters provided for in Part 2, 3 or 4 of this Act than the insured would be in by virtue of the provisions of those Parts (so far as relating to non-consumer insurance contracts) is to that extent of no effect, unless the requirements of section 17 have been satisfied in relation to the term.

(3) In this section references to a contract include a variation.

(4) This section does not apply in relation to a contract for the settlement of a claim arising under a non-consumer insurance contract.

16A Contracting out of the implied term about payment of claims: consumer and non-consumer insurance contracts[1]

(1) A term of a consumer insurance contract, or of any other contract, which would put the consumer in a worse position as respects any of the matters provided for in section 13A than the consumer would be in by virtue of the provisions of that section (so far as relating to consumer insurance contracts) is to that extent of no effect.

(2) A term of a non-consumer insurance contract, or of any other contract, which would put the insured in a worse position as respects deliberate or reckless breaches of the term implied by section 13A than the insured would be in by virtue of that section is to that extent of no effect.

(3) For the purposes of subsection (2) a breach is deliberate or reckless if the insurer—

a. knew that it was in breach, or

b. did not care whether or not it was in breach.

(4) A term of a non-consumer insurance contract, or of any other contract, which would put the insured in a worse position as respects any of the other matters provided for in section 13A than the insured would be in by virtue of the provisions of that section

1 Enterprise Act 2016, s.29.

(so far as relating to non-consumer insurance contracts) is to that extent of no effect, unless the requirements of section 17 have been satisfied in relation to the term.

(5) In this section references to a contract include a variation.

(6) This section does not apply in relation to a contract for the settlement of a claim arising under an insurance contract.

(7) In section 17(1) of that Act (the transparency requirements), after "16(2)" insert "or 16A(4)".

Contracting out of the Act

8.1 The Act permits parties to non-consumer insurance to contract out of the vast majority of the Act, subject to the fulfilment of two transparency requirements. This reflects the Law Commissions' acknowledgement that commercial parties must be able to agree to alternative arrangements in their contracts,[2] and their broad support for freedom of contract.[3] The Law Commissions have recognised that in certain cases such as large or unusual risks, contracting out may be appropriate.[4] This reality has already been reflected in certain quarters of the marine market, in which many of the P&I Clubs have decided to opt out of the Act to the fullest possible extent. However, the Act restricts contracting out in consumer insurance, which is not possible at all,[5] and to a lesser extent in non-consumer insurance. That reflects a desire on the part of the Law Commissions to ensure that parties do not contract out mindlessly or in a way that is unfair to insureds, particularly smaller businesses with limited expertise and bargaining power.[6] It also reflects the fact that a significant amount of non-consumer insurance is now purchased direct from the insurer and increasingly online, without much opportunity for the buyer of insurance to engage with the contract terms.[7] The Act therefore seeks to strike a balance between freedom of contract; a desire to prevent excessive contracting out; and to protect non-consumer insureds, particularly those that are less sophisticated.

8.2 Under the Act, contracting out means agreeing to terms which place the insured 'in a worse position' than it would enjoy under the Act.[8] Any such provision is a 'disadvantageous term' under section 16(2). For example, a term providing that breach of any warranty permanently discharges the insurer's liability regardless of whether the breach is remedied is 'disadvantageous', since it would place the insured in a worse position than it would enjoy under section 10.[9] Contrastingly, if a term is disadvantageous to the insurer, it is not a disadvantageous term under section 16(2), and the transparency requirements do not need to be fulfilled in order for the term to be effective. For example, a term providing that the insurer will have no remedy for any breach of the duty of fair presentation save in cases of fraud would place the insurer

2 July 2014 Report, para.29.3.

3 Ibid., para.29.18.

4 Ibid., para.29.32.

5 Insurance Act 2015, s.15(1).

6 July 2014 Report, paras 29.29–29.31.

7 Ibid.

8 Insurance Act 2015, s.16(2). The language of 'in a worse position' is the same as in Consumer Insurance (Disclosure and Representations) Act 2012, s.10.

9 Under which breach of a warranty suspends cover unless and until the breach is remedied. See Chapter 6.

in a worse position than under section 8, since it substantially restricts the remedies available to it. However, such a provision does not qualify as a 'disadvantageous term', because it does not put the insured in a worse position than under the Act.[10] This is consistent with the underlying philosophy of the Act, which is to attempt to level the playing field between the insurer and the insured.[11]

Meaning of 'consumer' and 'non-consumer' insurance

8.3 The Act distinguishes between consumer insurance contracts, in which contracting out of the Act is not possible, and non-consumer insurance contracts, in which contracting out is permitted, subject to certain restrictions and qualifications. It is therefore necessary to understand the difference between consumer and non-consumer insurance contracts, which is discussed in detail in Chapter 2. A 'consumer insurance contract' is one where 'the insured is an individual who enters into the contract wholly or mainly for purposes unrelated to that individual's business, trade or profession'.[12] Any insurance contract which is not a consumer contract will be a non-consumer contract.[13]

Contracting out in consumer insurance

8.4 Any attempt to contract out of those parts of the Act that apply to consumer insurance will be of no effect. For these purposes, the only relevant parts of the Act are: Part 3 (warranties and other risk mitigation terms,[14] including the provisions on late payment of insurance claims[15]) and Part 4 (fraudulent claims[16]). It should be noted that Part 2 of the Act (the duty of fair presentation) does not apply to consumer insurance contracts, since there is already a different and more lenient regime governing pre-contractual disclosure by consumer insureds under the Consumer Insurance (Disclosure and Representations) Act (CIDRA) 2012 (see paragraph 3.2 above). The overall effect of sections 15 and 16A(1), therefore, is that any attempt to contract out of any part of the Act which applies to consumer insurance contracts will be of no effect.

Contracting out in non-consumer insurance

8.5 Parties to a non-consumer insurance contract may contract out of any part of the Act, with two exceptions. Firstly, any attempt to contract out of section 9 (the abolition of basis clauses) will be of no effect.[17] Therefore, if a non-consumer insurance

10 Insurance Act 2015, s.16(2).
11 July 2014 Report, para.1.6.
12 Consumer Insurance (Disclosure and Representations) Act 2012, s.1. This definition applies under s.1 of the Act.
13 Insurance Act 2015, s.1: '"non-consumer insurance contract" means a contract of insurance that is not a consumer insurance contract".'
14 See Chapters 6 and 7.
15 Insurance Act 2015, s.16A(1).
16 See Chapter 9.
17 Insurance Act 2015, s.16(1).

contract contains a basis clause, it will be of no effect. Secondly, under section 13A there is an implied term in all insurance contracts requiring the insurer to pay sums due in respect of a claim within a reasonable time, failing which the insured may recover damages for foreseeable loss.[18] Any attempt to contract out of the insurer's liability for deliberate or reckless breach of this implied term will be of no effect in a non-consumer contract.[19]

8.6 For example, if a clause in a non-consumer insurance contract purports to limit the insurer's liability for any breach of the implied term, that clause would be of no effect as regards any deliberate or reckless breach of the implied term. However, the clause limiting the insurer's liability for breach of the implied term would be effective as regards any other breach of the implied term, provided the transparency requirements have been met.[20] The same analysis ought to apply where a contract contains an entire agreement clause which provides that no term is to be implied into the contract.[21] Whilst such a clause would normally bar the implication of any terms into the contract, it could not permit an insurer to evade liability for deliberate or reckless breach of the implied term, since that is impermissible under section 16A(2). The implied term will still be implied into the contract, but only to the effect that the insurer may be liable for deliberate or reckless breach of the duty to pay claims within a reasonable time, and not otherwise.

Disadvantageous terms

8.7 Subject to the exceptions noted above, the parties to a non-consumer insurance contract may contract out of any part of the Act, provided the insurer has fulfilled the transparency requirements. As has been seen, contracting out means agreeing to terms which place the insured in a worse position,[22] such terms being 'disadvantageous' under section 16(2), and effective only if the transparency requirements have been met. Whether a term is disadvantageous to the insured involves combined questions of contractual construction (i.e. what would the effect of the term be on the insured?) and statutory interpretation (i.e. what would the insured's position otherwise be under the Act?). Having answered these questions, it will in most cases be obvious whether the term puts the insured in a worse position than under the Act, as in the following examples.

(i) A term providing that the only remedy for any breach of the duty of fair presentation is avoidance. That is disadvantageous to the insured because

---

18 See Chapter 10.

19 Insurance Act 2015, s.16A(2).

20 Under Insurance Act 2015, s.16A(2), any term which puts the insured in a worse position as respects deliberate or reckless breach of the implied term is '*to that extent* of no effect' (emphasis added). It follows that such a term will be effective to the extent that it puts the insured in a worse position as regards any breach of the duty to pay claims within a reasonable time which is not deliberate or reckless, provided the transparency requirements are fulfilled. There is seemingly no need for a saving provision to make this point expressly in any case where the insurer seeks to exclude or limit its liability for late payment: see Law Com No 353, p.314 at fn.25.

21 Whether such a clause achieves this end is, of course, a question of construction of the particular clause.

22 Insurance Act 2015, s.16(2).

under Schedule 1 of the Act, if there is a breach of the duty of fair presentation which is neither deliberate nor reckless, the insurer may be entitled to a number of 'lesser' remedies, such as a proportionate reduction of the claim, or rewriting the terms of the contract. If avoidance is the only remedy, including where the insured's breach of the duty was neither deliberate nor reckless, the insured is in a worse position than under the Act, because the prospect that it will end up with no cover at all is higher.

(ii) A term providing that any breach of warranty by the insured will discharge the insurer's liability permanently. That is disadvantageous because, under section 10, breach of warranty suspends the insurer's liability unless and until the insured remedies its breach of warranty. The term is disadvantageous to the insured because it removes any possibility that the insured may remedy its breach of warranty and thereby restore cover.

(iii) A term excluding the effect of section 11, under which the insured may not rely upon breach of a risk mitigation term to escape liability if non-compliance with the term could not have increased the risk of the actual loss in the circumstances in which it occurred. The term would be disadvantageous to the insured, since it would enable the insurer to rely upon breach of a term notwithstanding that the breach could not have caused the loss which actually occurred.

(iv) A term limiting or excluding the insurer's liability for breach of the implied term requiring the insurer to pay sums due in respect of a claim within a reasonable time. This puts the insured in a worse position, since under section 13A the insured may otherwise recover all foreseeable loss caused by the insurer's breach of the implied term.

8.8 It may not always be obvious whether a contractual term puts the insured in a worse position than under the Act. For example, the parties may agree to contract out of section 4, which governs the insured's knowledge for the purpose of the duty of fair presentation. They elect instead to use the old law. The matter is covered in detail in Chapter 4 but, in broad summary, under the old law the insured knew what it ought to know 'in the ordinary course of business',[23] whereas under the Act it knows whatever 'should reasonably have been revealed by a reasonable search' of information.[24] It is likely that this reform has rendered the duty of disclosure more burdensome. On one view of the old law, the courts would consider the subjective characteristics of the insured in assessing what it ought to know 'in the ordinary course of business', meaning that if the insured ran its business in an inefficient manner, it might not be taken to have constructive knowledge of information which it overlooked through its inefficiency.[25] Under the Act, there is no such leniency, since the 'reasonable search' test is purely objective, based upon what 'should' have been revealed by a 'reasonable

23 Marine Insurance Act 1906, s.18(1).

24 Insurance Act 2015, s.4(6).

25 Particularly the dicta of McNair J in *Australia & New Zealand Bank Limited v Colonial & Eagle Wharves Limited* [1960] 2 Lloyd's Rep 241 at 252. See also *Simner v New India Assurance Co* [1995] LRLR 240, HHJ Diamond at 253–255. Note, however, that the opposite view is taken in Jonathan Gilman and others, *Arnould's Law of Marine Insurance and Average*, 17th edn (Sweet & Maxwell, London, 2008), para.16-46.

search'.[26] Because the Act takes no account of the subjective qualities of the insured, its burden of disclosure may in certain circumstance be increased, because it will be held to the higher standard of a reasonable insured for the purposes of determining its knowledge. A term which contracts on the basis of the old law might not be a disadvantageous term, therefore.

The transparency requirements

17 The transparency requirements

(1) In this section, 'the disadvantageous term' means such a term as is mentioned in section 16(2).
(2) The insurer must take sufficient steps to draw the disadvantageous term to the insured's attention before the contract is entered into or the variation agreed.
(3) The disadvantageous term must be clear and unambiguous as to its effect.
(4) In determining whether the requirements of subsections (2) and (3) have been met, the characteristics of insured persons of the kind in question, and the circumstances of the transaction, are to be taken into account.
(5) The insured may not rely on any failure on the part of the insurer to meet the requirements of subsection (2) if the insured (or its agent) had actual knowledge of the disadvantageous term when the contract was entered into or the variation agreed.

8.9 If a term is 'disadvantageous', it will be of no effect unless both of the transparency requirements have been fulfilled, namely:

(i) The insurer must take 'sufficient steps to draw the disadvantageous term to the insured's attention' before the contract (or variation) is entered into.[27]
(ii) The disadvantageous term must be 'clear and unambiguous as to its effect'.[28]

8.10 In determining whether the transparency requirements have been fulfilled, a court must take account of the characteristics of an insured of the kind in question, and the circumstances of the actual transaction.[29] This reflects the fact that there is one set of rules for contracting out of the Act which applies to all non-consumer insurance, notwithstanding there is a very wide spectrum of buyers of such insurance, from small businesses to large and sophisticated insureds operating through specialist insurance brokers. What is required to satisfy the transparency requirements for one insured will not necessarily be the same as for another, and section 17(4) is intended to introduce flexibility into the law on contracting out.[30]

First transparency requirement: sufficient steps to draw the term to the insured's attention

8.11 The first transparency requirement is that the insurer must take 'sufficient steps to draw the disadvantageous term to the insured's attention' before the contract (or variation) is entered into.[31] This is intended to provide the potential buyer of insurance

26 July 2014 Report, para.8.83.
27 Insurance Act 2015, s.17(2).
28 Insurance Act 2015, s.17(3).
29 Insurance Act 2015, s.17(4).
30 July 2014 Report, para.29.41.
31 Insurance Act 2015, s.17(2).

with a reasonable opportunity to know that the disadvantageous term exists before it enters into the contract.[32] It is not necessary that the insured has actual knowledge of the disadvantageous term, but merely that the insurer has taken sufficient steps to draw it to the insured's attention. The lengths to which the insurer must go to fulfil this requirement are uncertain, and will depend upon the nature of the insured and the circumstances surrounding the insurance. This is deliberate, since the first transparency requirement is intended to operate in a flexible way, reflecting the fact that what is sufficient for one insured may not be sufficient for another.[33]

8.12 The Law Commissions have suggested that, generally speaking, a disadvantageous term should not to be 'buried' in a policy document, without any further reference to it.[34] It follows that as a general rule, a disadvantageous term should be signposted by the insurer in a way which goes further than simply inserting the term into the policy in the normal way. However, the nature of the signposting that is required may vary substantially, depending upon the sophistication of the buyer and the circumstances in which it is buying insurance. To take a simple example, the owner of a small shop buying business interruption insurance online without a broker's assistance is very likely to require more comprehensive signposting than a multinational supermarket chain buying insurance from an expert insurance broker. At the lower end of the scale, the signposting could be as simple as marking the disadvantageous term with a distinguishing symbol within the policy wording,[35] or typing it in distinctive font. However, for a less sophisticated insured, it is probably necessary to provide clearer signposts, such as summarising or providing a cross-reference to the disadvantageous term in an outline of the key policy provisions. The Law Commissions have provided a number of examples to illustrate the differing standards of what could amount to 'sufficient steps', which are considered below.[36]

8.13 As a matter of general contract law, where a contract contains a term which is onerous or unusual, or which involves the abrogation of rights created by statute, the party tendering the onerous term must show that it has been brought fairly and reasonably to the other's attention.[37] The Law Commissions envisage that cases decided upon these principles may be pertinent when considering whether the first transparency requirement has been fulfilled.[38] Subject to one qualification, this appears to be correct. The qualification arises from the fact that non-consumer insurance is notable for the central role played by insurance brokers in many cases. The usual rule is that the insurance broker acts as agent for the insured.[39] It is important to appreciate that

32 Explanatory Notes to the Insurance Act 2015, para.125.
33 July 2014 Report, para.29.41.
34 July 2014 Report, para.29.37.
35 July 2014 Report, para.29.64.
36 Paras 8.14–8.17 below.
37 *Parker v South Eastern Ry* (1877) 2 CPD 416, 428; *Thornton v Shoe Lane Parking Ltd* [1971] 2 QB 163; *Hollingworth v Southern Ferries Ltd (The 'Eagle')* [1977] 2 Lloyd's Rep 70; *Interfoto Picture Library Ltd v Stiletto Visual Programmes Ltd* [1989] QB 433; *Dillon v Baltic Shipping Co (The Mikhail Lermontov)* [1991] 2 Lloyd's Rep 155; *AEG (UK) Ltd v Logic Resource Ltd* [1996] CLC 265; *Laceys Footwear (Wholesale) Ltd v Bowler International Freight Ltd* [1997] 2 Lloyd's Rep 369, 384–385; *Ocean Chemical Transport Inc v Exnor Craggs Ltd* [2000] 1 Lloyd's Rep. 446, 451; *Amiri Flight Authority v BAE Systems Plc* [2003] EWCA Civ 1447, [2003] 2 Lloyd's Rep 767; *Kaye v Nu Skin UK Ltd* [2009] EWHC 3509 (Ch.), [2011] 1 Lloyd's Rep 40.
38 July 2014 Report, paras 29.38–29.39.
39 *Re Great Western Assurance Co SA and Ors* [1999] 1 Lloyd's Rep IR 377.

where the insured is represented by a broker or other agent, the first transparency requirement may be fulfilled where the insurer takes sufficient steps to draw the disadvantageous term to the attention of that agent.[40] This is confirmed by section 22(4), which provides that reference to something being done by or in relation to the insured includes its being done by or in relation to the insured's agent. Moreover, if the insured or its agent has actual knowledge of the disadvantageous term before the contract is entered into, the insured will not be able to rely upon the insurer's failure to fulfil the first transparency requirement.[41] It is of course common for insurance wordings to be prepared by a broker. In those circumstances, the broker may have 'actual knowledge' of any disadvantageous term in the policy, if it has drafted the terms before the contract is entered into.

Examples applying the first transparency requirement[42]

8.14 The owner of a small business (B) visits an insurance company's (C) website to purchase public liability insurance. B fills in an online application, is given an automatically generated quote and is then asked to indicate whether or not he wishes to proceed. At this stage a large box appears on the screen showing the key terms of the policy: premium, extent of coverage, etc. B has to tick a box stating that he agrees to the standard terms and conditions attached to the insurance policy. There is a link next to the box which, if clicked, opens a window showing all of the standard terms, paragraph 24 of which is a term excluding liability for damages for late payment of an insurance claim. There is no other reference to the disadvantageous term. The insured is a small business unlikely to have expert knowledge of insurance, and operating without the assistance of a broker or any other intermediary. An insured with those characteristics is likely to require more comprehensive signposting towards a disadvantageous term, yet the insurer did not include any reference to the disadvantageous term in the box summarising the key terms of the policy, and to detect it the insured would have needed to click on a link and read through all the standard terms. The Law Commissions therefore concluded (correctly, it is suggested) that the first transparency requirement is unlikely to have been satisfied in this case,[43] meaning the disadvantageous term excluding liability for damages for late payment would be of no effect.[44] However, the outcome would be different if the large box summarising the key terms had summarised the effect of the disadvantageous term, and provided a cross-reference to paragraph 24 of the standard terms. In those circumstances, the insurer could have done little more to draw the term to the insured's attention, and the first transparency requirement would have been fulfilled.[45] If, in those circumstances, the actual insured was inefficient or careless such that it did not pay attention to the summary of key terms or paragraph 24 of the standard terms, this should be given little to no weight in

40 Explanatory Notes to the Insurance Act 2015, para.126; July 2014 Report, para.29.42.

41 Insurance Act 2015, s.17(5).

42 The examples set out below are adapted from July 2014 Report, and illustrate the way in which the first transparency requirement is expected to work in practice.

43 July 2014 Report, para.29.62.

44 The disadvantageous term could not in any event exclude liability for deliberate or reckless breach of the implied term: Insurance Act 2015, s,16A(2).

45 July 2014 Report, para.29.63.

determining whether the first transparency requirement was fulfilled, since those are subjective characteristics of the actual insured, and not 'the characteristics of insured persons of the kind in question'. Moreover, actual knowledge of the disadvantageous term by the insured is not required.

8.15 The managing director of a medium-sized enterprise (M) visits an insurance broker (IB) to discuss purchasing a bespoke liability policy to cover any liabilities arising from the manufacture, sale and use of a new product. IB discusses M's needs and agrees a set of requirements. IB then telephones a number of underwriters. Underwriter U offers the best price. IB and U discuss and negotiate certain terms of the insurance policy including price and coverage, and U states that the policy will, other than the negotiated terms, be on its standard terms and conditions. U emails a scanned copy of those conditions to IB. These include, at paragraph 24, a term stating that if any of M's employees have given a dishonest answer to M's reasonable search of information conducted pursuant to the duty of fair presentation, U is entitled to avoid the contract *ab initio*. This provision modifies the duty of fair presentation and U's remedies for its breach in a way that is disadvantageous to the insured. U did not mention the disadvantageous term on the telephone. Paragraph 24, along with a handful of other terms, is marked with an asterisk in the policy. IB consults with M, not mentioning paragraph 24. M is pleased with the price and instructs IB to purchase the policy. IB relays this to U, who asks whether IB has had a chance to go through the standard terms. IB replies in the affirmative and arranges for the policy to be entered into. The Law Commissions consider this to be 'at the limit' of what was sufficient to bring the term to the notice of the insured (through its agent), but that the steps taken would suffice.[46] That appears to be correct: the insured is represented by a broker; the insurer asks him whether he has read the policy; and the insurer has placed an asterisk by the disadvantageous term. Whilst this cannot (without more[47]) establish actual knowledge of the disadvantageous term by the broker, that is not a requirement to fulfil the first transparency requirement. If, in the same scenario, M dealt directly with U without the involvement of a broker, the Law Commissions consider that U had not done enough to draw the term to the insured's attention, because the insurer 'cannot assume that M will go through the standard terms, even when some were highlighted'.[48] Had U mentioned the term to M on the phone, or in the covering sheet or email with the scanned standard terms, they are of the view that the insurer would have satisfied the first transparency requirement.

8.16 The final example takes account of the standard wordings developed by Lloyd's underwriters and brokers to contract out of section 10 (so that breach of warranty permanently discharges the insurer's liability) and excluding liability for all but deliberate or reckless breach of the implied term to pay insurance claims within a reasonable time (i.e. contracting out of section 13A). These standard wordings have assigned codes of LMA5258 and LMA5277 respectively.[49] When a broker is negotiating a policy, if it is

---

46 July 2014 Report, para.29.64.

47 This is a question of evidence, as the Law Commissions rightly acknowledge.

48 July 2014 Report, para.29.65.

49 The Law Commissions did not refer to these clauses in their original example, but considering they have now in fact been developed by the Lloyd's Market Association, they have been introduced into the scenario.

agreed that any of the standard terms will apply, the broker writes the code down on the slip, and this is taken as evidence that the terms are agreed and incorporated into the policy. S has just chartered a ship to carry cargo, so it telephones its broker (IB) in London and asks IB to arrange cover for the voyage, which must be in place by the time the ship sails in 24 hours' time. U agrees to underwrite the voyage, but insists on excluding liability for damages for late payment. In the policy, S warrants that the ship will not deviate from its proposed course, and U wishes to contract out of section 10 as it would apply to that warranty, so that breach of that warranty will permanently discharge U's liability. IB, acting with authority to bind S, accepts these terms, and writes LMA5258 and LMA5277 on the slip, which is stamped by U. Both of those standard clauses are clear as to their effect.[50] In the Law Commissions' view, the first transparency requirement has been fulfilled. The insurance buyer is represented by a specialist broker buying insurance through Lloyd's, so the level of signposting required is at the lower end of the scale. The marine market must often operate at a fast pace,[51] and the actual transaction is on a very tight time scale. The Law Commissions place reliance upon the fact that the disadvantageous terms have been raised with the broker by the underwriter, and noted on the slip. The Law Commissions consider that the broker ought to know what the standard terms mean before binding the insured. Whilst this is correct, it should not be thought that section 17(2) requires the insurer to explain the meaning or purpose behind the disadvantageous term (particularly not in a sophisticated market such as this). All that is required are sufficient steps to draw the term to the broker's attention. In the authors' view, the fact that the broker wrote the terms LMA5258 and LMA5277 on the slip ought to be sufficient to establish actual knowledge of the disadvantageous terms on the part of the broker, which will prevent the insured from reliance on any failure to comply with the first transparency requirement.[52]

8.17 In a variation of the example above, the facts are the same, but U does not mention LMA5258 and LMA5277 to the broker, or its desire to contract out of certain provisions in the Act. Instead, U refers to its standard voyage conditions (coded U1VOY1). Those conditions have recently been updated to include terms substantively the same as LMA5258 and LMA5277. The broker writes a reference to the U1VOY1 conditions on the slip and the policy is concluded. In the Law Commissions' view, the first transparency requirement may not have been fulfilled in this case, because 'U has not done anything at all to bring IB's attention to the inclusion of the terms in its own standard terms'.[53] The Law Commissions acknowledge, however, that the answer is not clear, and would depend upon circumstances such as the extent to which the detail of U1VOY1, as recently modified, was known by brokers generally; the availability of U1VOY1 for inspection; and the extent to which other standard sets of voyage conditions would be known by brokers to include such exclusions. The Law Commissions consider that an insurer in such a situation would be 'well advised to mention the specific provisions to the broker, perhaps in an email or by having them

50 See paras 8.18–8.23 below.

51 The Law Commissions state that they 'would not want to interfere unnecessarily' with the operation of such a market.

52 Insurance Act 2015, s.17(5).

53 July 2014 Report, para.29.67.

specifically noted on the slip'.[54] Whilst the authors do not disagree with this advice, they consider that in a sophisticated insurance market such as this, the broker is likely to (and should) have actual knowledge of the terms of standard policies, including their recent amendments. This is a question of evidence, but if actual knowledge is established, the insured may not rely upon any failure to fulfil the transparency requirement by the insurer.[55]

Second transparency requirement: term must be clear and unambiguous as to effect

8.18 The second transparency requirement is that the disadvantageous term must be 'clear and unambiguous as to its effect'.[56] Whether this requirement has been fulfilled is an issue of construction of the term in question. It is probably not sufficient that the term is drafted in a way that is clear and unambiguous: the effect of the term must be clear and unambiguous.[57] That means that the effects of the disadvantageous term should be set out explicitly.[58] For example, a term providing that 'section 10 of the Insurance Act 2015 is excluded in its entirety' is clear, but it does not explain its effect, and therefore risks falling foul of the second transparency requirement.[59] In order to fulfil that requirement, the clause should also set out its effect in clear terms, as in the following example:

> Section 10 of the Insurance Act 2015 shall not apply to any warranty in this insurance contract. If any such warranty is breached, the Insurer's liability shall be discharged from the time of the breach of warranty, regardless of whether the breach is subsequently remedied.[60]

8.19 Similarly, if the insurer wished to contract out of section 11 in its entirety, the following clause is clear and unambiguous as to its effect:

> Section 11 of the Insurance Act 2015 shall not apply to any term of this insurance contract. Where this insurance contract contains any term which, if complied with, would tend to reduce the risk of loss of a particular kind or at a particular location or time, and such term is not complied with, the Insurer may rely upon such non-compliance to exclude, limit or discharge its liability, even if non-compliance with the term could not have increased the risk of the loss which actually occurred in the circumstances in which it occurred.[61]

8.20 If the parties agree to contract out of sections 10 and/or 11, there is a question whether it is necessary to state the effect of having done so in every single warranty or risk mitigation term[62] in the policy, particularly where the insured is less sophisticated.[63] The Law Commissions have suggested that where it is intended for breach of a term to have severe consequences, such as permanent discharge of the insurer's liability,

54 Ibid.
55 Insurance Act 2015, s.17(5).
56 Insurance Act 2015, s.17(3).
57 July 2014 Report, para.29.50.
58 Explanatory Notes to the Insurance Act 2015, para.128.
59 July 2014 Report, para.29.50.
60 LMA 5258, 16 March 2016.
61 LMA5260, 16 March 2016.
62 i.e. any term which is subject to s.11.
63 Dr George Leloudas, 'Contracting out of the Insurance Act 2015 in commercial insurance contracts' in Malcolm Clarke and Barış Soyer (eds), *The Insurance Act 2015: A New Regime for Commercial and Marine Insurance Law* (Informa, London, 2016), 104.

the insurer 'would be well-advised to spell out the desired consequences of breach within the term itself ...'.[64] This suggests that where the parties have contracted out of section 10, it could be necessary to set out the consequences of breach in each and every warranty in the policy. Whilst this could be necessary when dealing with an unsophisticated insured who is a quasi-consumer, it would be surprising if such an approach was necessary in every case. It would be unduly burdensome if each and every warranty and section 11 term had to spell out the consequences of its breach. There is also a risk that terms which were not on a true construction warranties or section 11 terms would be inadvertently elevated to that status. In view of this, provided that the language of the term contracting out of section 10 and/or 11 is clear as to its effect, it should not be necessary to state the effect on each and every term in the policy. However, this point is uncertain, particularly where the insured is unsophisticated. A potential solution to this uncertainty is for the insurer to consider which warranties or section 11 terms should not be subject to sections 10 and 11, and to apply the contracting out of those sections for those terms alone, as in the clauses set out below:

> Section 10 of the Insurance Act 2015 shall not apply to {this warranty/these warranties/refer to specific warranties}. If {this warranty/these warranties/refer to specific warranties} is breached, the Insurer's liability shall be discharged from the time of the breach of warranty, regardless of whether the breach is subsequently remedied.[65]
>
> Section 11 of the Insurance Act 2015 shall not apply to {this term/these terms/refer to specific terms}. If {this term/these terms/refer to specific terms} is not complied with, the Insurer may rely upon such non-compliance to exclude, limit or discharge its liability, even if non-compliance with {this term/these terms/refer to specific terms} could not have increased the risk of the loss which actually occurred in the circumstances in which it occurred.[66]

8.21 When it comes to contracting out of the insurer's potential liability under section 13A for breach of the implied term requiring payment of claims within a reasonable time, there are various potential approaches which may be taken. A basic approach is to adopt a term excluding the term which would otherwise be implied into every insurance contract under section 13A. Whilst the authors do not consider that such a term would be ineffective, it is not without potential difficulty. As has been explained, any term which puts the insured in a worse position than under the Act as regards deliberate or reckless breach of the implied term will be of no effect.[67] In view of this, a complete exclusion of the implied term cannot be fully effective, since it could not operate so as to exclude the implication of the implied term where the insured's breach was deliberate or reckless. It appears to the authors that if the parties have agreed to exclude the implied term altogether, that must itself be subject to an implied restriction in any case of deliberate or reckless breach of the implied term. However, a simpler and more attractive solution is not to exclude the implied term altogether, but to proceed on the basis that it will be implied into every contract of insurance, whilst limiting or excluding the insurer's liability in damages for any breach of the implied term which is neither deliberate nor reckless, as in LMA5277:

64 July 2014 Report, paras 17.73–17.75; see also para.18.53 (in the context of s.11).
65 LMA Model Clause 5259, 16 March 2016.
66 LMA Model Clause 5261, 16 March 2016.
67 Insurance Act 2015, s.16A(2).

The Insurer shall have no liability to pay damages to the Insured for late payment of a claim under this insurance contract, unless it fails deliberately or recklessly to pay the claim within a reasonable time.[68]

8.22 There are many possible variations on the theme of LMA5277, such as limiting liability for non-deliberate or non-reckless breach to a specified sum, or excluding liability for certain types of loss. For example, some of the possibilities are contained in LMA 5278:

1. The Insurer's liability to pay damages to the Insured for late payment of a claim under this insurance contract is limited as follows:
   {The Insurer's liability is limited to £X.} {OR}
   {The Insurer's liability is limited to a multiple of {X} times the premium charged under this insurance contract.} {OR}
   {The Insurer's liability is limited to interest on the amount which should have been paid, at a rate of 2% above LIBOR. The interest shall be payable from the date when payment should reasonably have been made until the date of actual payment.}
2. If the Insurer has underwritten a proportion of this insurance contract, its liability for any late payment shall be no greater than that proportion of any damages suffered by the insured, subject always to clause 1 above.
3. Clause 1 above does not apply if the Insurer fails deliberately or recklessly to pay the claim within a reasonable time.[69]

8.23 The lengths to which an insurer must go in spelling out the consequences of a disadvantageous term will vary depending on the nature of the insured and the extent to which they could be expected to understand the consequences of such a term.[70] As with the first requirement, what is sufficient for one insured might not be sufficient for another.[71] That said, it is difficult to see how the sophistication of the insured is as relevant to the second transparency requirement as the first. Generally speaking, a disadvantageous term either is or is not clear as to its effect. In cases where the disadvantageous term is arguably ambiguous as to its effect, the courts are likely to be less forgiving if the insured is sophisticated, or where a broker is involved. But in general, whether a term is unambiguous as to its effect is a matter of contractual construction, and the sophistication of the insured is unlikely to make much difference to the resolution of this question.

Contracting out: group insurance

18 Contracting out: group insurance contracts

(1) This section applies to a contract of insurance referred to in section 13(1)(a); and in this section—

(2) "A" and "the Cs" have the same meaning as in section 13,
"consumer C" means an individual who is one of the Cs, where the cover provided by the contract for that individual would have been a consumer insurance contract if entered into by that person rather than by A, and
"non-consumer C" means any of the Cs who is not a consumer C.

68 LMA Model Clause 5277, 12 October 2016.
69 LMA 5278, 12 October 2016.
70 July 2014 Report, para.29.62 *et seq*.
71 Explanatory Notes to the Insurance Act 2015, para.129.

(3) A term of the contract of insurance, or any other contract, which puts a consumer C in a worse position as respects any matter dealt with in section 13 than that individual would be in by virtue of that section is to that extent of no effect.

(4) A term of the contract of insurance, or any other contract, which puts a non-consumer C in a worse position as respects any matter dealt with in section 13 than that person would be in by virtue of that section is to that extent of no effect, unless the requirements of section 17 have been met in relation to the term.

(5) Section 17 applies in relation to such a term as it applies to a term mentioned in section 16(2), with references to the insured being read as references to A rather than the non-consumer C.

(6) In this section references to a contract include a variation.

(7) This section does not apply in relation to a contract for the settlement of a claim arising under a contract of insurance to which this section applies.

8.24 The Act makes specific provision for contracting out in 'group insurance', which means a situation in which the contract is entered into between the insurer and another, but the contract provides cover for other persons who are not parties to the contract.[72] In those circumstances, if any of the non-parties for whom cover is provided under the contract are consumers, then any disadvantageous term in the contract will be of no effect as regards those consumers. For example, the landlord of a block of flats takes out a contract of insurance under which each of the occupants is entitled to cover for the contents of their flat. The contract between the landlord and the insurer is a non-consumer contract, because the landlord takes it out for purposes wholly or mainly related to his business letting out flats.[73] However, if any of the tenants had taken out the insurance individually, it would have been a consumer contract, since it would have been taken out for private personal reasons. In those circumstances, any disadvantageous term in the contract will not apply to any of the tenants.[74] However, if one of the tenants used his flat as his full-time office, had he taken out the insurance himself it would have been a non-consumer contract. In that case, the disadvantageous term will have effect in respect of the non-consumer tenant, provided the transparency requirements in section 17 have been met.[75] However, the person to whom sufficient notice of the disadvantageous term must have been given is not the non-consumer tenant, but the landlord.[76]

72 Insurance Act 2015, s.18(1).
73 Insurance Act 2015, s.18(3).
74 Insurance Act 2015, s.18(3).
75 Insurance Act 2015, s.18(4).
76 Insurance Act 2015, s.18(5).

CHAPTER 9

Fraudulent claims

12 Remedies for fraudulent claims

(1) If the insured makes a fraudulent claim under a contract of insurance –
  (a) the insurer is not liable to pay the claim,
  (b) the insurer may recover from the insured any sums paid by the insurer to the insured in respect of the claim, and
  (c) in addition, the insurer may by notice to the insured treat the contract as having been terminated with effect from the time of the fraudulent act.

(2) If the insurer does treat the contract as having been terminated –
  (a) it may refuse all liability to the insured under the contract in respect of a relevant event occurring after the time of the fraudulent act, and
  (b) it need not return any of the premiums paid under the contract.

(3) Treating a contract as having been terminated under this section does not affect the rights and obligations of the parties to the contract with respect to a relevant event occurring before the time of the fraudulent act.

(4) In subsections (2)(a) and (3), "relevant event" refers to whatever gives rise to the insurer's liability under the contract (and includes, for example, the occurrence of a loss, the making of a claim, or the notification of a potential claim, depending on how the contract is written).

13 Remedies for fraudulent claims: group insurance

(1) This section applies where –
  (a) a contract of insurance is entered into with an insurer by a person ("A"),
  (b) the contract provides cover for one or more other persons who are not parties to the contract ("the Cs"), whether or not it also provides cover of any kind for A or another insured party, and
  (c) a fraudulent claim is made under the contract by or on behalf of one of the Cs ("CF").

(2) Section 12 applies in relation to the claim as if the cover provided for CF were provided under an individual insurance contract between the insurer and CF as the insured; and, accordingly –
  (a) the insurer's rights under section 12 are exercisable only in relation to the cover provided for CF, and
  (b) the exercise of any of those rights does not affect the cover provided under the contract for anyone else.

(3) In its application by virtue of subsection (2), section 12 is subject to the following particular modifications –
  (a) the first reference to "the insured" in subsection (1)(b) of that section, in respect of any particular sum paid by the insurer, is to whichever of A and CF the insurer paid the sum to; but if a sum was paid to A and passed on by A to CF, the reference is to CF,
  (b) the second reference to "the insured" in subsection (1)(b) is to A or CF,

(c) the reference to "the insured" in subsection (1)(c) is to both CF and A,
(d) the reference in subsection (2)(b) to the premiums paid under the contract is to premiums paid in respect of the cover for CF.

9.1 The making of a fraudulent claim under an insurance contract has wider implications than the consequences that arise between the parties to the contract, since it involves dishonest and potentially criminal behaviour by or on behalf of the insured, which engages the public interest. It is common for policies to contain a clause setting out the insurer's remedies should the insured make a fraudulent claim.[1] In the absence of such a clause, the courts have struggled over time with the principles to apply where the insured has behaved dishonestly, given the mix of insurance contract law and public policy involved. The Law Commissions described the law in this area as 'convoluted and confused' in their July 2014 Report,[2] and it was therefore considered ripe for clarification and reform in the Insurance Act. Sections 12 and 13 of the Insurance Act contain the new law and apply to both consumer and non-consumer insurance contracts.

9.2 Under the old law:

(i) The policy of the law was to discourage the making of fraudulent claims. As Lord Hobhouse said in *Manifest Shipping Co Ltd v Uni-Polaris Shipping Co Ltd (The Star Sea)*:[3] 'The fraudulent insured must not be allowed to think: if the fraud is successful, then I will gain; if it is unsuccessful, I will lose nothing.'

(ii) A fraudulent claim involved the insured acting dishonestly to get him something under the insurance contract to which he was not entitled. If the insured told a lie, or committed some other dishonest act which was irrelevant to the existence or amount of the insurer's liability under the contract, that 'fraudulent device' was in itself not to be treated as a fraudulent claim.[4] This is likely to remain the position in relation to the meaning of a fraudulent claim in sections 12 and 13 Insurance Act.

(iii) If the insured made a fraudulent claim (including by exaggerating the amount of an otherwise legitimate claim), the whole claim was forfeited (and not just the exaggerated part).[5] The fraudulent part of the claim had to be substantial 'in the sense of not being insubstantial or immaterial or *de minimis*', although this was 'not a high threshold'.[6]

(iv) Although the making of a fraudulent claim was a clear breach of the insured's duty of good faith, the remedy under section 17 Marine Insurance Act 1906

1 See, for example, *Joseph Fielding Properties (Blackpool) Ltd v Aviva Insurance Ltd* [2010] EWHC 2192; [2011] Lloyd's Rep IR 238 (QB); *Nsubuga v Commercial Union Assurance Co PLC* [1998] 2 Lloyd's Rep 682 (Com Ct).

2 July 2014 Report, para.19.3.

3 *Manifest Shipping Co Ltd v Uni-Polaris Shipping Co Ltd (The Star Sea)* [2001] UKHL 1, [2003] 1 AC 469, [62].

4 The so-called 'collateral lie': see the judgments of Lord Sumption [25], [36] and Lord Toulson [105] in *Versloot Dredging BV & Anor v HDI Gerling Industrie Versicherung AG & Ors (The DC Merwestone)* [2016] UKSC 45, [2016] 3 WLR 543.

5 *Goulstone v Royal Insurance Co* 175 ER 725, 1 F&F 276; *Britton v Royal Insurance Co* 176 ER 843 (1866) 4 F&F 905; and *Galloway v Guardian Royal Exchange (UK) Ltd* [1999] Lloyd's Rep IR 209 (CA).

6 *Versloot Dredging BV & Anor v HDI Gerling Industrie Versicherung AG & Ors (The DC Merwestone)* [2013] EWHC 1666 (Comm), [2013] 2 Lloyd's Rep 131, [156], [157] (Popplewell J).

for breach of that duty, being the avoidance of the insurance contract by the insurer *ab initio*, has more recently been regarded as one not available to the insurer in these circumstances, or is at least a remedy that the courts have been reluctant to apply. This was because any breach would have occurred after the insurance contract was entered into, but the remedy would apply retrospectively to avoid the contract, which would be penal in its effect.[7] Recent cases tended to treat the breach of duty as one incidental to the contract, rather than a breach of a separate duty of good faith.[8]

(v) If the insured's breach of its duty of good faith was sufficiently serious, the breach might be treated as repudiatory of the insurance contract. If accepted by the insurer, this would terminate cover from the date of acceptance, with the consequences that valid claims made before the acceptance were covered, but those arising thereafter were not since such a release would only apply prospectively and not affect accrued rights to be indemnified.[9] In *Axa General Insurance v Gottlieb*,[10] Mance LJ said that the fraudulent act had the effect of forfeiting the whole of the claim to which the fraud related, including any valid interim payments made prior to the fraud.[11]

(vi) If the remedies for the making of a fraudulent claim were contract-based, the insurer ought also to have had a right to claim damages for the breach of contract (for example, in respect of the costs incurred in investigating the claim), but this would not be consistent with the remedy for breach of the duty of utmost good faith, which was one of avoidance only.[12] In *London Assurance v Clare*,[13] Goddard J held that the cost of investigation of a fraudulent claim was not recoverable as damages for breach of contract, although he said that there might be something to be said for a claim for damages for fraud. In *Insurance Corporation of Ireland v McHugh*[14] it was acknowledged by Mance J that a claim in damages for deceit might lie against a fraudulent insured.

(vii) The duty of good faith under section 17 Marine Insurance Act 1906 ceased to apply after litigation between the insured and the insurer in respect of the claim had commenced.[15]

9.3 The uncertainties in the case law justified the Law Commissions' decision to review the law in this area, and Section 12 Insurance Act brings a welcome degree of clarity to the remedies for a fraudulent claim. Those remedies are in line with the

7 *Manifest Shipping Co Ltd v Uni-Polaris Shipping Co Ltd (The Star Sea)* [2001] UKHL 1 (CA), [2003] 1 AC 469, [51] (Hobhouse L).

8 Lord Hobhouse in *The Star Sea*, ibid., [50]–[57] and Mance LJ in *Agapitos v Agnew (The Aegon)* [2002] EWHC 1558 (Comm), [2002] 2 Lloyd's Rep 42, [13], [45]. Lord Sumption suggested *obiter* in *Versloot Dredging* [2016] UKSC 45, [2016] 3 WLR 543, [8], that although he tended to agree with Lord Hobhouse that the 'fraudulent claims rule' should be regarded as an incident of the contract, he left open the question whether there was a remedy of avoidance *ab initio* for breach of the insured's duty of utmost good faith.

9 Lord Hobhouse in *The Star Sea*, ibid., [50].

10 [2005] EWCA Civ 112, [2005] Lloyd's Rep IR 369.

11 Ibid., [26], [32].

12 *Banque Keyser Ullman SA v Skandia (UK) Insurance Co Ltd* [1991] 2 AC 249 (CA), [1990] 3 WLR 364.

13 (1937) 57 Ll L Rep 254 (KB).

14 [1997] LRLR 94 (Com Ct).

15 *The Aegon* [2002] EWHC 1558 (Comm), [2002] 2 Lloyd's Rep 42, [53].

trends in the case law outlined in paragraph 9.2. The Law Commissions were of the view that there was a clear case for strong remedies given the moral hazard involved in fraud by policyholders,[16] and that the civil law had an important role in deterring insureds from making fraudulent claims.[17] The Insurance Act does not define what is meant by a 'fraudulent claim' and the July 2014 Report[18] and Explanatory Notes[19] make it clear that whether or not a claim is fraudulent will depend on common law principles, as to which see sub-paragraphs 9.2(i)–9.2(iii) above.

9.4 By abolishing any remedy for breach of the duty of utmost good faith under Section 17 Marine Insurance Act,[20] it is no longer arguable that the making of a fraudulent claim entitles the insurer to avoid the insurance contract *ab initio*. Section 12(1) Insurance Act provides that an insurer has three remedies available to it if the insured makes a fraudulent claim:

(a) The insurer is not liable to pay the claim. Applying the previous case law, this means that the entire claim is forfeit, not just the exaggerated part (see sub-paragraph 9.2(iii) above).
(b) Any sums previously paid by the insurer in respect of the same claim are recoverable from the insured, even where those sums were in respect of a valid part of the claim. This reflects the position set out by the Court of Appeal in *AXA v Gottlieb*[21] (see sub-paragraph 9.2(v) above).
(c) The insurer may elect to give notice to terminate the insurance contract with effect from the time of the fraudulent act. If the insurer does treat the contract as having been terminated, it will not be liable in respect of a 'relevant event' occurring after the fraudulent act and will not be liable to return any premiums paid for the contract.[22] This introduces new remedies and is considered in paragraphs 9.5–9.8 below.

The right to terminate

9.5 The uncertainties under the old law concerning the effect of a fraudulent claim on other claims and on the insurance contract are summarised in sub-paragraphs 9.2(iv) and (v) above. The remedy provided in section 12(1) Insurance Act is to entitle the insurer to terminate the insurance contract with effect from the date of the insured's fraudulent act. The election to terminate may be made at any time (subject to waiver or estoppel) and will be retrospective in effect so that the contract will be deemed terminated as at the time of the fraudulent act. This has the consequence that valid claims for which the insurer would have been liable under the contract will not be recoverable if those claims arise from a 'relevant event' occurring after the time of the fraudulent act, but will be covered if the 'relevant event' occurs prior to that time. This gives rise to the following issues:

16 July 2014 Report, para.21.23.
17 July 2014 Report, para.21.24.
18 July 2014 Report, paras 22.17–24.
19 Explanatory Notes to the Insurance Act 2015, para.99.
20 Insurance Act 2015, s.14(3)(a) and para.3.11 above.
21 [2005] EWCA Civ 112, [2005] Lloyd's Rep IR 369.
22 Insurance Act 2015, s.12(2).

- What is the relevant fraudulent act?
- What is the 'relevant event' giving rise to a claim?
- Can the insurer waive its right to terminate?

9.6 The Law Commissions described a fraudulent act as 'the behaviour which makes a claim fraudulent',[23] which the Explanatory Notes say may be after the initial submission of the claim.[24] An 'act' on the part of the insured, for example the addition of a fabricated head of loss, is required, not just an intention to submit a fabricated claim, or the avoidance of answering the insurer's questions about the claim. The Supreme Court judgment in *Versloot Dredging*,[25] the effect of which is described in sub-paragraph 9.2(ii) above and which was given after the Insurance Act was enacted, has complicated the application of this remedy. In accordance with that judgment, if the insured tells a lie in support of his claim, that is a fraudulent act, but the claim may not be a fraudulent claim if that lie is collateral to the claim itself in that it did not result in the insured getting something under the insurance contract to which he was not entitled (even if the purpose of telling the lie was to induce the insurer to pay the claim). If the insurer discovers that the insured has committed a fraudulent act in relation to a claim, it will be entitled to decline the claim and terminate the insurance contract only if it can establish that the act affected the quantum or validity of the claim under the contract once finally adjusted. Exaggeration of the value of goods lost by, for example, fabricating an invoice for non-existent goods, would constitute a fraudulent act making the claim fraudulent, but fabrication of an invoice in respect of goods actually stolen would not, because the insured would in the latter case be seeking only that which it was entitled to under the contract. The distinction between the use of a fraudulent device to exaggerate the insured's claim and one used to speed up payment of the claim is a fine one which does not fit comfortably with the overriding purpose of the law, as set out in paragraph 9.2(i) above. Insurers have introduced terms in their policies that give them the right to refuse to pay a claim whose presentation or furtherance has been supported by a fraudulent device,[26] although there may be an issue about whether this is contracting out of the Insurance Act, particularly if used in consumer insurance contracts (see Chapter 8 above).

9.7 Section 12(4) Insurance Act defines a 'relevant event' as meaning 'whatever gives rise to the insurer's liability under the contract', including 'the occurrence of a loss, the making of a claim, or the notification of a potential claim, depending on how the contract is written'. The Explanatory Notes provide the following commentary:

> 'Relevant event', as defined in section 12(4), refers to any event that would trigger the insurer's liability under the particular insurance contract. Usually, this will be the occurrence of loss or damage which is insured under the contract. However, some insurance contracts, such as professional indemnity insurance contracts, are written on the basis of a 'claims made' policy. In such cases, the 'relevant event' may be the notification of a claim against the professional, even where no loss has actually occurred.[27]

---

23 July 2014 Report, para.22.7.
24 Explanatory Notes to the Insurance Act 2015, para.102.
25 Ibid.
26 See for example AVN 100A dated 26 July 2016.
27 Explanatory Notes to the Insurance Act 2015, para.104.

The meaning of a claim arising out of a 'relevant event' is considered in paragraphs 5.32–5.34 above. The examples given in the Explanatory Notes suggest that determining whether the 'relevant event' occurred before or after the fraudulent act will be relatively straightforward. However, any claim under a professional indemnity 'claims made' policy is predicated on an actual or alleged error or omission by the insured, which is as much a 'relevant event' for the purposes of cover under the policy as the making of a claim against the insured, or notifying the claim to the insurer, which is also often a requirement of cover. The authors of *Arnould* suggest that it should be the later of the relevant events that should determine whether the claim is covered once the insurer has terminated the contract.[28] *MacGillivray* would appear to support this approach in describing the claims that should be covered after termination as those for which 'liability had crystallised before the fraudulent act'.[29]

9.8 When considering the position under liability insurance, although giving notice of a claim to the insurer may trigger the insurer's liability to indemnify the insured in respect of costs incurred in defending the claim, the insurer's liability to indemnify the insured in respect of the damages claimed by the third party only arises on judgment or settlement,[30] and that would be the relevant event for the purposes of section 12(4) Insurance Act.

9.9 The insurer's right to terminate the insurance contract where there has been a fraudulent claim may be exercised at any time, although clearly it can only be exercised once the insurer is aware of the fraud, and presumably also aware that the fraud is material to the claim, rather than a 'collateral lie'.[31] Since the insurer will be entitled to keep the premium and will cease to be liable for claims arising out of a relevant event occurring after the fraudulent act, there will generally be an incentive to terminate the contract once there is evidence of fraud. The insurer may, however, delay giving notice to terminate, for example, in circumstances where it is uncertain whether the fraud is material, or it may still need the insured to comply with a contractual obligation to provide information, or it wishes to continue to have control over other, non-fraudulent claims which may or may not continue to be covered after termination. Delay in terminating the contract may prejudice the insured since, for example, it may lose the opportunity to obtain alternative insurance. The authors of *Arnould* suggest that the right to terminate should be exercised within a reasonable time, lest the insurer should waive its right to terminate, as it may previously have lost its right to avoid for breach of the duty of good faith if, having knowledge of that right, the insurer nonetheless treated the contract as continuing.[32]

9.10 By way of example, an insured firm of solicitors gives notices to its professional indemnity insurers of a number of circumstances that it believes may give rise to claims against it by its clients including Client A. These notices trigger cover under

28 Jonathan Gilman and others, *Arnould's Law of Marine Insurance and Average*, 1st supp., 18th edn (Sweet & Maxwell, London, 2016) (hereafter *Arnould*, supp. to 18th edn), para.1.4-21.

29 John Birds, Ben Lynch, Simon Milnes, *MacGillivray on Insurance Law*, 1st supp., 13th edn (Sweet & Maxwell, London, 2016), para.21-069.

30 *Post Office v Norwich Union Fire Insurance Society Ltd* [1967] 1 Lloyd's Rep 216.

31 *Versloot Dredging BV & Anor v HDI Gerling Industrie Versicherung AG & Ors (The DC Merwestone)* [2016] UKSC 45, [2016] 3 WLR 543.

32 *Arnould*, supp. to 18th edn, paras 1.4-15–17 and Mance J in *ICCI and Royal Insurance (UK) Ltd v The Royal Hotel Ltd* [1998] Lloyd's Rep IR 151 (Com Ct), [161].

the current policy. Client A eventually makes a claim against the firm for negligence in respect of a transaction. In collusion with Client A, the firm exaggerates the amount of the claim and persuades its insurers to authorise settlement of the claim. The insurers subsequently discover the fraud and elect to terminate the policy with effect from the date that the firm colluded with the client to present the exaggerated claim. The authors consider that there would be no cover under the policy for any of the notifications of circumstances given by the firm, unless claims had been brought in respect of those circumstances prior to policy termination (in which case the insurers might be liable for defence costs), or a claim had resulted in judgment or settlement prior to policy termination (in which case the insurer might be liable for the amount of the judgment or settlement).

Attribution of fraudulent intent

9.11 Although the Insurance Act provides a new scheme for determining the knowledge of the insured for purposes of the duty of fair presentation (see Chapter 4), it does not do so in relation to knowledge (or intent) in relation to a fraudulent claim. In their July 2014 Report, the Law Commissions say that in the context of post-contract fraud, 'the existing rules of attribution are relatively clear'.[33] Accordingly it is the common law which will determine whether the insured will be fixed with the knowledge or intention of the individual(s) involved in presenting or furthering the fraudulent claim. Where the insured is not a natural person, as in *Meridian Global Funds Management Asia Ltd v Securities Commission*,[34] Lord Hoffmann pointed out that the rules by which the acts and omissions of natural persons are attributed to a company depend on the proper interpretation of the policy underlying the substantive rules of law to which they relate. He said:

> The company's primary rules of attribution together with the general principles of agency, vicarious liability and so forth are usually sufficient to enable one to determine its rights and obligations. In exceptional cases, however, they will not provide an answer. This will be the case when a rule of law, either expressly or by implication, excludes attribution on the basis of the general principles of agency or vicarious liability. For example, a rule may be stated in language primarily applicable to a natural person and requires some act or state of mind on the part of that person 'himself', as opposed to his servants or agents. This is generally true of rules of criminal law, which ordinarily impose liability only for the *actus reus* and *mens rea* of the defendant himself. How is such a rule to be applied to a company?
>
> One possibility is that the court may come to the conclusion that the rule was not intended to apply to companies at all; for example, a law which created an offence for which the only penalty was community service. Another possibility is that the court might interpret the law as meaning that it could apply to a company only on the basis of its primary rules of attribution, i.e. if the act giving rise to liability was specifically authorised by a resolution of the board or an unanimous agreement of the shareholders. But there will be many cases in which neither of these solutions is satisfactory; in which the court considers that the law was intended to apply to companies and that, although it excludes ordinary vicarious liability, insistence on the primary rules of attribution would in practice defeat that intention. In such a case, the court must fashion a special rule of attribution for the particular substantive rule.

33 July 2014 Report, para.22.26.

34 *Meridian Global Funds Management Asia Ltd v Securities Commission* [1995] 2 AC 500 (PC), [1995] 3 WLR 413.

This is always a matter of interpretation: given that it was intended to apply to a company, how was it intended to apply? Whose act (or knowledge, or state of mind) was for this purpose intended to count as the act etc. of the company? One finds the answer to this question by applying the usual canons of interpretation, taking into account the language of the rule (if it is a statute) and its content and policy.

9.12 The authors suggest that in the context of section 12 Insurance Act, whether or not a claim is fraudulent will depend on the conduct of the individual insured, the senior management of a corporate insured, and any individual given authority by the insured to present and negotiate the claim with the insurer on the insured's behalf, which may include an employee of the insured or a loss adjuster.

Group insurance

9.13 Section 13 Insurance Act provides for the remedies for a fraudulent claim under so-called 'group insurance' by which the policy provides cover to persons who are not parties to the contract of insurance (and are accordingly not 'insureds' for the purposes of the Insurance Act: see paragraphs 3.5–3.7 above). If such a third-party beneficiary makes a fraudulent claim under the policy, the insurer's remedies will lie against that person, such that the claim will be forfeited and the insurer will be able to terminate the insurance for that person, but the policy will otherwise be unaffected. If money has been paid in respect of the fraudulent claim to the policyholder, it will be refundable to the insurer by the policyholder, as it would be if the fraudulent third-party beneficiary had received payment. The inclusion of specific remedies in respect of fraudulent claims by third-party beneficiaries of a group insurance raises the question why the position of such beneficiaries in relation to the duty of fair presentation was not also addressed in the Act.

CHAPTER 10

Damages for late payment

PART 5 ENTERPRISE ACT 2016
LATE PAYMENT OF INSURANCE CLAIMS

28 Insurance contracts: implied term about payment of claims

(1) After section 13 of the Insurance Act 2015 (remedies for fraudulent claims: group insurance) insert –

"PART 4A
LATE PAYMENT OF CLAIMS

13A Implied term about payment of claims

(1) It is an implied term of every contract of insurance that if the insured makes a claim under the contract, the insurer must pay any sums due in respect of the claim within a reasonable time.

(2) A reasonable time includes a reasonable time to investigate and assess the claim.

(3) What is reasonable will depend on all the relevant circumstances, but the following are examples of things which may need to be taken into account –

(a) the type of insurance,
(b) the size and complexity of the claim,
(c) compliance with any relevant statutory or regulatory rules or guidance,
(d) factors outside the insurer's control.

(4) If the insurer shows that there were reasonable grounds for disputing the claim (whether as to the amount of any sum payable, or as to whether anything at all is payable) –

(a) the insurer does not breach the term implied by subsection (1) merely by failing to pay the claim (or the affected part of it) while the dispute is continuing, but
(b) the conduct of the insurer in handling the claim may be a relevant factor in deciding whether that term was breached and, if so, when.

(5) Remedies (for example, damages) available for breach of the term implied by subsection (1) are in addition to and distinct from –

(a) any right to enforce payment of the sums due, and
(b) any right to interest on those sums (whether under the contract, under another enactment, at the court's discretion or otherwise)."

(2) In section 22 of that Act (application etc. of Parts 2 to 5), after subsection (3) insert –

"(3A) Part 4A applies only in relation to contracts of insurance entered into after that Part has come into force, and variations to such contracts."

29 Contracting out of the implied term about payment of claims

(1) After section 16 of the Insurance Act 2015 (contracting out: non-consumer contracts) insert –

"16A Contracting out of the implied term about payment of claims: consumer and non-consumer insurance contracts

(1) A term of consumer insurance contract, or of any other contract, which would put the consumer in a worse position as respects any of the matters provided for in section 13A than the consumer would be in by virtue of the provisions of that section (so far as relating to consumer insurance contracts) is to that extent of no effect.

(2) A term of a non-consumer insurance contract, or of any other contract, which would put the insured in a worse position as respects deliberate or reckless breaches of the term implied by section 13A than the insured would be in by virtue of that section is to that extent of no effect.

(3) for the purposes of subsection (2) a breach is deliberate or reckless if the insurer –

(a) knew that it was in breach, or

(b) did not care whether or not it was in breach

(4) A term of a non-consumer insurance contract, or of any other contract, which would put the insured in a worse position as respects any of the other matters provided for in section 13A than the insured would be in by virtue of the provisions of that section (so far as relating to non-consumer insurance contracts) is to that extent of no effect, unless the requirements of section 17 have been satisfied in relation to the term.

(5) In this section references to a contract include a variation.

(6) This section does not apply in relation to a contract for the settlement of a claim arising under an insurance contract."

(2) In section 17(1) of that Act (the transparency requirements), after "16(2)" insert "or 16A(4)".

30 Additional time limit for actions for damages for late payment of insurance claims
After section 5 of the Limitation Act 1980 insert –

"5A Additional time limit for actions for damages for late payment of insurance claims

(1) An action in respect of breach of the term implied into a contract of insurance by section 13A of the Insurance Act 2015 (late payment of claims) may not be brought after the expiration of one year from the date on which the insurer has paid all the sums referred to in subsection (1) of that section.

(2) Any payment which extinguishes an insurer's liability to pay a sum referred to in section 13A of the Insurance Act 2015 is to be treated for the purposes of this section as payment of that sum."

The insurer's liability for late payment of a claim

10.1 It is an established principle of English law that 'there is no such thing as a cause of action in damages for late payment of damages'.[1] A contracting party may, however, be entitled to recover damages for late payment of a debt due under a contract, subject to the ordinary principles of remoteness and mitigation.[2] Prior to the Enterprise Act 2016, whether an insurer could be held liable in damages for late payment of a claim accordingly turned on the question whether a claim under an insurance contract was one for unliquidated damages for breach of contract or one for liquidated damages. Again, as a matter of established principle, 'a contract of

1 *President of India v Lips Maritime* [1998] AC 395 (HL), [425] (Lord Brandon).

2 *Sempra Metals Ltd v Inland Revenue Commissioners* [2007] UKHL 34, [2008] 1 AC 561 and *Equitas Ltd v Walsham Brothers & Co Ltd* [2013] EWHC 3264 (Comm), [2014] Lloyd's Rep IR 398.

indemnity gives rise to an action for unliquidated damages, arising from the failure of the indemnifier to prevent the indemnified person from suffering damage, for example, by having to pay a third party'.[3] A contract of insurance is an archetypal contract of indemnity and is accordingly subject to the legal fiction that an insurer is in breach of contract if it fails to prevent the insured from suffering harm, and the insured's claim is one in unliquidated damages for that breach. There is accordingly no basis on which the insured could claim damages for late payment of those damages absent a term to the contrary in the contract of insurance.[4] In their July 2014 Report, the Law Commissions said that this rule had not been followed in other common law jurisdictions, or in Scotland,[5] that it was unprincipled and unfair, and should be reformed.[6]

10.2 Rather than abrogate the principle that a contract of insurance is a contract of indemnity by which the insurer undertakes to prevent the insured from suffering harm, the Law Commissions determined that the appropriate way to reform the law was to provide that the contract should contain an implied term that the insurer would pay sums due within a reasonable time.[7] A clause to this effect was included in the draft Insurance Contracts Bill appended to the July 2014 Report. The clause was removed from the Bill that was introduced in the House of Lords, but amendments were moved to reinstate it at the proceedings of the Special Public Bill Committee on 15 December 2014. Concerns were expressed that the proposed clause might encourage speculative litigation, or be used to exert undue pressure to expedite settlement of claims.[8] As the procedure used to introduce the Bill was that reserved for legislation recommended by the Law Commission, there is a requirement that such proposed legislation should not be controversial. The Government was of the view that the proposed clause was controversial and accordingly it was not included in the Insurance Bill that eventually became law.[9] The Government did, however, support the policy behind the late payment provision, and took the opportunity to include the relevant clauses in the Enterprise Bill introduced in 2015, which received Royal Assent as the Enterprise Act on 4 May 2016. It came into force in respect of contracts of insurance (and reinsurance) entered into on or after 4 May 2017.[10]

Part 5 Enterprise Act 2016

10.3 Part 5 of the Enterprise Act introduced new sections into the Insurance Act and those section numbers will be used when discussing the new law. Section 13A(1) Insurance Act sets out the term that is implied into all contracts of insurance (and reinsurance) entered into on or after 4 May 2017: if the insured makes a claim under

3 *Firma C-Trade SA v Newcastle P&I Assn. The Fanti & Padre Island* [1991] 2 AC 1 (HL) 35 (Lord Goff).

4 *Sprung v Royal Insurance (UK) Ltd* [1999] Lloyd's Rep IR 111 (CA); *Ventouris v Mountain (The Italia Express) (No 3)* [1992] 2 Lloyd's Rep 281 (Com Ct) (Hirst J), [292].

5 July 2014 Report, para.25.31.

6 July 2014 Report, para.25.32.

7 July 2014 Report, para.27.2.

8 House of Lords Special Public Bill Committee, *Insurance Bill* (HL), 15 December 2014, Lord Newby, [123].

9 Special Public Bill Committee, *Insurance Bill* (HL), 15 December 2014, Lord Newby, [124]–[125].

10 Enterprise Act 2016, s.44(3).

the insurance contract, the insurer must pay any sums due within a reasonable time. The implied term applies only to sums due under the contract. It does not affect the insurer's duties to the insured in handling the claim unless and until the claim is for payment of a monetary amount. Accordingly, the liability insurer's duties in handling claims made against the insured remain unaffected until the point at which the insured pays or is liable to pay the third party's claim (as a consequence of settlement, judgment or award[11]).

A 'reasonable time'

10.4 Once an amount becomes payable by the insurer in respect of a claim, in accordance with the implied term, it has a 'reasonable time' within which to make payment. Section 13A(2)–(4) sets out some guidance as to what constitutes a reasonable time, but it is not exhaustive, and each case will turn on its own facts. Clearly an amount may become payable by the insurer before the insurer is aware that an amount is payable. As set out in paragraph 10.1 above, an insurer may be liable to pay a claim immediately the event causing loss has occurred, but an insurer will not be in a position to pay that claim until it has had the opportunity to investigate and assess the claim. Section 13A(2) recognises that a reasonable time must include the time taken to do that, provided the time taken is reasonable.

10.5 Section 13A(3) sets out examples of things that may need to be taken into account in assessing whether the time taken by the insurer is reasonable. The type of insurance and the size and complexity of the claim are two such things.[12] In *Brit v F&B Trenchless*,[13] there was an issue as to whether the insurer had waived its right to avoid the policy for non-disclosure by taking four to five months to determine whether or not it had evidence that would support an avoidance case. The court considered it was reasonable for an insurer to take four to five months to investigate and determine its position on coverage for a complex construction claim. Whilst this case does not concern the Insurance Act, it may provide some guidance on what a court might consider to be a reasonable time to investigate and assess a complex claim. In *Gentry v Miller*,[14] the judge thought that a period of two months over Christmas was a reasonable time to investigate a motor claim involving personal injury. Factors outside the insurer's control are also matters to take into account:[15] those would include lack of cooperation by the insured, or the imposition of trade sanctions by the authorities that might make the payment of an insurance claim illegal.

10.6 A further matter which section13A(3) provides should be taken into account is 'compliance with any relevant statutory or regulatory rules or guidance'. This implicitly recognises that insurers and their agents are subject to regulatory oversight of their claims-handling practices and processes.[16] Failure to comply with regulatory

11 *Post Office v Norwich Union Fire Insurance Society Ltd* [1967] 1 Lloyd's Rep 216.
12 Insurance Act 2015, s.13A(3)(a) and s.13A (3)(b).
13 [2015] EWHC 2237 (Comm), [2016] Lloyd's Rep IR 69.
14 [2016] EWCA Civ 141, [2016] 1 WLR 2696.
15 Insurance Act 2015, s.13A(3)(d).
16 This was one of the reasons why it was thought that the introduction of the implied term was unnecessary as insurers were already under statutory obligations to handle claims fairly.

rules may result in disciplinary action being taken by the regulator (the Financial Conduct Authority (FCA) in the UK), but is also a matter which may affect the court's view of whether the insurer has taken a reasonable time to pay a claim. The 'relevant statutory or regulatory rules or guidance' is not limited to the legislative or regulatory requirements of the UK and will include whatever legislation or rules may apply to the insurer in the particular jurisdiction. In the UK, the following statutory or regulatory rules or guidance are likely to be relevant.

FCA Principles for Business[17]

A firm must:

- conduct its business with due skill, care and diligence (Principle 2);
- observe proper standards of market conduct (Principle 5);
- pay due regard to the interests of its customers and treat them fairly (Principle 6);
- pay due regard to the information needs of its clients, and communicate information to them in a way which is clear, fair and not misleading (Principle 7).

Insurance Conduct of Business Sourcebook (ICOBS) Chapter 8[18]

An insurer must:

- handle claims promptly and fairly (ICOBS 8.1.1(1));
- provide reasonable guidance to help a policyholder make a claim (ICOBS 8.1.1(2));
- provide appropriate information on the progress of the claim (ICOBS 8.1.1(2));
- not unreasonably reject a claim (including by terminating or avoiding the policy) (ICOBS 8.1.1(3));
- settle claims promptly once terms are agreed (ICOBS 8.1.1(4)).

Lloyd's Minimum Standards for Conduct Risk (MS 11)[19]

Lloyd's syndicates must:

- pay due regard to the interests of Lloyd's customers and treat them fairly at all times (CR 1.1);
- properly assess the complexity of the insurance product they are offering (CR 5.3);
- ensure that the product can be properly serviced (CR 7.9);
- ensure that claims are handled fairly (CR 11);
- ensure that complaints are handled fairly (CR 12).

Lloyd's Minimum Standards 2 – Claims Management[20]

Lloyd's syndicates must:

- have a claims management philosophy by which there is effective claims management ensuring that claims are adjusted on their merits (CLM 1.1);

17 FCA 'Principles for Business' (30 March 2016).
18 FCA 'ICOBS Insurance: Conduct of Business Sourcebook' (Release 11, November 2016).
19 Lloyd's 'Minimum Standards MS11 – Conduct Risk' (July 2014).
20 Lloyd's 'Minimum Standards MS2 Claims Management' (July 2014).

- ensure there is performance and resource management so that performance is measured against key indicators, staff are properly trained and sufficient resource is available to handle claims properly (CLM 2.2 and CLM 3.2);
- have clear processes and procedures for the handling of claims (CLM 4.1);
- ensure that claims managed on behalf of the syndicates by third parties are handled in accordance with the Claims Management principles applicable to the syndicates (CLM 6.1).

10.7 Whilst it is impossible to provide an exhaustive list of other factors which may be relevant in deciding whether an insurer has breached the implied term, the following is a list of factors which may be relevant, depending upon the facts and circumstances of each case:

- The time of year. If part of the claims handling process takes place at a time when large numbers of staff are either absent from work or particularly busy (such as Christmas), payment of the claim might reasonably take longer than at other times. However, an insurer's regulatory obligation to ensure that the handling of claims is properly resourced will be a factor in assessing whether the time taken was reasonable (see paragraph 10.6 above).
- The occurrence of other losses. If there is a loss-causing event which affects a large number of policyholders simultaneously, such as flooding or other natural disasters, an insurer may come under intense pressure to handle a large number of claims. In those circumstances, it is expected that the length of time considered reasonable for payment of claims will be longer.[21] However, the insurer may be expected to take reasonable steps to ensure that if there is a sudden high volume of claims, it has adequate measures in place to handle those claims within a reasonable time.
- The non-availability of relevant staff. If one or more of the insurer's claims-handling staff with responsibility for the claim are absent for a prolonged period, it may be reasonable to expect that the claims handling process will be delayed. However, if the insurer fails to take reasonable steps to ensure that contingency plans are in place for handling claims in the absence of key individuals, this could be a relevant factor in showing that the implied term was breached.
- The difficulty of investigating the loss. If the loss has taken place in circumstances which make it difficult to investigate and assess, the process will reasonably take longer. For example, if the loss occurs in a distant or remote location, it will take longer for the insurer to investigate.[22] Similarly, if the site of the loss has been secured due to risks of contamination, or because of an investigation by the police, it will be difficult or impossible for the insurer to investigate until the restrictions are lifted.
- Suspicion of fraud. If the insurer has reasonable grounds to suspect that the insured has committed fraud, either in the course of the risk presentation or

21 July 2014 Report, para.28.38.
22 Explanatory Notes to the Enterprise Act 2016, para.266.

in making the claim, it is reasonable to expect that the insurer should take more time to investigate the matter fully.[23]

Reasonable grounds for disputing a claim

10.8 If the insurer has reasonable grounds for disputing the claim (whether over liability or quantum), the insurer will not breach the implied term by failing to make payment of that part of the claim that is disputed while the dispute is continuing.[24] This is not intended to be an onerous requirement,[25] and clearly it is not necessary for the insurer to be successful in its dispute (since there would be no claim to pay in that circumstance). However, the availability to the insurer of the defence that it had reasonable grounds for disputing the claim is qualified by section 13A(4)(b) Insurance Act which provides that the conduct of the insurer in handling the claim may be a relevant factor in determining whether the insurer is in breach of the implied term, presumably even though the insurer had reasonable grounds for disputing the claim. Thus a court may take account of the insurer's behaviour towards the insured, including by reference to statutory or regulatory rules or guidance, including those set out in paragraph 10.6 above.

10.9 Whether there are reasonable grounds for disputing a claim is a matter of objective assessment of the arguments advanced by the insurer by reference to the available facts. Ultimately this will be a matter for the court or tribunal that is asked to determine whether or nor not the insurer is liable for the claim and, if it is, whether there were reasonable grounds for contesting liability. As the insurer will usually have received legal advice on the merits of the insured's claim, the court or tribunal will in effect be determining whether that advice was correct when addressing the question whether or not the insurer is liable for the claim. This can be done without sight of the advice actually given, but if the advice was wrong and effectively found to have been negligent (because it was not reasonable), it may still be open to the insurer to argue that it had reasonable grounds for disputing the claim because it had reasonably acted on the advice of its legal advisers, albeit the advice was wrong. If it is to take that course, it seems to be unavoidable that the insurer will have to produce the legal advice on which it relied to establish that it was advised that there was a defence to the claim, and did not appreciate that the advice was wrong. If the insurer elects to disclose the effect of privileged legal advice, there is a risk that it will thereby waive privilege in that advice, and therefore be required to disclose the content of the entire advice.[26] In order to safeguard against this risk, it is necessary that the disclosure of the effect of the advice is done on terms which are carefully drawn.[27] To ensure that the insurer can rely on the effect of its legal advice without waiving privilege, the LMA has suggested the following Model Clause for insertion in the policy:

23 July 2014 Report, para.28.46.
24 Insurance Act 2015, s.13A(4)(a).
25 July 2014 Report, para.28.85.
26 *Mid-East Sales Limited v United Engineering & Trading Company Limited* [2014] EWHC 892 (Comm).
27 *B v Auckland District Law Society* [2003] UKPC 38, [2003] 2 AC 736.

The Insurer is entitled to give evidence that it obtained legal advice that there were reasonable grounds for disputing any claim under this insurance contract, for the purposes of section 13A(4) Insurance Act 2015. If it does so:

(a) the Insurer will not thereby waive privilege in the content of that legal advice to any person;
(b) the existence of the advice shall be not be disclosed by any person for any purpose other than showing that the Insurer had reasonable grounds for disputing a claim under this insurance contract; and,
(c) the insured and the insurer shall at all times preserve confidence in the existence of the advice.[28]

10.10 One of the concerns about the new implied term is that the insured's claim that it has been breached is likely to be brought at the same time as the insured's action for payment of the claim in dispute. It would obviously be unfortunate for the insurer if it produces privileged legal advice concerning the merits of the underlying claim in defending the claim for late payment, and that advice is considered at the same trial at which the underlying claim is adjudicated. It will be a matter for careful case management to avoid the risk of prejudice in these circumstances, but also to ensure that the conduct of the litigation is proportionate and cost efficient.

Remedies

10.11 The insurer's obligation to pay a claim within a reasonable time arises out of a term implied into the contract of insurance. Any breach of the term accordingly gives rise to a claim for breach of contract, which will usually mean a claim in damages. Section 13A(5) Insurance Act confirms that the claim for breach of the implied term is in addition to any right to enforce payment of the claim and any right to interest that arises under a term of the contract, any other enactment, or at the court's discretion (which would include an arbitration tribunal's discretion to award interest, including compound interest, on a claim[29]). Where a court or tribunal exercises its discretion to award interest to the claimant, it is to be assumed that the claimant will not be entitled to recover interest twice by pursuing a claim for late payment based on breach of the implied term by the insurer.

10.12 As the duty to pay a claim within a reasonable time is a contractual one, whether or not the insurer is under a liability to pay a claim for late payment damages will depend on the usual rules applicable to the payment of damages for breach of contract.[30] The insured will have to establish that its damages were caused by the late payment and that it mitigated its loss. Of particular importance will be whether the losses that occurred were reasonably foreseeable at the time the insurance contract was entered into. A party may recover damages for breach of contract only if they may fairly and reasonably be said to have arisen naturally ('according to the normal course of things') or from special circumstances communicated at the time the contract was entered into (per *Hadley v Baxendale*[31]). While it would be reasonably foreseeable that

28 LMA Model Clause 5279, 12 October 2016.
29 Pursuant to Arbitration Act 1996, s.49(3).
30 Acknowledged by the Law Commissions in the July 2014 Report, para.26.37.
31 (1854) 9 341, 156 ER 145.

the insured would suffer a loss of interest on the amounts claimed if they were not paid on time,[32] it would be more difficult for an insured to show that, say, its insolvency was the reasonably foreseeable consequence of a breach at the time the insurance was concluded.

10.13 The requirement for foreseeability can be illustrated by the case of *Sprung v Royal Insurance (UK) Ltd*.[33] In that case, Mr Sprung owned a factory, which was insured against 'sudden and unforeseen damage'. Vandals broke in, causing severe damage which put the factory out of use. The insurer refused to pay the claim, on the basis that it was not covered under the policy. The insured was unable to raise a loan to repair the factory, and went out of business, suffering additional losses of £75,000 (which was the amount he could have obtained had he been able to sell his business). Four years later, the insurer abandoned its coverage defence, and paid the insurance claim. Under the old law, the insured was unable to recover damages for his consequential loss (i.e. the additional £75,000), because they amounted to damages for late payment of damages (see paragraph 10.1 above). Under section 13A of the Insurance Act, the insured could in theory recover this additional loss as damages. It is, however, arguable that the insured in *Sprung* would not have been assisted by the implied term. That is because the cause of the insured's consequential loss was his own decision not to reinstate the factory, itself a product of the insured's weak financial position, and his inability to raise a loan. It is now likely that, in a tort claim, the insured's impecuniosity does not break the chain of causation,[34] though this is not necessarily the position in contract.[35] In other words, the implied term might not have made any difference to Mr Sprung, since his claim may have foundered on causation.

10.14 In light of these limitations on recoverable loss for breach of contract, it is likely that even if the insured can establish breach of the implied term by the insurer, its recoverable damages will usually be limited to compound interest on the claim from the date when it would have been reasonable to make payment to the date of

32 A claim for compound interest reflects the cost of borrowing where a debt has not been paid on time and may now be regarded as an established head of recoverable damages for late payment of a debt: *Equitas v Walsham Brothers & Co Ltd* [2014] EWHC 3264 (Comm), [2014] Lloyd's Rep IR 398 (Males J), [123(ii)]–[123(iii)].

33 [1999] 1 Lloyd's Rep IR 111 (CA).

34 *Lagden v O'Connor* [2003] UKHL 64, [2004] 1 AC 1067.

35 The issue of remoteness of damages in tort is key to the decision in *Lagden v O'Connor*, ibid. In this case, an innocent party was involved in a car accident. As a result of their impecuniosity, they were unable to hire a car through a hire company and instead had to rely on a credit hire company, at a higher cost. The question at hand was whether the victim was entitled to recover the full costs of the credit hire company (the only option available to them), or only the lower costs they would have incurred through a regular hire company (an option unavailable to them). The test of remoteness is set out in *Overseas Tankship (UK) Ltd v Morts Dock and Engineering Co Ltd (The Wagon Mound No 1)* [1961] AC 388 (PC). The question is whether the kind of damage suffered was reasonably foreseeable by the defendant at the time of the breach of duty. If it was, the damages are not too remote, and the defendant will be liable. *Heron II Koufos v C Czarnikow Ltd (The Heron II)* [1969] 1 AC 350 (HL) expanded on this, stating that the defendant will be liable 'for any type of damage which is reasonably foreseeable as liable to happen even in the most unusual case unless the risk is so small that a reasonable man would in the whole circumstances feel justified in neglecting it'. Additionally, as long as the kind of damage is reasonably foreseeable, it does not matter if the manner of infliction or its extent was unforeseeable (*Vacwell Engineering Co Ltd v BDH Chemicals Ltd* [1971] 1 QB 88 (QB)). Damages for breach of contract are recoverable in respect of losses 'such as may fairly and reasonably be considered either arising naturally, i.e. according to the usual course of things, from such breach of contract itself, or such as may reasonably be supposed to have been in the contemplation of both parties at the time they made the contract, as the probable result of the breach of it'. (*Hadley v Baxendale* [1854] 9 Ex 341, 156 ER 145).

actual payment of the claim.[36] To recover damages other than for loss of interest, the insured is probably going to have to show that at the time of underwriting, the insurer was aware of special circumstances such that it could be contemplated that delay in settlement of a claim could result in the damages suffered by the insured. Such special circumstances could include the size of the insured's business (a small business is likely to find it more difficult to raise finance if a significant insured asset is lost, which may have an impact upon the ability of the insured to replace the asset and continue in business) or the fact that the insured owns only the insured asset, such that the loss of that asset will prevent the insured from continuing in business (for example a one-ship company which is not in a position to replace the vessel that is its only asset if she is lost). The damages suffered by the insureds in these circumstances are similar to those insured by a business interruption policy where cover is provided for the loss of business resulting from physical loss or damage to the insured's property.

Reinsurance

10.15 The introduction of the implied term gives rise to particular issues for reinsurance contracts. The term is implied into contracts of reinsurance and accordingly the reinsurer may be liable in damages to the reinsured for late payment of a reinsurance claim, although establishing the foreseeability of losses beyond compound interest may be particularly challenging (see paragraph 10.14 above). The implication of the term into underlying contracts of insurance does, however, give rise to questions about the liability of the reinsurer to indemnify the reinsured in respect of damages paid by the reinsured for late payment both generally and where the reinsurer's conduct has resulted in the late payment.

10.16 A typical reinsurance contract will provide for the indemnification by the reinsurer of the reinsured in respect of a loss falling within the terms and conditions of the reinsured's policies.[37] As the reinsured's liability for damages for late payment arises out of an implied term in the underlying policies, any reinsurance that reinsures the reinsured's liability under those policies is likely to provide cover for such damages, subject to any excess and limits of the reinsurance. If the reinsurance provides cover for losses arising out of an event, there may be an issue as to whether the reinsured's liability for damages for late payment of a claim arises out of that event depending on the particular terms of the reinsurance contract.

10.17 Some reinsurance contracts provide that the reinsurer has control over the reinsured's handling and settlement of underlying claims. In *Eagle Star Insurance Co Ltd v JN Cresswell*,[38] the Court of Appeal considered a claims cooperation clause in

36 *Equitas Ltd v Walsham Brothers* [2014] EWHC 3264 (Comm), [2014] Lloyd's Rep IR 398, [123(ii)]–[123(iii)] (Males J).

37 For example:

The Reinsurer shall indemnify the Reinsured in respect of any loss and interest which falls within the terms and conditions of the original policy.

The reinsurers hereon shall reimburse the reassured to the extent that its net loss under business reinsured by this contract exceeds the reassured's retention … 'Loss' means loss, damages, liability or expense or a series thereof arising from one event.

38 [2004] EWCA Civ 602, [2004] Lloyd's Rep IR 573.

the following terms and held that compliance with the second sentence was a condition precedent to the reinsurer's liability in respect of any claim whose negotiation and settlement they did not control:

> [The Reinsurers] shall control the negotiations and settlements of any claims under this Policy. In the event [the Reinsurers] hereon will not be liable to pay any claim not controlled as set out above.

10.18 In *Gan Insurance Company v Tai Ping Insurance Company (Nos 2 and 3)*,[39] the Court of Appeal rejected the suggestion that the reinsurer had to act reasonably in its control of the underlying claim where that was not a requirement of the claims control clause, although Mance LJ said:

> I would therefore accept as a general qualification, that any withholding of approval by reinsurers should take place in good faith after consideration of and on the basis of the facts giving rise to the particular claim and not with reference to considerations wholly extraneous to the subject-matter of the particular reinsurance.[40]
>
> If there is any further implication, it is along the lines that the reinsurer will not withhold approval arbitrarily, or (to use what I see as no more than an expanded expression of the same concept) will not do so in circumstances so extreme that no reasonable company in its position could possibly withhold approval. This will not ordinarily add materially to the requirement that the reinsurer should form a genuine view as to the appropriateness of settlement or compromise without taking into account considerations extraneous to the subject-matter of the reinsurance.[41]

10.19 In light of these decisions it is accordingly quite possible that a reinsured may be held liable to pay damages for late payment of a claim where the late payment has resulted from decisions made in good faith by the reinsurer in the handling of the claim. It is unlikely that the reinsurer's conduct of the claim in these circumstances would be a 'factor outside the insurer's control' so as to excuse the delay in paying.[42] The reinsurer might be liable to indemnify the reinsured in respect of those damages under a standard reinsuring clause, but subject to the excess and limits of the reinsurance (see paragraph 10.16 above).[43] It may also be argued that the damages for late payment are an incident of the costs of defending the insured's claim for coverage, and ought therefore to be paid by the reinsurer if it is liable for such costs under the reinsurance.

Limitation period

10.20 Breach of the implied term by the insurer to pay a claim within a reasonable time gives rise to a cause of action that is independent of the insured's cause of action for payment of the claim itself. Accordingly, time within which to bring proceedings in respect of the breach of the implied term does not depend on the limitation period applicable to the underlying claim, but would ordinarily start to run from the point at which the underlying claim should have been paid had the insurer complied with

39 [2001] EWCA Civ 1047, [2001] Lloyd's Rep IR 667.
40 Ibid., [67].
41 Ibid., [73].
42 Insurance Act 2015, s.13A(3)(d): see para.10.5 above.
43 LMA Model Clause 5283, 12 October 2016, expressly provides that the reinsurer should indemnify the reinsured in full in these circumstances.

the implied term. If the usual six-year limitation period for the bringing of a claim for breach of contract were to apply, this would extend significantly the period during which an insurer might have to reserve for the financial consequences of the underlying claim. Section 30 Enterprise Act amends the Limitation Act 2016 by providing that the time limit for actions for damages for breach of the implied term may not be brought more than one year after the insurer's liability to pay all of the sums due in respect of the underlying claim has been extinguished (which would usually be by way of payment of the underlying claim by the insurer).[44] Although unlikely to arise in practice, the claim for breach of the implied term would, however, become time-barred if proceedings in respect of the breach were not commenced within six years of the date when the insurer should have paid the underlying claim, even if the underlying claim was actually paid less than one year before proceedings were commenced.

Contracting out

10.21 The provisions of section 16A Insurance Act concerning contracting out of the implied term are considered in Chapter 8.

44 Limitation Act 1980, s.5A.

CHAPTER 11

Utmost good faith

14 Good faith

(1) Any rule of law permitting a party to a contract of insurance to avoid the contract on the ground that the utmost good faith has not been observed by the other party is abolished.

(2) Any rule of law to the effect that a contract of insurance is a contract based on the utmost good faith is modified to the extent required by the provisions of this Act and the Consumer Insurance (Disclosure and Representations) Act 2012.

(3) Accordingly –

(a) in section 17 of the Marine Insurance Act 1906 (marine insurance contracts are contracts of the utmost good faith), the words from ", and" to the end are omitted, and

(b) the application of that section (as so amended) is subject to the provisions of this Act and the Consumer Insurance (Disclosure and Representations) Act 2012.

(4) In section 2 of the Consumer Insurance (Disclosure and Representations) Act 2012 (disclosure and representations before contract or variation), subsection (5) is omitted.

11.1 Section 17 Marine Insurance Act codified the common law and provided that a contract of insurance is a contract of the utmost good faith. It further provided that '… if the utmost good faith be not observed by either party, the contract may be avoided by the other party'.[1] This draconian remedy had been the source of much of the concern over the old law which resulted in law reform through the Insurance Act. The obligation on the insured to disclose material information, which is one facet of the duty of utmost good faith, has been retained in the duty of fair presentation, but the scope of that duty is now to be found in section 3 of the Insurance Act.[2] The remedy of avoidance for breach of the duty of utmost good faith at the time of underwriting the contract of insurance has been replaced by the proportionate remedies set out in Schedule 1 of the Insurance Act.[3] The considerable doubt that surrounded the application of the remedy of avoidance to post-contractual breaches of the duty of utmost good faith[4] has been clarified, at least in relation to fraudulent claims, by section 12 Insurance Act.[5]

---

1 Marine Insurance Act, s,17.

2 See Chapter 3, above.

3 See Chapter 5, above.

4 *Manifest Shipping Co Ltd v Uni-Polaris Shipping Co Ltd (The Star Sea)* [2001] UKHL 1, [2003] 1 AC 469 [62].

5 See Chapter 9, above.

11.2 These changes to the duty of utmost good faith are reflected in section 14 Insurance Act. Section 14(1) provides that the remedy of avoidance for breach of the utmost good faith is abolished and the relevant part of section 17 Marine Insurance Act quoted in paragraph 11.1 above is omitted by section 14(3)(a) Insurance Act. However, the rule of law that a contract of insurance is one of utmost good faith remains in place, save as modified by CIDRA 2012 and the Insurance Act.[6] There is, however, no longer a statutory remedy for breach of the duty of utmost good faith beyond the remedies set out in CIDRA 2012 and the Insurance Act. This gives rise to a number of issues.

No remedy for insurer's breach

11.3 Under the old law, as the duty of utmost good faith was (and remains) reciprocal, an insured was entitled to avoid the insurance contract for breach of the duty of good faith by the insurer. However, avoidance was the insured's only remedy,[7] and in most circumstances it was unlikely that the insured would want to avoid the insurance contract and recover its premium for breach of the duty of utmost good faith by the insurer, if the insured had a claim under the contract. In considering whether to provide the insured with a remedy for the insurer's breach of duty of good faith, the Law Commissions gave the example of an insurer knowingly selling a worthless policy,[8] but accepted representations that this would best be dealt with by regulators (or the Financial Ombudsman Service, in the case of consumers) rather than by giving the insured a remedy for the insurer's breach of duty.[9] Accordingly, the remedy of avoidance for breach of the duty of good faith by the insurer is no longer available to the insured.

11.4 The Law Commissions suggested that the courts might revisit the question of a remedy in damages for breach of duty of utmost good faith by the insurer, particularly in an extreme case,[10] but this seems unlikely given the clear position of the House of Lords in *Banque Financiere de la Cité*[11] that damages are not an available remedy. Where the insurer's breach of the duty of utmost good faith consists of a misrepresentation to the putative insured, the latter's remedy may be one for damages or rescission under the Misrepresentation Act 1967, or for deceit.[12]

Tool of interpretation

11.5 The Law Commissions recognised the importance of the status of an insurance contract as one of the utmost good faith when interpreting the contract and applying the remedies in the Insurance Act.[13] They gave the example of an intentional decision by the insured to disclose only the bare minimum of information on placing

6 Insurance Act, s.14(2).
7 *Banque Financiere de la Cité v Westgate Insurance* [1991] 2 AC 249.
8 July 2014 Report, para.30.33.
9 Ibid., para.30.34.
10 Ibid., para.30.53.
11 *Banque Financiere de la Cité v Westgate Insurance* [1991] 2 AC 249.
12 See paras 5.28 and 5.29 above.
13 July 2014 Report, para.30.23.

in the hope that the insurer would fail to ask questions. To the extent that the insured had not acted in good faith, the Law Commissions thought that the presentation would not be fair.[14] For the reasons given in paragraph 3.36(ii) above, this may not necessarily be the right approach since it would only apply where breach of the duty of good faith was fraudulent, rather than innocent or negligent, and there seems to be no basis in the Insurance Act for drawing that distinction. A better example may be the application of the duty of good faith to the insurer's conduct when dealing with a breach of the duty of fair presentation by the insured.[15]

11.6 The fact that the contract is one of utmost good faith is likely to be relevant to the interpretation of the terms of the contract. In *Gan Insurance Company Ltd v Tai Ping Insurance Company Ltd (Nos 2 and 3)*,[16] the Court of Appeal considered a claims cooperation clause in a contract of reinsurance where the reinsurer's approval of a settlement was a condition precedent to its liability for that settlement. Mance LJ accepted that, as a general qualification, any withholding of approval by the reinsurer 'should take place in good faith after consideration of and on the basis of the facts giving rise to the particular claim and not with reference to considerations wholly extraneous to the subject-matter of the particular reinsurance'.[17] The Law Commissions thought that good faith would provide a background when considering whether it was necessary to imply a term into an insurance contract[18] and might provide judicial flexibility to deal with a particularly hard case.[19]

Remedies for post-contractual breach

11.7 In *The Mercandian Continent*[20] Longmore LJ listed various situations in which it was said that the duty of good faith might arise post-contract.[21] They included where the contract is varied and where a fraudulent claim is made, both of which are addressed expressly by the Insurance Act.[22] The remaining matters largely concerned the performance of the contract, including the provision of information to the insurer and the insurer's right to cancel. Any doubt about whether the insurer has a right to avoid the contract for any breach of the insured's duty of good faith in respect of its performance of the contract has been removed by section 14(1) Insurance Act. Any remedy for breach will depend on the ordinary rules of contract law, allowing for the special status of warranties in insurance law[23] and the effect of the duty of good faith on the interpretation of the contract.[24]

14 Ibid., para.30.23(1).

15 See *Drake Insurance plc v Provident Insurance plc* [2003] EWCA Civ 1834, [2004] 1 Lloyd's Rep 268 and para.5.10 above.

16 [2001] Lloyd's Rep IR 667.

17 Ibid., [67].

18 July 2014 Report, para.30.24(2) and paras 30.57–30.60.

19 Ibid., para.30.24(3).

20 *K/S Merc-Scandia XXXXII v Certain Lloyd's Underwriters* [2001] EWCA Civ 1275, [2001] 2 Lloyd's Rep 563.

21 Ibid., [22].

22 By Part 2 of Schedule 1 in respect of variations (see paras 5.30–5.38 above) and by s.12 in respect of fraudulent claims (see Chapter 9).

23 See Chapter 6 above.

24 See para.11.6 above.

APPENDIX

Insurance Act 2015 c. 4

An Act to make new provision about insurance contracts; to amend the Third Parties (Rights against Insurers) Act 2010 in relation to the insured persons to whom that Act applies; and for connected purposes. [12th February 2015]

BE IT ENACTED by the Queen's most Excellent Majesty, by and with the advice and consent of the Lords Spiritual and Temporal, and Commons, in this present Parliament assembled, and by the authority of the same, as follows: –

Part 1

Insurance contracts: main definitions

1 Insurance contracts: main definitions

In this Act (apart from Part 6)—

"consumer insurance contract" has the same meaning as in the Consumer Insurance (Disclosure and Representations) Act 2012;

"non-consumer insurance contract" means a contract of insurance that is not a consumer insurance contract;

"insured" means the party to a contract of insurance who is the insured under the contract, or would be if the contract were entered into;

"insurer" means the party to a contract of insurance who is the insurer under the contract, or would be if the contract were entered into;

"the duty of fair presentation" means the duty imposed by section 3(1).

Part 2

The duty of fair presentation

2 Application and interpretation

(1) This Part applies to non-consumer insurance contracts only.

(2) Part applies in relation to variations of non-consumer insurance contracts as it applies to contracts, but—

(a) references to the risk are to be read as references to changes in the risk relevant to the proposed variation, and

(b) references to the contract of insurance are to the variation.

3 The duty of fair presentation

(1) Before a contract of insurance is entered into, the insured must make to the insurer a fair presentation of the risk.

(2) The duty imposed by subsection (1) is referred to in this Act as *"the duty of fair presentation"*.

(3) A fair presentation of the risk is one—

(a) which makes the disclosure required by subsection (4),

(b) which makes that disclosure in a manner which would be reasonably clear and accessible to a prudent insurer, and

(c) in which every material representation as to a matter of fact is substantially correct, and every material representation as to a matter of expectation or belief is made in good faith.

(4) The disclosure required is as follows, except as provided in subsection (5)—

(a) disclosure of every material circumstance which the insured knows or ought to know, or

(b) failing that, disclosure which gives the insurer sufficient information to put a prudent insurer on notice that it needs to make further enquiries for the purpose of revealing those material circumstances.

(5) In the absence of enquiry, subsection (4) does not require the insured to disclose a circumstance if—

(a) it diminishes the risk,

(b) the insurer knows it,

(c) the insurer ought to know it,

(d) the insurer is presumed to know it, or

(e) it is something as to which the insurer waives information.

(6) Sections 4 to 6 make further provision about the knowledge of the insured and of the insurer, and section 7 contains supplementary provision.

4 Knowledge of insured

(1) This section provides for what an insured knows or ought to know for the purposes of section 3(4)(a).

(2) An insured who is an individual knows only—

(a) what is known to the individual, and

(b) what is known to one or more of the individuals who are responsible for the insured's insurance.

(3) An insured who is not an individual knows only what is known to one or more of the individuals who are—

(a) part of the insured's senior management, or

(b) responsible for the insured's insurance.

(4) An insured is not by virtue of subsection (2)(b) or (3)(b) taken to know confidential information known to an individual if—

(a) the individual is, or is an employee of, the insured's agent; and

(b) the information was acquired by the insured's agent (or by an employee of that agent) through a business relationship with a person who is not connected with the contract of insurance.

(5) For the purposes of subsection (4) the persons connected with a contract of insurance are—

(a) the insured and any other persons for whom cover is provided by the contract, and

(b) if the contract re-insures risks covered by another contract, the persons who are (by virtue of this subsection) connected with that other contract.

(6) Whether an individual or not, an insured ought to know what should reasonably have been revealed by a reasonable search of information available to the insured (whether the search is conducted by making enquiries or by any other means).

(7) In subsection (6) *"information"* includes information held within the insured's organisation or by any other person (such as the insured's agent or a person for whom cover is provided by the contract of insurance).

(8) For the purposes of this section—

(a) *"employee"*, in relation to the insured's agent, includes any individual working for the agent, whatever the capacity in which the individual acts,

(b) an individual is responsible for the insured's insurance if the individual participates on behalf of the insured in the process of procuring the insured's insurance (whether the individual does so as the insured's employee or agent, as an employee of the insured's agent or in any other capacity), and

(c) *"senior management"* means those individuals who play significant roles in the making of decisions about how the insured's activities are to be managed or organised.

5 Knowledge of insurer

(1) For the purposes of section 3(5)(b), an insurer knows something only if it is known to one or more of the individuals who participate on behalf of the insurer in the decision whether to take the risk, and if so on what terms (whether the individual does so as the insurer's employee or agent, as an employee of the insurer's agent or in any other capacity).

(2) For the purposes of section 3(5)(c), an insurer ought to know something only if—

(a) an employee or agent of the insurer knows it, and ought reasonably to have passed on the relevant information to an individual mentioned in subsection (1), or

(b) the relevant information is held by the insurer and is readily available to an individual mentioned in subsection (1).

(3) For the purposes of section 3(5)(d), an insurer is presumed to know—

(a) things which are common knowledge, and

(b) things which an insurer offering insurance of the class in question to insureds in the field of activity in question would reasonably be expected to know in the ordinary course of business.

6 Knowledge: general

(1) For the purposes of sections 3 to 5, references to an individual's knowledge include not only actual knowledge, but also matters which the individual suspected, and of which the individual would have had knowledge but for deliberately refraining from confirming them or enquiring about them.

(2) Nothing in this Part affects the operation of any rule of law according to which knowledge of a fraud perpetrated by an individual ("F") either on the insured or on the insurer is not to be attributed to the insured or to the insurer (respectively), where—

(a) if the fraud is on the insured, F is any of the individuals mentioned in section 4(2)(b) or (3), or

(b) if the fraud is on the insurer, F is any of the individuals mentioned in section 5(1).

7 Supplementary

(1) A fair presentation need not be contained in only one document or oral presentation.
(2) The term *"circumstance"* includes any communication made to, or information received by, the insured.
(3) A circumstance or representation is material if it would influence the judgement of a prudent insurer in determining whether to take the risk and, if so, on what terms.
(4) Examples of things which may be material circumstances are—
 (a) special or unusual facts relating to the risk,
 (b) any particular concerns which led the insured to seek insurance cover for the risk,
 (c) anything which those concerned with the class of insurance and field of activity in question would generally understand as being something that should be dealt with in a fair presentation of risks of the type in question.
(5) A material representation is substantially correct if a prudent insurer would not consider the difference between what is represented and what is actually correct to be material.
(6) A representation may be withdrawn or corrected before the contract of insurance is entered into.

8 Remedies for breach

(1) The insurer has a remedy against the insured for a breach of the duty of fair presentation only if the insurer shows that, but for the breach, the insurer—
 (a) would not have entered into the contract of insurance at all, or
 (b) would have done so only on different terms.
(2) The remedies are set out in Schedule 1.
(3) A breach for which the insurer has a remedy against the insured is referred to in this Act as a *"qualifying breach"*.
(4) A qualifying breach is either—
 (a) deliberate or reckless, or
 (b) neither deliberate nor reckless.
(5) A qualifying breach is deliberate or reckless if the insured —
 (a) knew that it was in breach of the duty of fair presentation, or
 (b) did not care whether or not it was in breach of that duty.
(6) It is for the insurer to show that a qualifying breach was deliberate or reckless.

9 Warranties and representations

(1) This section applies to representations made by the insured in connection with—
 (a) a proposed non-consumer insurance contract, or
 (b) a proposed variation to a non-consumer insurance contract.
(2) Such a representation is not capable of being converted into a warranty by means of any provision of the non-consumer insurance contract (or of the terms of the variation), or of any other contract (and whether by declaring the representation to form the basis of the contract or otherwise).

Part 3

Warranties and other terms

10 Breach of warranty

(1) Any rule of law that breach of a warranty (express or implied) in a contract of insurance results in the discharge of the insurer's liability under the contract is abolished.

(2) An insurer has no liability under a contract of insurance in respect of any loss occurring, or attributable to something happening, after a warranty (express or implied) in the contract has been breached but before the breach has been remedied.

(3) But subsection (2) does not apply if—

(a) because of a change of circumstances, the warranty ceases to be applicable to the circumstances of the contract,

(b) compliance with the warranty is rendered unlawful by any subsequent law, or

(c) the insurer waives the breach of warranty.

(4) Subsection (2) does not affect the liability of the insurer in respect of losses occurring, or attributable to something happening—

(a) before the breach of warranty, or

(b) if the breach can be remedied, after it has been remedied.

(5) For the purposes of this section, a breach of warranty is to be taken as remedied—

(a) in a case falling within subsection (6), if the risk to which the warranty relates later becomes essentially the same as that originally contemplated by the parties,

(b) in any other case, if the insured ceases to be in breach of the warranty.

(6) A case falls within this subsection if—

(a) the warranty in question requires that by an ascertainable time something is to be done (or not done), or a condition is to be fulfilled, or something is (or is not) to be the case, and

(b) that requirement is not complied with.

(7) In the Marine Insurance Act 1906—

(a) in section 33 (nature of warranty), in subsection (3), the second sentence is omitted,

(b) section 34 (when breach of warranty excused) is omitted.

11 Terms not relevant to the actual loss

(1) This section applies to a term (express or implied) of a contract of insurance, other than a term defining the risk as a whole, if compliance with it would tend to reduce the risk of one or more of the following—

(a) loss of a particular kind,

(b) loss at a particular location,

(c) loss at a particular time.

(2) If a loss occurs, and the term has not been complied with, the insurer may not rely on the non-compliance to exclude, limit or discharge its liability under the contract for the loss if the insured satisfies subsection (3).

(3) The insured satisfies this subsection if it shows that the non-compliance with the term could not have increased the risk of the loss which actually occurred in the circumstances in which it occurred.

(4) This section may apply in addition to section 10.

PART 4

FRAUDULENT CLAIMS

12 Remedies for fraudulent claims

(1) If the insured makes a fraudulent claim under a contract of insurance—
  (a) the insurer is not liable to pay the claim,
  (b) the insurer may recover from the insured any sums paid by the insurer to the insured in respect of the claim, and
  (c) in addition, the insurer may by notice to the insured treat the contract as having been terminated with effect from the time of the fraudulent act.

(2) If the insurer does treat the contract as having been terminated—
  (a) it may refuse all liability to the insured under the contract in respect of a relevant event occurring after the time of the fraudulent act, and
  (b) it need not return any of the premiums paid under the contract.

(3) Treating a contract as having been terminated under this section does not affect the rights and obligations of the parties to the contract with respect to a relevant event occurring before the time of the fraudulent act.

(4) In subsections (2)(a) and (3), *"relevant event"* refers to whatever gives rise to the insurer's liability under the contract (and includes, for example, the occurrence of a loss, the making of a claim, or the notification of a potential claim, depending on how the contract is written).

13 Remedies for fraudulent claims: group insurance

(1) This section applies where—
  (a) a contract of insurance is entered into with an insurer by a person ("A"),
  (b) the contract provides cover for one or more other persons who are not parties to the contract ("the Cs"), whether or not it also provides cover of any kind for A or another insured party, and
  (c) a fraudulent claim is made under the contract by or on behalf of one of the Cs ("CF").

(2) Section 12 applies in relation to the claim as if the cover provided for CF were provided under an individual insurance contract between the insurer and CF as the insured; and, accordingly—
  (a) the insurer's rights under section 12 are exercisable only in relation to the cover provided for CF, and
  (b) the exercise of any of those rights does not affect the cover provided under the contract for anyone else.

(3) In its application by virtue of subsection (2), section 12 is subject to the following particular modifications—
  (a) the first reference to *"the insured"* in subsection (1)(b) of that section, in respect of any particular sum paid by the insurer, is to whichever of A and CF the insurer paid the sum to; but if a sum was paid to A and passed on by A to CF, the reference is to CF,
  (b) the second reference to *"the insured"* in subsection (1)(b) is to A or CF,
  (c) the reference to *"the insured"* in subsection (1)(c) is to both CF and A,
  (d) the reference in subsection (2)(b) to the premiums paid under the contract is to premiums paid in respect of the cover for CF.

PART 4A

LATE PAYMENT OF CLAIMS

13A Implied term about payment of claims

(1) It is an implied term of every contract of insurance that if the insured makes a claim under the contract, the insurer must pay any sums due in respect of the claim within a reasonable time.

(2) A reasonable time includes a reasonable time to investigate and assess the claim.

(3) What is reasonable will depend on all the relevant circumstances, but the following are examples of things which may need to be taken into account—

(a) the type of insurance,

(b) the size and complexity of the claim,

(c) compliance with any relevant statutory or regulatory rules or guidance,

(d) factors outside the insurer's control.

(4) If the insurer shows that there were reasonable grounds for disputing the claim (whether as to the amount of any sum payable, or as to whether anything at all is payable)—

(a) the insurer does not breach the term implied by subsection (1) merely by failing to pay the claim (or the affected part of it) while the dispute is continuing, but

(b) the conduct of the insurer in handling the claim may be a relevant factor in deciding whether that term was breached and, if so, when.

(5) Remedies (for example, damages) available for breach of the term implied by subsection (1) are in addition to and distinct from—

(a) any right to enforce payment of the sums due, and

(b) any right to interest on those sums (whether under the contract, under another enactment, at the court's discretion or otherwise).

PART 5

GOOD FAITH AND CONTRACTING OUT

14 Good faith

(1) Any rule of law permitting a party to a contract of insurance to avoid the contract on the ground that the utmost good faith has not been observed by the other party is abolished.

(2) Any rule of law to the effect that a contract of insurance is a contract based on the utmost good faith is modified to the extent required by the provisions of this Act and the Consumer Insurance (Disclosure and Representations) Act 2012.

(3) Accordingly—

(a) in section 17 of the Marine Insurance Act 1906 (marine insurance contracts are contracts of the utmost good faith), the words from ", and" to the end are omitted, and

(b) the application of that section (as so amended) is subject to the provisions of this Act and the Consumer Insurance (Disclosure and Representations) Act 2012.

(4) In section 2 of the Consumer Insurance (Disclosure and Representations) Act 2012 (disclosure and representations before contract or variation), subsection (5) is omitted.

15 Contracting out: consumer insurance contracts

(1) A term of a consumer insurance contract, or of any other contract, which would put the consumer in a worse position as respects any of the matters provided for in Part 3 or 4 of this Act than the consumer would be in by virtue of the provisions of those Parts (so far as relating to consumer insurance contracts) is to that extent of no effect.
(2) In subsection (1) references to a contract include a variation.
(3) This section does not apply in relation to a contract for the settlement of a claim arising under a consumer insurance contract.

16 Contracting out: non-consumer insurance contracts

(1) A term of a non-consumer insurance contract, or of any other contract, which would put the insured in a worse position as respects representations to which section 9 applies than the insured would be in by virtue of that section is to that extent of no effect.
(2) A term of a non-consumer insurance contract, or of any other contract, which would put the insured in a worse position as respects any of the other matters provided for in Part 2, 3 or 4 of this Act than the insured would be in by virtue of the provisions of those Parts (so far as relating to non-consumer insurance contracts) is to that extent of no effect, unless the requirements of section 17 have been satisfied in relation to the term.
(3) In this section references to a contract include a variation.
(4) This section does not apply in relation to a contract for the settlement of a claim arising under a non-consumer insurance contract.

16A Contracting out of the implied term about payment of claims: consumer and non-consumer insurance contracts

(1) A term of a consumer insurance contract, or of any other contract, which would put the consumer in a worse position as respects any of the matters provided for in section 13A than the consumer would be in by virtue of the provisions of that section (so far as relating to consumer insurance contracts) is to that extent of no effect.
(2) A term of a non-consumer insurance contract, or of any other contract, which would put the insured in a worse position as respects deliberate or reckless breaches of the term implied by section 13A than the insured would be in by virtue of that section is to that extent of no effect.
(3) For the purposes of subsection (2) a breach is deliberate or reckless if the insurer—
    (a) knew that it was in breach, or
    (b) did not care whether or not it was in breach.
(4) A term of a non-consumer insurance contract, or of any other contract, which would put the insured in a worse position as respects any of the other matters provided for in section 13A than the insured would be in by virtue of the provisions of that section (so far as relating to nonconsumer insurance contracts) is to that extent of no effect, unless the requirements of section 17 have been satisfied in relation to the term.
(5) In this section references to a contract include a variation.
(6) This section does not apply in relation to a contract for the settlement of a claim arising under an insurance contract.

17 The transparency requirements

(1) In this section, *"the disadvantageous term"* means such a term as is mentioned in section 16(2).
(2) The insurer must take sufficient steps to draw the disadvantageous term to the insured's attention before the contract is entered into or the variation agreed.

(3) The disadvantageous term must be clear and unambiguous as to its effect.

(4) In determining whether the requirements of subsections (2) and (3) have been met, the characteristics of insured persons of the kind in question, and the circumstances of the transaction, are to be taken into account.

(5) The insured may not rely on any failure on the part of the insurer to meet the requirements of subsection (2) if the insured (or its agent) had actual knowledge of the disadvantageous term when the contract was entered into or the variation agreed.

18 Contracting out: group insurance contracts

(1) This section applies to a contract of insurance referred to in section 13(1)(a); and in this section—

"A" and *"the Cs"* have the same meaning as in section 13,

"consumer C" means an individual who is one of the Cs, where the cover provided by the contract for that individual would have been a consumer insurance contract if entered into by that person rather than by A, and

"non-consumer C" means any of the Cs who is not a consumer C.

(2) A term of the contract of insurance, or any other contract, which puts a consumer C in a worse position as respects any matter dealt with in section 13 than that individual would be in by virtue of that section is to that extent of no effect.

(3) A term of the contract of insurance, or any other contract, which puts a non-consumer C in a worse position as respects any matter dealt with in section 13 than that person would be in by virtue of that section is to that extent of no effect, unless the requirements of section 17 have been met in relation to the term.

(4) Section 17 applies in relation to such a term as it applies to a term mentioned in section 16(2), with references to the insured being read as references to A rather than the non-consumer C.

(5) In this section references to a contract include a variation.

(6) This section does not apply in relation to a contract for the settlement of a claim arising under a contract of insurance to which this section applies.

Part 6

Amendment of the Third Parties (Rights Against Insurers) Act 2010

19 Power to change meaning of "relevant person" for purposes of 2010 Act

For section 19 of the Third Parties (Rights against Insurers) Act 2010 (power to amend sections 4 to 6 of the Act) substitute—

"19 Power to change the meaning of "relevant person"

(1) The Secretary of State may by regulations make provision adding or removing circumstances in which a person is a "relevant person" for the purposes of this Act, subject to subsection (2).

(2) Regulations under this section may add circumstances only if, in the Secretary of State's opinion, the additional circumstances—

(a) involve actual or anticipated dissolution of a body corporate or an unincorporated body,

(b) involve actual or anticipated insolvency or other financial difficulties for an individual, a body corporate or an unincorporated body, or

(c) are similar to circumstances for the time being described in sections 4 to 7.

(3) Regulations under this section may make provision about—

(a) the persons to whom, and the extent to which, rights are transferred under section 1 in the circumstances added or removed by the regulations (the "affected circumstances"),

(b) the re-transfer of rights transferred under section 1 where the affected circumstances change, and

(c) the effect of a transfer of rights under section 1 on the liability of the insured in the affected circumstances.

(4) Regulations under this section which add or remove circumstances involving actual or anticipated dissolution of a body corporate or unincorporated body may change the cases in which the following provisions apply so that they include or exclude cases involving that type of dissolution or any other type of dissolution of a body—

(a) section 9(3) (cases in which transferred rights are not subject to a condition requiring the insured to provide information or assistance to the insurer), and

(b) paragraph 3 of Schedule 1 (notices requiring disclosure).

(5) Regulations under this section which add circumstances may provide that section 1 of this Act applies in cases involving those circumstances in which either or both of the following occurred in relation to a person before the day on which the regulations come into force—

(a) the circumstances arose in relation to the person;

(b) a liability against which the person was insured under an insurance contract was incurred.

(6) Regulations under this section which—

(a) add circumstances, and

(b) provide that section 1 of this Act applies in a case involving those circumstances in which both of the events mentioned in subsection (5)(a) and (b) occurred in relation to a person before the day on which the regulations come into force, must provide that, in such a case, the person is to be treated for the purposes of this Act as not having become a relevant person until that day or a later day specified in the regulations.

(7) Regulations under this section which remove circumstances may provide that section 1 of this Act does not apply in cases involving those circumstances in which one of the events mentioned in subsection (5)(a) and (b) (but not both) occurred in relation to a person before the day on which the regulations come into force.

(8) Regulations under this section may—

(a) include consequential, incidental, supplementary, transitional, transitory or saving provision,

(b) make different provision for different purposes, and

(c) make provision by reference to an enactment as amended, extended or applied from time to time,

(and subsections (3) to (7) are without prejudice to the generality of this subsection).

(9) Regulations under this section may amend an enactment, whenever passed or made, including this Act.

(10) Regulations under this section are to be made by statutory instrument.

(11) Regulations under this section may not be made unless a draft of the statutory instrument containing the regulations has been laid before, and approved by a resolution of, each House of Parliament."

20 Other amendments

Schedule 2 amends the Third Parties (Rights against Insurers) Act 2010 in relation to the insured persons to whom the Act applies.

PART 7

GENERAL

21 Provision consequential on Part 2

(1) The provision made by this section is consequential on Part 2 of this Act.

(2) In the Marine Insurance Act 1906, sections 18 (disclosure by assured), 19 (disclosure by agent effecting insurance) and 20 (representations pending negotiation of contract) are omitted.

(3) Any rule of law to the same effect as any of those provisions is abolished.

(4) In section 152 of the Road Traffic Act 1988 (exceptions to duty of insurers to satisfy judgment against persons insured against third-party risks)—

(a) in subsection (2)—

(i) in paragraph (a), for "it either under the Consumer Insurance (Disclosure and Representations) Act 2012 or, if that Act does not apply," substitute "the policy under either of the relevant insurance enactments, or the security",

(ii) in paragraph (b), for "or security under that Act or" substitute "under either of the relevant insurance enactments, or the security";

(b) in subsection (3), after "specifying" insert "the relevant insurance enactment or, in the case of a security,";

(c) after subsection (4) add—

"(5) In this section, *"relevant insurance enactment"* means the Consumer Insurance (Disclosure and Representations) Act 2012 or Part 2 of the Insurance Act 2015."

(5) In Article 98A of the Road Traffic (Northern Ireland) Order 1981 (S.I. 1981/154 (N.I.)) (exceptions to duty of insurers to satisfy judgement against persons insured against third party risks)—

(a) in paragraph (2)—

(i) in paragraph (a), for "it either under the Consumer Insurance Act (Disclosure and Representations) Act 2012 or, if that Act does not apply," substitute "the policy under either of the relevant insurance enactments, or the security";

(ii) in paragraph (b), for "or security under that Act or" substitute "under either of the relevant insurance enactments, or the security";

(b) in paragraph (3), after "specifying" insert "the relevant insurance enactment or, in the case of a security,";

(c) after paragraph (4) add—

"(5) In this Article, *"relevant insurance enactment"* means the Consumer Insurance (Disclosure and Representations) Act 2012 or Part 2 of the Insurance Act 2015."

(6) In section 11 of the Consumer Insurance (Disclosure and Representations) Act 2012 (consequential provision), subsections (1) and (2) are omitted.

22 Application etc. of Parts 2 to 5

(1) Part 2 (and section 21) and section 14 apply only in relation to—

(a) contracts of insurance entered into after the end of the relevant period, and

(b) variations, agreed after the end of the relevant period, to contracts of insurance entered into at any time.

(2) Parts 3 and 4 of this Act apply only in relation to contracts of insurance entered into after the end of the relevant period, and variations to such contracts.

(3) In subsections (1) and (2) *"the relevant period"* means the period of 18 months beginning with the day on which this Act is passed.

(4) Unless the contrary intention appears, references in Parts 2 to 5 to something being done by or in relation to the insurer or the insured include its being done by or in relation to that person's agent.

23 Extent, commencement and short title

(1) This Act extends to England and Wales, Scotland and Northern Ireland, except for—

(a) section 21(4), which does not extend to Northern Ireland; and

(b) section 21(5), which extends to Northern Ireland only.

(2) This Act (apart from Part 6 and this section) comes into force at the end of the period of 18 months beginning with the day on which it is passed.

(3) In Part 6—

(a) section 19 comes into force at the end of the period of two months beginning with the day on which this Act is passed; and

(b) section 20 and Schedule 2 come into force on the day appointed under section 21(2) of the Third Parties (Rights against Insurers) Act 2010 for the coming into force of that Act.

(4) This section comes into force on the day on which this Act is passed.

(5) This Act may be cited as the Insurance Act 2015.

SCHEDULES

Schedule 1

INSURERS' REMEDIES FOR QUALIFYING BREACHES

PART 1

CONTRACTS

General

1 This Part of this Schedule applies to qualifying breaches of the duty of fair presentation in relation to non-consumer insurance contracts (for variations to them, see Part 2).

Deliberate or reckless breaches

2 If a qualifying breach was deliberate or reckless, the insurer—

(a) may avoid the contract and refuse all claims, and

(b) need not return any of the premiums paid.

Other breaches

3 Paragraphs 4 to 6 apply if a qualifying breach was neither deliberate nor reckless.

4 If, in the absence of the qualifying breach, the insurer would not have entered into the contract on any terms, the insurer may avoid the contract and refuse all claims, but must in that event return the premiums paid.

5 If the insurer would have entered into the contract, but on different terms (other than terms relating to the premium), the contract is to be treated as if it had been entered into on those different terms if the insurer so requires.

6 (1) In addition, if the insurer would have entered into the contract (whether the terms relating to matters other than the premium would have been the same or different), but would have charged a higher premium, the insurer may reduce proportionately the amount to be paid on a claim.

(2) In sub-paragraph (1), *"reduce proportionately"* means that the insurer need pay on the claim only X% of what it would otherwise have been under an obligation to pay under the terms of the contract (or, if applicable, under the different terms provided for by virtue of paragraph 5), where—(Equation not available. Please see original printed copy.)

Part 2

Variations

General

7 This Part of this Schedule applies to qualifying breaches of the duty of fair presentation in relation to variations to non-consumer insurance contracts.

Deliberate or reckless breaches

8 If a qualifying breach was deliberate or reckless, the insurer—

(a) may by notice to the insured treat the contract as having been terminated with effect from the time when the variation was made, and

(b) need not return any of the premiums paid.

Other breaches

9 (1) This paragraph applies if—

(a) a qualifying breach was neither deliberate nor reckless, and

(b) the total premium was increased or not changed as a result of the variation.

(2) If, in the absence of the qualifying breach, the insurer would not have agreed to the variation on any terms, the insurer may treat the contract as if the variation was never made, but must in that event return any extra premium paid.

(3) If sub-paragraph (2) does not apply—

(a) if the insurer would have agreed to the variation on different terms (other than terms relating to the premium), the variation is to be treated as if it had been entered into on those different terms if the insurer so requires, and

(b) paragraph 11 also applies if (in the case of an increased premium) the insurer would have increased the premium by more than it did, or (in the case of an unchanged premium) the insurer would have increased the premium.

10 (1) This paragraph applies if—

(a) a qualifying breach was neither deliberate nor reckless, and

(b) the total premium was reduced as a result of the variation.

(2) If, in the absence of the qualifying breach, the insurer would not have agreed to the variation on any terms, the insurer may treat the contract as if the variation was never made, and paragraph 11 also applies.

(3) If sub-paragraph (2) does not apply—

(a) if the insurer would have agreed to the variation on different terms (other than terms relating to the premium), the variation is to be treated as if it had been entered into on those different terms if the insurer so requires, and

(b) paragraph 11 also applies if the insurer would have increased the premium, would not have reduced the premium, or would have reduced it by less than it did.

Proportionate reduction

11 (1) If this paragraph applies, the insurer may reduce proportionately the amount to be paid on a claim arising out of events after the variation.

(2) In sub-paragraph (1), *"reduce proportionately"* means that the insurer need pay on the claim only Y% of what it would otherwise have been under an obligation to pay under the terms of the contract (whether on the original terms, or as varied, or under the different terms provided for by virtue of paragraph 9(3)(a) or 10(3)(a), as the case may be), where—(Equation not available. Please see original printed copy.)

(3) In the formula in sub-paragraph (2), "P"—

(a) in a paragraph 9(3)(b) case, is the total premium the insurer would have charged,

(b) in a paragraph 10(2) case, is the original premium,

(c) in a paragraph 10(3)(b) case, is the original premium if the insurer would not have changed it, and otherwise the increased or (as the case may be) reduced total premium the insurer would have charged.

PART 3

SUPPLEMENTARY

Relationship with section 84 of the Marine Insurance Act 1906

12 Section 84 of the Marine Insurance Act 1906 (return of premium for failure of consideration) is to be read subject to the provisions of this Schedule in relation to contracts of marine insurance which are non-consumer insurance contracts.

Schedule 2

RIGHTS OF THIRD PARTIES AGAINST INSURERS: RELEVANT INSURED PERSONS

1 The Third Parties (Rights against Insurers) Act 2010 is amended as follows.

Individuals subject to debt relief orders in Northern Ireland

2 (1) Section 4 (relevant persons: individuals) is amended as follows.

(2) In subsection (3), after paragraph (b) (deed of arrangements registered under the Insolvency (Northern Ireland) Order 1989) insert—

"(ba) subject to subsection (4), a debt relief order made under Part 7A of that Order,".

(3) In subsection (4) (individuals who are relevant persons for the purposes of section 1(1)(b) only), after "(1)(d)" insert "or (3)(ba)".

Corporate bodies etc in administration

3 (1) Section 6 (corporate bodies etc.) is amended as follows.

(2) In subsection (2) (events under the Insolvency Act 1986), for paragraph (b) substitute—
"(b) the body is in administration under Schedule B1 to that Act,".

(3) In subsection (4) (events under the Insolvency (Northern Ireland) Order 1989), for paragraph (b) substitute—
"(b) the body is in administration under Schedule B1 to that Order,".

Transitional cases

4 In section 1(5)(b) (definition of "relevant person"), at the end insert "(and see also paragraph 1A of Schedule 3)".

5 (1) Schedule 3 (transitory, transitional and saving provision) is amended as follows.

(2) At the beginning insert—
"Application of this Act"

(3) After paragraph 1 insert—
Relevant persons

1A (1) An individual, company or limited liability partnership not within sections 4 to 7 is to be treated as a relevant person for the purposes of this Act in the following cases.

(2) The first case is where an individual—
(a) became bankrupt before commencement day, and
(b) has not been discharged from that bankruptcy.

(3) The second case is where—
(a) an individual made a composition or arrangement with his or her creditors before commencement day, and
(b) the composition or arrangement remains in force.

(4) The third case is where—
(a) a winding-up order was made, or a resolution for a voluntary winding-up was passed, with respect to a company or limited liability partnership before commencement day, and
(b) the company or partnership is still wound up.

(5) The fourth case is where a company or limited liability partnership—
(a) entered administration before commencement day, and
(b) is still in administration.

(6) The fifth case is where—
(a) a receiver or manager of the business or undertaking of a company or limited liability partnership was appointed before commencement day, and
(b) the appointment remains in force.

(7) In those cases, the person is a relevant person only in relation to liabilities under a contract of insurance under which the person was insured at the time of the event mentioned in sub-paragraph (2)(a), (3)(a), (4)(a), (5)(a) or (6)(a) (as appropriate)."

(4) Before paragraph 2 insert—
"Bankruptcy and Diligence etc. (Scotland) Act 2007"

(5) Before paragraph 3 insert—
"Application of 1930 Acts"

(6) Before paragraph 5 insert—
"Interpretation"

Interpretation

6 After section 19 insert—

"19A.— Interpretation

(1) The references to enactments in sections 4 to 7, 9(7) and 14(4) and paragraph 3(2)(b), (4) and (5) of Schedule 1 are to be treated as including references to those enactments as amended, extended or applied by another enactment, whenever passed or made, unless the contrary intention appears.

(2) In this Act, *"enactment"* means an enactment contained in, or in an instrument made under, any of the following—

(a) an Act;
(b) an Act or Measure of the National Assembly for Wales;
(c) an Act of the Scottish Parliament;
(d) Northern Ireland legislation."

INDEX

For Product Safety Concerns and Information please contact our
EU representative GPSR@taylorandfrancis.com Taylor & Francis
Verlag GmbH, Kaufingerstraße 24, 80331 München, Germany